Walnut Creek Valley

Cookbook

**A collection of
744 recipes from the
Walnut Creek Amish Church**
Holmes County, Ohio

First Printing 1995-5m
Second Printing 1997-5m
Third Printing 1999-5m
Fourth Printing 2000-5m
Fifth Printing 2003-5m
Sixth Printing 2005-5m
Seventh Printing 2009-5m
Eighth Printing 2012-2.5m

ISBN - 978-1-933753-14-0
        1-933753-14-5

Cover photo by: Larry McBride

2673 TR 421
Sugarcreek, OH 44681
Phone: 1.800.852.4482

Carlisle Press
WALNUT CREEK

Acknowledgements

We wish to extend a sincere thank you to all who donated recipes for the Walnut Creek Valley Cookbook. And a special thank you to Maria Miller for the artwork on the divider pages.

We hope you enjoy these recipes from the Amish Church ladies of Walnut Creek Valley, in Holmes County, Ohio.

Mrs. Naomi Mast
Twila Beachy

Abbreviations Used

T. . . . . tablespoon
t. . . . . teaspoon
C. . . . . cup
qt. . . . . quart
pt. . . . . pint
lb. . . . . pound
oz. . . . . ounce

Table of Contents

- Notes -

Appetizers, Beverages, Dips & More

FRENCH TOAST
Mrs. Jay Miller

½ C. all-purpose flour
2 C. milk
1½ T. sugar
¼ t. salt

6 eggs
18 slices French bread
  (1" thick)
1 T. butter

Beat flour, milk, sugar, salt and eggs with beater until smooth. Soak bread in egg mixture until saturated. Heat butter in skillet until melted. Cook bread until golden brown, about 12 minutes on each side.

GARLIC TOAST
Mrs. Mark Hochstetler

Spread one side of a slice of bread with butter. Sprinkle with garlic salt, garlic powder and oregano. Toast on griddle. Try using hot dog buns, tastes great with spaghetti.

BUTTERMILK PANCAKES
Mrs. Crist Miller

1 egg
1 C. buttermilk
2 T. vegetable oil
1 C. flour

1 T. white sugar
1 t. baking powder
½ t. baking soda
½ t. salt

Beat egg, buttermilk and soda with wire whip. Then add rest of ingredients, beat until smooth. Fry on greased skillet. Makes 10 - 4" pancakes.

Pancake Syrup

½ C. brown sugar
1 C. water

Boil together and thicken with clear-jel.

WHOLE WHEAT PANCAKES
Mrs. Robert J. Yoder

1 egg
1 C. buttermilk
2 T. oil
¾ C. whole wheat flour

½ t. salt
1 T. sugar
1 t. baking powder
½ t. soda

Mix all ingredients and fry on hot skillet.

PANCAKES
Twila Beachy

1 C. buttermilk
1 C. flour
1 egg

1 t. soda
pinch of salt

Mix well, makes 7 pancakes. Fry on greased skillet.

HOMEMADE PANCAKE MIX
Bethany Miller

10 C. all-purpose flour
1/2 C. sugar
2 1/2 C. instant nonfat dry milk

1/4 C. baking powder
2 T. salt

Combine all ingredients in a large bowl. Stir together to blend well. Put in large airtight container. Store in a cool, dry place. Use within 6 - 8 months. Makes about 13 C. mix.

AMERICAN CHEESE SPREAD
Mrs. Henry Beachy

1 lb. white American cheese
1 C. milk

Melt in double boiler.

QUICK RELISH
Mrs. Henry Beachy

1 pt. sweet pickles
1 medium onion

Chop together. Good on hot dogs.

SPICED PECANS
Mrs. Mark Hochstetler

1 egg white
1 t. cold water
4 C. pecan halves

1/2 C. sugar
1/4 t. salt
1/2 t. ground cinnamon

In mixing bowl, beat egg white lightly. Add water, beat until frothy but not stiff. Add pecans, stir until well coated. Combine sugar, salt and cinnamon. Sprinkle over pecans. Toss to mix. Spread in 10" x 15" greased baking pan. Bake at 250° for 45 minutes, stirring occasionally.

RICE KRISPIE BARS

Mrs. Henry Beachy

$1/4$ C. butter
4 C. marshmallows
6 C. Rice Krispies

Melt butter in large saucepan over low heat. Add marshmallows and stir till completely melted. Remove from heat, add Rice Krispies. Stir until well coated. Spread evenly into buttered 9" x 13" pan.

SIMPLE CARAMELS

Mrs. Josiah Miller

$2^2/3$ C. brown sugar
1 C. light Karo

1 can Eagle Brand milk
1 C. butter

Boil for 15 minutes, stirring constantly. Pour into greased pan, cool, cut and wrap.

BUTTER CREAMS

Mrs. David Ray Yoder

2 C. white sugar
$1/4$ t. cream of tartar

1 C. cream
$1/2$ C. butter

Mix sugar, butter and cream in saucepan. Bring to a boil over medium heat and boil for 5 minutes. Sprinkle cream of tartar over boiling syrup, and continue to boil to soft ball stage. Do not stir while cooking. Remove from heat and let cool completely. When cold beat with spoon until creamy. Shape into balls and dip into melted chocolate.

FANTASTIC BUTTER TOFFEE

Mrs. Mark Hochstetler

2 C. whole unblanched almonds
11 oz. milk chocolate
1 C. sweet cream butter

1 C. sugar
3 T. cold water

Spread almonds in a pan and toast at 350° for about 10 minutes, shaking pan occasionally. Cool nuts. Grind milk chocolate fine in food processor, set aside. Chop nuts coarsely and sprinkle 1 C. over bottom of greased 10" x 15" jelly roll pan. Sprinkle 1 C. ground chocolate over nuts. Set aside. In heavy saucepan combine butter, sugar and water. Cook over medium heat, stirring occasionally, until the mixture reaches 290° (soft crack stage). Very quickly pour mixture over nuts and chocolate. Then top with remaining nuts. Chill and break into pieces.

❧

The Christian life is like tea, its full strength
comes out when its in hot water!

FANTASY FUDGE

Mrs. Henry Beachy

3 C. sugar
³/₄ C. oleo
²/₃ C. evaporated milk
12 oz. chocolate chips

2 C. marshmallow creme
1 t. vanilla
1 C. chopped nuts

Combine sugar, oleo and milk, bring to a rolling boil, stirring constantly. Boil for 5 minutes over medium heat. Remove from heat, stir in chocolate chips until melted. Add marshmallow creme, nuts and vanilla. Beat until well blended, pour into greased 9" x 13" pan. Cool to room temperature, cut into squares.

CARAMEL CANDY APPLES

Barbara Schrock

12 medium red apples
12 wooden skewers
1 lb. light colored caramels
¹/₄ C. light cream

Wash and dry apples, stick skewers in stem end. Put caramels and cream in top of double boiler. Cook, stirring occasionally until caramels are melted. Dip apples into syrup, twirl once or twice to cover evenly. Place on tray and cover with wax paper or foil, put in refrigerator for 2 hours. Yield:12

TAFFY

Leona Yoder
Mrs. Joe Miller Jr.

1 qt. white sugar
1 pt. cream
1 T. paraffin

1 pt. light Karo
1 T. gelatin dissolved in
    ¹/₂ C. cold water

Combine all ingredients and boil to 250° or until it forms a hard ball when a little is dropped into cold water. Pour into 3 large well greased pie pans. When cool enough to handle, butter hands and start pulling. When an ivory color is obtained, twist and cut with the kitchen shears. 1 pt. sugar may be used instead of 1 qt. for taffy that is not so sweet.

WHITE TRASH

Mrs. Jake Hershberger

6 C. Crispix
4 C. small pretzels
2 C. dry roasted peanuts

1 lb. M&M's
1¹/₄ lb. white dipping
    chocolate (melted)

Mix all ingredients and cover with white chocolate. Spread into cookie sheet and cool.

HOMEMADE SWEETENED CONDENSED MILK   Mrs. Nathan Miller

1 C. instant dry milk $^1/_3$ C. boiling water
$^2/_3$ C. white sugar   3 T. butter

Mix together, beat until smooth. Use in recipes that ask for 1 can condensed milk.

3 LAYER FINGER JELLO   Dorothy Yoder

1st layer
   3 small boxes jello   4 C. boiling water
   3 pkgs. Knox gelatin
Mix jello then add water.

2nd layer
   3 pkgs. Knox gelatin - wet with cold water then add
   2 C. boiling water
Cool slightly then add
   1 can Eagle Brand milk

3rd layer
   Repeat first layer.

Divide each layer in 2 sheet cake pans.

MINI CRACKER PIZZAS   Mrs. Mark Hochstetler

Place Ritz crackers on cookie sheet. Top each cracker with one pepperoni and a small amount of pizza sauce and Mozzarella cheese. Bake at 350° until cheese is melted, no longer or crackers will become soggy. (Can also be made without pizza sauce.)

MINI APPLE PIZZAS   Mrs. Mark Hochstetler

10 refrigerator biscuits   1 t. cinnamon
$^1/_2$ C. packed brown sugar   2 cooking apples peeled,
2 T. flour   cored and shredded

Roll or pat biscuits into $3^1/_2$" circles, place on lightly greased baking sheet. In mixing bowl, combine brown sugar, flour and cinnamon, mix well. Add apples and mix well. Spoon rounded tablespoonfuls onto biscuits. Bake at 350° for 15 - 20 minutes or until edges begin to brown. Serve warm.

BACON CHESTNUTS

Leona Yoder

1 lb. bacon
2 cans whole water chestnuts

Sauce
1 C. ketchup
1 C. brown sugar

Wrap a piece of bacon around each water chestnut and secure with toothpick. Bake at 350° for 30 minutes. Drain off fat. Pour sauce over chestnuts and bake another 30 minutes. Baking them on a cooling rack in a cake pan works well, so the fat can drain off.

HAM ROLL UPS

Orpha Peachey

8 oz. cream cheese
1 pkg. sliced ham

dill pickle spears

Let cream cheese set at room temperature. Dry ham with paper towels. Spread cream cheese on sliced layer of ham. Place long quarter wedge of dill pickle on the ham, roll up like a jelly roll. Spear a toothpick about every 1" through the rolled up pickle. Cut into 1" wedges. Place on pretty platter. These can be prepared the day before. Makes 50.

OVENFRIED QUESADILLAS

Mrs. Matthew Miller

8 flour tortillas
1 can pizza sauce
1 sm. green pepper
1 can mushrooms
1 pkg. sausage
1 pkg. shredded cheese

Preheat oven to 450°. Take one tortilla and brush with butter. Layer toppings as you would for pizza. Then top with another tortilla. Bake for 10 minutes or until tops are lightly browned. Let set 3 - 5 minutes. Cut each Quesadilla into 8 wedges.

CHURCH PEANUT BUTTER

Mrs. Crist Beachy

2 C. brown sugar
1 C. water
2 T. light Karo
2 C. peanut butter
2 C. marshmallow creme

Mix together brown sugar, water and Karo and bring to a boil. Cool. Add peanut butter and marshmallow creme. Mix well.

PEANUT BUTTER FOR CHURCH

Mrs. Willis Karen Miller
Mrs. Ben Troyer, Jr.

Bring to a boil:
4 C. brown sugar
2 C. boiling water

1/4 C. light Karo
2 t. maple flavoring

Cool, then add 2 1/2 lbs. peanut butter and 1 qt. marshmallow creme. If this recipe is double plus a half it will take 5 to 6 pounds of peanut butter and 2 qts. marshmallow creme. This will almost fill an 8 qt. bowl. A little pancake syrup may be added for a different taste. If it is too stringy add a bit of cold water.

PEANUT BUTTER

Mrs. John Troyer

10 C. brown sugar
5 C. water
Cook, cool then add:
7 1/2 lbs. peanut butter
4 qt. marshmallow creme

1 1/4 C. Karo
2 t. maple flavoring

WHITE CHOCOLATE PARTY MIX

Mrs. Willis Karen Miller

3 C. Rice Chex
3 C. Corn Chex
3 C. Cheerios
1 C. peanuts

1 lb. M&Ms
1 C. broken pretzel sticks
1 1/2 lbs. melted white
   chocolate

Stir all together and put on wax paper until cool.

PARTY MIX

Mrs. Mark Hochstetler

7 1/2 sticks oleo
12 T. Worcestershire sauce
3 t. celery salt
3 t. Lawry's seasoning salt
3 t. salt
1 box Corn Chex

1 box Rice Chex
1 box Honey Nut Cheerios
1 can shoestring potatoes
2 bags pretzels
1 box cinnamon teddies
2 lbs. peanuts

Melt oleo, while this melts mix cereal, peanuts, pretzels and teddies together. Mix salts and Worcestershire sauce with melted oleo. Pour this mixture over cereal mixture toss lightly to avoid crumbling the cereals. But mix thoroughly. Divide evenly in top and bottom of Lifetime roaster or other large baking dishes. Bake at 250° for 1 1/2 hours. Stirring every 15 minutes. When cooled add M&Ms.

PARTY MIX   Maria Miller

2 sticks butter
1 tsp. onion salt
1 t. garlic salt
1 t. celery salt
1/2 t. Tabasco sauce
1 t. Worcestershire sauce
shoestring potatoes

2 C. Cheerios
2 C. Rice Chex
2 C. Wheat Chex
2 C. Corn Chex
1 bag pretzels
2 C. nuts

Melt butter and add salts and sauces, pour over mixed cereals and toss together. Bake at 200° for 1 1/2 hours, stirring every 30 minutes. Add M&Ms after it is cooled.

HOMEMADE PRETZELS   Barbara Schrock

2 T. dry yeast
1 1/2 C. warm water
2 T. sugar

1 t. salt
4 C. flour

Mix yeast and water in bowl, add sugar, salt and flour, mix well. Put dough on waxed paper and knead until it is smooth. Cut thin strips and make into shapes of your choice. If you make them too thick they will be doughy and if you make them too thin they will become brittle. Place on cookie sheet and brush with beaten egg (be sure to cover the whole top) and sprinkle with coarse salt. Bake at 425° for 12 to 15 minutes or until golden brown.

SOFT PRETZELS   Mrs. Josiah Miller
                                                             Maria Miller

1 T. yeast
1 t. sugar
4 t. soda

2 t. salt
4 - 5 C. flour
butter as needed

Dissolve yeast in 1/4 C. warm water. Then stir in additional cup of warm water and sugar, add salt. Beat in flour to make dough stiff. Knead for 10 minutes or until dough is elastic. Place into bowl and spread with butter, cover and let rise for 45 minutes or until double. Cut 1/2" strips, shape into sticks or twists. Bring to a boil 4 C. water and 4 t. soda. Drop 3 pretzels in at one time. Boil for 1 minute or until they float. Remove and drain. Place on buttered cookie sheets. Sprinkle with coarse salt. Bake at 375° for 12 minutes or until golden brown. To make crisp pretzels put on cookie sheet and place in 200° oven for 2 hours.

೭ఊ

"A man of words and not of deeds
is like a garden full of weeds!"

SOFT PRETZELS

Mrs. Alfred Miller
Mrs. Willis Karen Miller

1¹/₂ C. warm water
2 T. dry yeast
¹/₂ t. salt

4¹/₂ C. flour
1 T. sugar

Dissolve yeast in warm water, add sugar, mix well, add rest of ingredients. Let rise in warm place for 15 minutes. Roll out and shape pretzels. Dip into soda solution of 3 C. boiling water and 4 t. soda, keep this on low heat as you dip them. Drain (they can be drained on a towel). Place on cookie sheet and sprinkle with salt, garlic salt, etc. Let rise 5 minutes. Then bake at 550° - 600° till golden brown, brush with melted butter.

HOT FUDGE SAUCE

Mrs. Eli B. Yoder
Mrs. Crist Beachy

3 T. oleo
1 C. sifted powdered sugar
3 T. cocoa

1 C. evaporated milk
1 t. vanilla

Melt oleo in saucepan over medium heat. Add powdered sugar and cocoa alternately with milk. Beat until smooth. Bring to a boil over medium heat, stirring constantly. Cook for 2 minutes. Add 1 t. vanilla. Serve hot over ice cream!

CHOCOLATE TOPPING

Mrs. Dean Wengerd

¹/₃ C. Hershey's cocoa
1 C. white sugar
³/₄ C. evaporated milk

¹/₄ C. butter or margarine
¹/₈ t. salt
¹/₂ t. vanilla

Combine cocoa and sugar in saucepan, blend in evaporated milk. Add butter or margarine and salt. Cook and stir constantly until mixture begins to boil. Remove from heat add vanilla. Serve warm over ice cream and other desserts.

REFRIGERATOR CHOCOLATE SYRUP

Mrs. Eddie Miller

1 C. white sugar
¹/₃ C. cocoa
3 T. flour
¹/₄ t. salt

1 C. boiling water
1 T. butter or oleo
¹/₂ t. vanilla

Mix sugar, cocoa, flour and salt in saucepan. Stir in boiling water, add butter, cook, stirring constantly 3 or 4 minutes until slightly thickened. Remove from heat, add vanilla. Store in covered jar in refrigerator.

HOT CHOCOLATE MIX

Mrs. Mark Hochstetler

1 lb. powdered sugar
2 lbs. Nestle's Quik

6 oz. Coffee Mate
8 qt. powdered milk

Mix all ingredients together. Makes about 1 gallon mix. Put ⅓ C. of mix in a cup and fill with boiling water. Miniature marshmallows may be added.

HOT CHOCOLATE MIX

Annalisa Miller

28 oz. Nestle's Quik
11 oz. instant coffee creamer

8 qt. box powdered milk
1 lb. powdered sugar

Mix thoroughly. Fill cup ½ full of mix, add boiling water and stir. Delicious on cold winter nights after coming home from youth meeting or singing.

BANANA PUNCH

Rosanna Miller

2 C. sugar
3 C. water
¼ can frozen orange juice

46 oz. pineapple juice
3 bananas
2 liter ginger ale

Mix sugar and water, boil for 10 minutes, cool and add ¼ can frozen orange juice, pineapple juice, and bananas. Freeze, to serve thaw slightly and add ginger ale.

ICED TEA

Mrs. Josiah Miller

Boil 4 C. water add 1½ qt. tea, tightly packed. Turn off heat and let steep for 15 minutes add 1½ C. sugar. Put in freezer boxes. Use 3 parts water to 1 part tea.

PARTY PUNCH

Twila Beachy

1 pkg. cherry Kool-Aid
1 pkg. strawberry Kool-Aid
6 oz. frozen orange juice
6 oz. frozen lemonade

1½ C. sugar
3 qt. water
2 C. ginger ale

Ginger ale may be added just before serving.

❧

*"The full use of today is the best
preparation for tomorrow."*

FROZEN RHUBARB PUNCH

Mrs. Josie Miller

2 qt. rhubarb juice
6 oz. frozen orange juice
1 pkg. raspberry Kool-Aid

6 oz. ReaLemon
2 C. sugar
3 qts. water

Cut 10 - 12 C. rhubarb, cover with water and bring to a boil. Let stand for a 1/2 hour then drain for juice. Mix all ingredients. Freeze. To serve mix 1 part punch with 1 part 7-Up or Sprite. Serve while still slushy.

ROOTBEER

Mrs. Levi Miller
Naomi Engbretson

2 C. white sugar
2 T. rootbeer extract

1 t. yeast
1 gal. lukewarm water

Mix yeast and sugar with a little water. Let set for 5 minutes then add rest of the water, set in the sun or in the oven above the pilot light for 3 - 4 hours. Do not turn lid tight. Then set in cold place.

ICE SLUSH

Mrs. Jake Hershberger

2 - 3 oz. jello (cherry, orange, lemon or lime)
2 C. sugar
1 qt. boiling water
Dissolve then add:
2 C. cold water
46 oz. pineapple juice

Freeze. Fill glass 3/4 full with slush, then fill it up with 7-Up. Refreshing in 90° weather.

VINTAGE COOLER

Mrs. Matthew Miller

1/2 gal. grape juice
1 qt. raspberry sherbet

2 liter 7-Up or Sprite

Mix together in punch bowl, very refreshing.

SLUSHY DRINK

Yvonne Miller

6 oz. jello, any flavor
4 C. hot water

8 C. cold water
2 C. white sugar

Freeze. Thaw till slush. Add 46 oz. pineapple juice. Fill glasses 3/4 full of slush then fill with pop.

VEGETABLE DIP

Rosanna Miller

²/₃ C. spin blend
²/₃ C. sour cream
1 T. minced dry onion
1 T. parsley
2 - 5 drops Tabasco sauce

1 t. Lawry's seasoning salt
1 t. dill seed
¹/₂ t. Worcestershire sauce
¹/₂ t. accent

Mix all ingredients together. Great with vegetables or potato chips.

MALLOW FRUIT DIP

Barbara Schrock

2 - 8 oz. cream cheese
13 oz. marshmallow topping
2 T. orange juice

2 t. grated orange rind
¹/₈ t. ground ginger

Mix all together, beat until well blended. Serve with fruit.

FRUIT DIP

Mrs. Mark Hochstetler

8 oz. cream cheese
8 oz. marshmallow creme

12 oz. Cool Whip

Mix all ingredients together. Add food coloring if desired. Serve with fresh fruit.

FRUIT DIP

Mrs. Martha Sue Miller

¹/₂ C. white sugar
2 T. orange rind
1 egg beaten

8 oz. cream cheese
12 oz. Cool Whip

Boil together first 3 ingredients. Cream together cream cheese and ¹/₂ C. white sugar. Add Cool Whip. Mix all together.

FRUIT DIP

Mrs. Josie Miller

14 oz. sweetened condensed milk
6 oz. frozen pink lemonade
12 oz. Cool Whip

Mix and serve with fresh fruits.

ঐ

Little boy helping his grandfather dig potatoes:
"Whatever made you bury these in the first place?"

FLUFFY CITRUS DIP

Mrs. Aaron Coblentz
Mrs. Ben Troyer, Jr.

1 egg
1/2 C. sugar
2 t. grated orange peel
3 oz. cream cheese

2 T. pineapple juice
add more if needed
1 C. whipping cream

In saucepan beat 1 egg, add sugar, orange peel and pineapple juice. Cook and stir over low heat until thickened, about 5 minutes. Add 3 oz. cream cheese, cool thoroughly. Fold in whipping cream. Chill. Makes 2 1/2 C.

CHEESE BALL

Mrs. Josiah Miller

2 - 8 oz. cream cheese
1 pkg. Cheddar cheese
1/2 t. garlic salt
1/2 t. onion salt

2 C. chopped onions
1 T. Worcestershire sauce
1/4 C. parsley flakes
1/4 C. chopped nuts

Mix cheeses together, then add rest of ingredients except for parsley flakes and nuts. Shape into a ball and roll in parsley flakes and nuts.

CHEESE BALL

Mrs. Dan J. Yoder

12 oz. cream cheese
4 oz. Bleu cheese dressing
6 oz. Cheddar cheese
6 T. chopped onion

1 t. Worcestershire sauce
a little green pepper
some Velveeta cheese
nuts if desired

CHEESE BALL

Janice Schlabach

2 - 8 oz. cream cheese
2 C. Cracker Barrel
   sharp cheddar cheese, shredded

1 t. lemon juice
Lawry's seasoning salt
2 t. Worcestershire sauce

Finely chopped pecans or walnuts. Mix together and chill. Form into a ball and roll in nuts.

CHOCOLATE DROPS

Twila Beachy

2 C. white sugar
1 C. cream

1/4 t. cream of tartar
1 t. vanilla

Boil cream and sugar to 230°. Immediately pour, and don't scrape, into 9" x 13" pan. Don't move pan. Sprinkle cream of tartar on top of sugar and cream mixture. Stir when lukewarm, then add vanilla. Stir until creamy. Form into balls and dip into melted chocolate.

MINI-CHEESECAKE TARTS   Dorothy Yoder
                                                        Mrs. Dan J. Yoder

16 oz. cream cheese, softened   2 eggs
1 box vanilla wafers   1 T. lemon juice
$^1/_2$ - $^3/_4$ C. sugar   1 t. vanilla

Place vanilla wafers in bottom of a cupcake liner. Combine remaining ingredients until creamy. Fill liners $^2/_3$ full and bake at 375° for 12 - 15 minutes. Serve warm or cold with a generous dab of pie filling of your choice. Makes 24.

CRISPY CARAMEL CORN   Twila Beachy
                                                    Mrs. David Schlabach

8 qts. popped corn   1 C. oleo
2 C. brown sugar $^1/_2$ t. soda
$^1/_2$ C. light Karo   1 t. vanilla
1 t. salt

Boil sugar, Karo, salt and oleo, cook for 5 minutes. Remove from stove, add soda and vanilla, pour over popped corn, stir. Bake 1 hour at 250° stirring every 15 minutes.

CARAMEL CORN   Mrs. Dean Wengerd
                                                        Mrs. Nathan Mast
                                                 Mrs. Willis Karen Miller

7 qts. popped corn   2 sticks oleo
2 C. brown sugar $^1/_2$ t. baking soda
$^1/_2$ C. light Karo or white sugar   1 t. vanilla
1 t. salt

Boil sugar, Karo, oleo and salt for 5 minutes. Remove from heat, add soda and vanilla. Pour over the popped corn and mix well. Pour into pans and bake at 250° for 1 hour. Stir several times during baking.

CARAMEL CORN   Naomi Engbretson

1 C. oleo   1 t. soda
2 C. brown sugar   1 t. vanilla
$^1/_2$ C. light Karo   1$^1/_2$ C. unpopped corn

Pop popcorn. Melt butter, add sugar and Karo, boil for 5 minutes. Add soda and vanilla. Bake at 200° for 1 hour stirring every 15 minutes.

CRACKER JACK

Mrs. John Mark Troyer

¹/₄ lb. butter
2¹/₂ C. white sugar (scant)
1 pt. light Karo

¹/₄ t. cream of tartar
6 qts. popped corn

Boil first 3 ingredients to soft crack stage 285°, then add cream of tartar, boil until just a little over 300° then pour over popcorn. Flatten on buttered counter top until cool.

MEX TEX DIP

Twila Beachy

1ˢᵗ layer
1 can refried beans and 1 can bean dip, (mixed)
2ⁿᵈ layer
¹/₂ C. mayonnaise, ¹/₂ C. sour cream, 1 pkg. taco seasoning, (mixed)
3ʳᵈ layer
¹/₂ lb. Mozzarella cheese, ¹/₂ lb. Cheddar cheese, (grated)
4ᵗʰ layer
tomatoes (chopped), green onions (chopped)

TACO DIP

Mrs. Leroy Yoder

8 oz. cream cheese
16 oz. sour cream

1 pkg. taco seasoning

Cream together when ingredients are at room temperature. Top with: shredded cheese, tomatoes and lettuce. Serve with taco chips.

HOT TACO DIP

Mrs. Firman Miller

1 lb. hamburger, browned
1 t. chili powder
¹/₂ t. garlic powder

8 oz. mild taco sauce
1 t. Worcestershire sauce
1 lb. Velveeta cheese

Mix all together and heat. Serve with taco chips.

DILL DIP

Mrs. Alfred Miller
Ruby Beachy

1 C. sour cream
1 C. mayonnaise
1 t. chopped onions

1 t. parsley flakes
1 t. dill weed
1 t. beau monde seasoning

Mix and enjoy.

HAMBURGER CHEESE DIP

Twila Beachy

1 – 1½ lb. hamburger
1 onion
8 oz. taco sauce
1 can mushroom soup
1 can tomato soup

1 t. chili powder
1 t. Worcestershire sauce
½ t. garlic powder
1 – 1½ lb. Velveeta cheese

Brown hamburger with onion, salt and pepper to taste. Add remaining ingredients. Heat till cheese is melted. Serve warm with corn tortilla chips.

HAMBURGER CHEESE DIP

Joanna Miller

1 lb. hamburger
1 can tomato soup
1 t. chili powder
½ t. garlic powder

1 lb. Velveeta cheese
1 can mushroom soup
1 t. Worcestershire sauce
1 C. peppers

Heat until cheese is melted. Serve warm with nacho chips.

WARM TACO DIP

Janice Schlabach

2 lbs. hamburger
1 lb. Velveeta cheese
1 can tomato soup
1 can mushroom soup
1 t. chili powder

1 t. Worcestershire sauce
1 t. onion powder
1 t. garlic salt
green peppers
onions

Fry hamburger, add spices and soups then add Velveeta cheese. Serve with a large bowl of taco chips.

TORTILLA PINWHEELS

Elaine Wengerd

16 oz. sour cream
4 oz. cream cheese
8 pack flour tortillas

1 pkg. Hidden Valley Ranch
  dip mix

Mix all ingredients except tortillas. Then spread over tortillas.

Top with:
broccoli
cauliflower
onions

grated Cheddar cheese
crumbled bacon

Salsa Master works well to chop broccoli and cauliflower. Roll up and chill overnight. Slice ½" thick. Enjoy!

CORNMEAL MUSH

Mrs. Jay Mark Miller

3 C. water
1 C. cornmeal
1 t. salt

1 t. flour
1 C. cold water

In a saucepan heat water to boiling. Mix together cornmeal, salt, flour and 1 C. water. Pour into boiling water, stirring constantly. Cook until thickened, stirring frequently. Cover, continue cooking over low heat for 5 minutes or longer, pour into loaf pan. Cool and chill. Cut into 1/4" thick slices and fry. Serve with ham or dried beef gravy.

GUNK OR GAK

Mrs. Willis Karen Miller
Mrs. Josiah Miller
Elaine Wengerd

1st Bowl:
Mix together 2 C. Elmers glue and 1 1/2 C. water.

2nd Bowl:
Dissolve 2 level t. of 20 Mule Team Borax in 1 C. water. Slowly add and stir this to the glue mixture. You may have to use hands to mix thoroughly. Store in refrigerator in ziplock bag or in glass jar.

MAGIC BUBBLES

Mrs. Linus Troyer

2 C. Joy dishwashing soap
6 C. water

3/4 C. light Karo

Combine ingredients, shake well then let settle for 4 hours before using. Store in refrigerator. Warm before using. We've used it cold and it works too.

SHAVING CREAM BATH PAINT

Mrs. Nathan Miller

Squirt shaving cream dallop into each section of muffin tin, add a couple drops of food coloring to each section, mix together with spoon. The children will love to create pictures on the tub and tile during bathtime. Be sure to rinse after each bathtime.

KNOX GELATIN FOR HOUSEPLANTS

Mrs. David Schlabach

Dissolve 1 pkg. Knox gelatin in 1/2 C. cold water. Add 3 cups hot water. Let cool. Use to water houseplants once a month.

PEANUT BUTTER SUET FOR BIRDS
Debra Kay Miller

1 C. crunchy peanut butter
2 C. quick oats
2 C. cornmeal

1 C. lard (no substitute)
1 C. white flour
$^1/_3$ C. sugar

Melt lard and peanut butter, then stir in remaining ingredients. Pour into square freezer containers about 1½" thick. Store in freezer. Hang them on a tree and let the birds enjoy.

FEED YOUR BIRDS THIS MIX
Mrs. Willis Karen Miller

$^1/_2$ C. peanut butter
2$^1/_2$ C. cornmeal

1 C. bird seed
$^1/_2$ C. melted suet

The birds really like this. We have a log which we drilled holes into and then we fill it with this mixture. You can also hang it up and enjoy watching the birds.

FOR HUMMINGBIRDS
Debra Kay Miller

1 C. water

$^1/_3$ C. sugar

Bring water and sugar to a boil, let cool, add red food coloring and serve.

❧

My Kitchen Prayer

Man shall not live by bread alone,
Our Lord and Master said.
But by the living word of God,
Our souls must feed instead.

So as I cook and serve the meals
I sincerely pray,
That I shall give, along with food,
Some Christlike love today.

❧

- Notes -

Breads, Rolls & Cereals

WHOLE WHEAT BREAD

Mrs. Marcus Mast

1 T. yeast
2 C. warm water
1 T. white sugar
6 C. (more or less) Thesco flour
2 C. whole wheat flour

$\frac{1}{2}$ C. milk
$\frac{1}{2}$ C. brown sugar
$\frac{1}{2}$ C. vegetable oil
4 t. salt

Dissolve yeast in warm water. Add white sugar, salt and wheat flour. Stir till thoroughly mixed. Add only 1 C. of Thesco flour, cover and let rise till light and bubbly. Approximately $\frac{1}{2}$ - 1 hour. Meanwhile dissolve brown sugar with $\frac{1}{2}$ C. milk warmed. Milk and sugar mixture will get curdly if mixed too hot. Add the oil. Add this to the first mixture after it is light and bubbly. Add rest of flour 1 C. at a time and work well with hands. Do not add too much flour. Just add enough so you can form a ball and the dough does not stick to your hands. Pour a little oil over the dough. Cover and let rise in a warm place until double. Punch down dough and cut into 4 equal parts. Work into balls and let set for 5 minutes. Roll out and shape into loaves. Bake at 325° for 35 to 40 minutes. Yield: 4 loaves. Or you can make 2 large loaves baking for 50 - 55 minutes.

WHOLE WHEAT BREAD

Mrs. Aaron Coblentz

2 C. warm water
1 T. yeast
1 T. salt
1 T. sugar
2 C. whole wheat flour
$\frac{1}{4}$ C. oat bran

$\frac{1}{2}$ C. milk
$\frac{1}{2}$ C. vegetable oil
$\frac{1}{2}$ C. honey or brown sugar
1 T. lecithin
6 C. Thesco flour

Mix water, yeast, salt and sugar until dissolved, add whole wheat flour and oat bran. Keep in warm place for 1 hour. Heat milk to scalding, cool to warm. If using sugar, add sugar to milk, add to flour mixture, add lecithin and oil. Then knead in flour 1 C. at a time. Cover and let rise till double in size. Punch down cut into 4 equal parts, and work it a little. Let rest 5 to 10 minutes, shape and let rise in warm place. Bake at 300° for 45 minutes.

WHOLE WHEAT BREAD

Mrs. Ben Troyer, Jr.

$\frac{2}{3}$ C. white sugar
$\frac{2}{3}$ C. brown sugar
2 T. salt
$\frac{1}{2}$ C. flour
2 C. boiling water

4 C. cold water
4 T. yeast
16 C. flour
   (some wheat flour)
$1\frac{1}{2}$ C. cooking oil

Mix sugar, salt and flour. Pour hot water over mixture, stir well. Add cold water and yeast. Let stand till foamy. Add 4 C. whole wheat and rest of white flour. Add oil, let rise once, work out dough, put in pans and let rise till double in size. Makes 8 large loaves. Bake at 300° for 30 minutes.

WHOLE WHEAT BREAD   Deborah Troyer

2½ C. milk   1½ t. salt
¼ C. oil   2 T. dry yeast
1 egg   3 C. whole wheat flour
½ C. molasses   approx. 4 C. unbleached flour

Heat the milk until it is warm and pour it into a large mixing bowl. Add the yeast
and stir till it is dissolved, then add oil, egg, molasses, salt and all of the whole
wheat flour. Beat for 2 or 3 minutes with mixer or egg beater. Add enough of
the unbleached flour to make a soft dough, knead the dough adding flour as
necessary till dough is smooth and elastic. Let rise till double in size. Shape
into 3 loaves and place into pans to rise again until nearly double. Bake at 375°
for about 30 minutes.

WHEAT BREAD   Mrs. Roman Coblentz

2 T. yeast   ¾ C. honey
¾ qt. warm water   4 C. whole wheat flour
¾ C. oil

Mix first 5 ingredients and let set for 20 minutes. Then add enough Sapphire flour
to make a soft dough. Knead and let rise twice. Bake at 350° for 30 minutes.

WHOLE WHEAT BREAD   Mrs. Josiah Miller

3 C. warm water   ¾ C. honey
2 T. yeast   1 T. salt
¾ C. lard   7 – 8 C. flour
                                       (2 C. whole wheat)

Dissolve yeast in water, add lard, honey, salt, and wheat flour. Let set for ½
hour. Add rest of flour and knead well. Let rise till double and put in pans. Bake
at 300° for 30 - 35 minutes. Makes 3 loaves.

WHITE BREAD   Mrs. James Troyer

4 C. warm water   ½ C. vegetable oil
2 t. salt   2 T. yeast
½ C. white sugar   enough flour so
                                       you can handle the dough

Put water in large bowl, add salt, sugar and oil. Then stir in about 3 C. flour.
Next add yeast then add more flour to make a soft but not sticky dough. Let rise
twice in the bowl and also once in the pans. Bake at 350° for 30 minutes.

FRENCH BREAD

Mrs. Moses S. Miller

2 T. white sugar
2 t. salt

2 T. shortening

Pour 2 C. boiling water over above ingredients then cool. Dissolve 2 pkg. dry yeast and 1 T. sugar in ½ C. warm water. Add to shortening mixture. Add 2½ C. flour and beat until smooth. Add approximately 4 more C. of flour. Punch down 4 or 5 times every 10 minutes. Divide in half and roll out to ½" thickness. Roll up tightly like a jelly roll. Seal the ends. Place on cookie sheet and slash tops ¼" deep. Let rise, brush with a mixture of 1 egg and 1 T. milk beaten. Bake at 400° for 10 minutes then reduce heat to 350° and bake another 20 minutes.

OATMEAL BREAD

Mrs. Henry Beachy

2 C. boiling water
1 C. quick oats
½ C. whole wheat flour

½ C. brown sugar
1 T. salt
2 T. butter

Pour 2 C. boiling water over rest of ingredients. Mix together and let set until lukewarm. Dissolve 1 T. yeast in ½ C. warm water, add to batter. Add Robin Hood flour until thick enough to knead, using enough to make a smooth and elastic dough, about 5 C. Place in greased bowl and let rise till double in bulk. Shape into loaves and place into greased loaf pans, 5" x 9" x 3". Let rise until nicely rounded in pan. Bake at 350° for about 30 minutes. Bread is done when a dull sound is heard when loaf is tapped lightly. Makes 2 loaves.

RAISIN BREAD

Mrs. Henry Beachy

2 T. yeast
1½ C. warm water
1½ C. boiling water
1½ C. raisins
1 C. oatmeal

½ C. light Karo
2 t. salt
2 T. shortening
7½ C. Robin Hood flour

Mix 2 T. yeast and warm water, let set. Mix 1½ C. boiling water, raisins, oatmeal and shortening, let set till cool. Add Karo and salt. Mix all together and add flour. Let rise then punch down, put in 2 loaf pans, let set 1 hour. Bake at 350° for 30 minutes.

ح

The measure of a man's real character is
what he would do if he knew he'd never be found out.

SOUR CREAM CORN BREAD

Mary A. Kaufman

³/₄ C. cornmeal
1 t. cream of tartar
2¹/₂ t. sugar
1 egg well beaten
1 C. thick sour cream

1 C. flour
1 t. soda
1 t. salt
2 t. melted butter
4 t. milk

Sift flour, cornmeal, soda, cream of tartar, salt and sugar add beaten egg, cream, milk and melted butter. Beat thoroughly. Pour into greased 9" square pan. Bake at 400° for 20 minutes.

WHEAT CHEX BREAD

Mrs. Eli A. Mast

2 C. milk
3 C. water
4 C. Wheat Chex
¹/₂ C. sugar

¹/₂ C. shortening
9 C. flour
4 t. salt
2 T. yeast

Heat milk and 2¹/₂ C. water to boiling. Pour over Wheat Chex, salt, sugar and shortening. Cool till lukewarm. Then add ¹/₂ C. water and 2 T. yeast last. Makes 4 loaves. Bake at 350° for 30 minutes.

ZUCCHINI BREAD

Melva Schrock

1 C. oil
2 C. sugar
3 eggs (1 at a time)
1 t. salt
1 t. cinnamon
2 t. vanilla

1 t. soda
1 t. baking powder
3 C. flour
2 C. zucchini
  grated fine

Mix and bake at 350° for approximately 45 minutes.

❧

There is no sense in advertising your troubles.
There's no market for them.

FAVORITE GRAPENUTS

Mrs. Ray N. Troyer

2¹/₂ lbs. brown sugar
4 lbs. whole wheat flour
³/₄ T. salt
1 T. soda

1¹/₂ sticks oleo (melted)
³/₄ t. maple flavoring
1 T. vanilla
1¹/₄ qt. buttermilk
or sour milk

Put dry ingredients in a bowl, except for soda which should be added to buttermilk before adding to dry ingredients. Last add oleo and flavorings. Put in 2 big cookie sheets and bake at 325°. Cut and cool, put through Salad Master and dry in oven.

GRAPENUTS

Mrs. Wally Detweiler

8 C. whole wheat flour
4 C. brown sugar
2 T. salt
3¹/₃ C. sour milk or buttermilk

1 stick oleo melted
¹/₂ t. maple flavoring
1 T. vanilla
1 T. soda

Mix dry ingredients together. Mix soda in milk, add to dry ingredients. Add butter and flavorings, mix well. Spread in 2 greased 9" x 13" pans. Bake at 350° till done. Cool, cut in strips and put through Salad Master (shoestrings). Toast at 300° in shallow pans till golden brown, stirring often.

GRAPENUTS

Mrs. Levi Miller

4 C. brown sugar
8 C. whole wheat flour
1 t. salt
4 t. soda

³/₄ C. vegetable oil
4 C. milk
1¹/₄ t. maple flavoring
vanilla

Bake 45 minutes at 350°. This fills 2 - 9" x 13" pans. Cut in large pieces and grate when cooled. Layer crumbs in pan (shallow layer at a time) and toast till crisp.

GRAPENUTS

Mrs. David Ray Yoder

7 C. wheat flour
3 C. brown sugar
2 t. salt
4 t. soda
1 t. maple flavoring

2 C. wheat germ
4 C. buttermilk
1 C. melted oleo
1 t. vanilla

Mix ingredients and spread on greased baking sheets. Bake at 325° for 40 minutes. Cool then grind cake using the shredder cone on the Salad Master. Spread on cookie sheets and toast in 250° oven till dry.

GRANOLA

Mrs. Marion Miller

1½ C. butter or oleo (or a little of both)
3¼ C. brown sugar   2 t. salt
Combine and heat to boiling, pour over:
4 C. coconut   14 C. oatmeal

Mix until crumbly and bake at 250° until golden brown 2½ to 3 hours.

GRANOLA

Mrs. Josiah Miller

6 C. rolled oats   1 C. oil
2 C. wheat germ   1 C. honey
1 C. coconut   4 t. vanilla
1 C. chopped nuts

Mix dry ingredients in large bowl. Mix oil, honey and vanilla and pour over dry mixture. Bake at 275° for 1 hour, stirring every 15 minutes. I like to sprinkle chocolate chips on top while still warm. A yummy breakfast!

GRANOLA

Mrs. Paul Mast

3 C. brown sugar   1 C. vegetable oil or
6 C. wheat germ   melted butter
12 C. oatmeal   1½ t. salt
3 T. vanilla or maple flavoring   6 C. coconut

Mix everything together and toast in oven until coconut is brown. Sunflower seeds and mini chocolate chips may also be added once cereal is cooled.

HOMEMADE GRANOLA

Mrs. Roman Coblentz

6 C. oatmeal   3 C. nuts
3 C. brown sugar   1 C. melted oleo
3 C. wheat germ   3 C. coconut

Mix all together and toast in oven for 1 hour at 275°.

&

You give but little when you give of your possessions.
It is when you give of yourself that you truly give.

GRANOLA CEREAL

Mrs. Crist Beachy

6 C. quick oatmeal
4 C. whole wheat flour
2 C. brown sugar
1 C. coconut, optional

2 t. salt
1^1/$_2$ t. soda
1^1/$_2$ C. melted butter
1 C. chocolate chips

Mix dry ingredients together, add melted butter and mix well. Place on 2 cake pans and toast in oven at 400°, stirring every 5 - 10 minutes. Add chocolate chips after slightly cooled.

GRANOLA

Mrs. Willis Priscilla Miller

15 C. old fashioned oatmeal
3 C. wheat germ
3 C. coconut
2 C. brown sugar

^{3}/$_4$ C. vegetable oil
^{3}/$_4$ C. honey
3 t. vanilla
1^1/$_2$ t. salt

Mix dry ingredients. Stir together oil, honey, and vanilla, mix into dry ingredients. Rub together with hands until evenly mixed. Pour into shallow pans and toast at 300° until golden brown. About 1 hour. Stir often as it can burn easily, cool.

BREAKFAST CEREAL

Mrs. Jay Miller

1^1/$_2$ C. brown sugar
8 C. oatmeal
4 C. whole wheat flour
2 t. salt

3 t. soda
2^1/$_2$ C. melted butter
4 C. coconut
2 pkgs. graham crackers
crushed

Mix all together, bake at 250° for 45 minutes. Stir often. Right after taking from oven add 1 lb. chocolate chips and 1 lb. butterscotch chips. This cereal can be eaten on top of other cereals such as Bran Flakes.

FRIED OAT CEREAL

Mrs. David Schlabach

3 C. oatmeal
^{1}/$_2$ C. butter
^{1}/$_2$ C. brown sugar
^{1}/$_2$ t. vanilla
pinch of salt

Any of these may be added:
^{1}/$_2$ C. nuts
^{1}/$_2$ C. coconut
^{1}/$_2$ C. wheat germ
^{1}/$_2$ C. dried fruit

Fry in skillet stirring constantly until golden brown.

GRAHAM CEREAL

Anna Fern Troyer

2 C. sugar
4 C. graham flour (sifted)
1 t. soda
1 t. vanilla
1 t. salt

2 C. flour
1 C. shortening
1 t. baking powder
1 C. milk

Mix ingredients and roll out thin on 2 cookie sheets. Prick with fork. Bake at 350° till brown. Cut in small squares while still warm.

BAKED OATMEAL

Mary Miller
Mrs. Nathan Miller

1 C. brown sugar
1/2 C. melted butter
2 eggs beaten
3 C. oatmeal

2 t. baking powder
1 t. salt
1 C. milk

Stir together, bake at 350° for 30 minutes. Delicious with fruit or milk. Serves 7.

BAKING POWDER BISCUITS

Mrs. Joe Miller, Jr.

2 C. all-purpose flour
3 t. baking powder
1/2 t. salt

1/4 C. shortening
2/3 – 3/4 C. milk

Stir dry ingredients in a bowl. Cut in shortening till it forms coarse crumbs. Make a well; add milk all at one time, stir quickly with fork, just till dough follows fork around the bowl. Knead gently 10 – 12 strokes. Pat dough to 1/2" thick. Cut. If you use this recipe for drop biscuits increase milk to 1 C. Bake at 450°. Makes 16.

BISCUIT MIX

Mary A. Kaufman

8 C. flour
1/3 C. baking powder
8 t. sugar
2 t. cream of tartar

2 t. salt
1 C. powdered milk
1 3/4 C. shortening

Sift dry ingredients and cut in shortening. Bake at 450° for 10 – 12 minutes. Pack coarsely into airtight container. When ready to serve use 1 C. mix to 1/3 C. water. Powdered milk may be omitted, when ready to mix you can use milk instead of water.

BUTTERMILK BISCUITS

Janice Schlabach

2 C. flour
2 1/4 t. baking powder
1 t. salt

1/4 t. soda
6 level T. shortening
3/4 C. buttermilk

Sift flour, baking powder, salt and soda together. Cut in shortening with pastry blender. Add buttermilk. Form into balls. Bake at 450° for 12 – 15 minutes. Makes 20 small biscuits.

BISQUICK BISCUITS

Mrs. Charles Karn

2 C. flour
4 t. baking powder
2 t. sugar
1/2 t. cream of tartar

1/2 t. salt
1/2 C. margarine
2/3 C. milk

Mix first 5 ingredients. Cut in margarine. Add milk. Drop by tablespoons onto greased cookie sheet. Bake at 375° till golden brown.

EMERGENCY BISCUITS

Mrs. Crist Beachy

2 C. flour
1 t. salt
4 t. baking powder

4 T. shortening
1 C. milk

Mix first four ingredients well. Add milk and stir. Drop on cookie sheet. Bake at 350° until well done, 15 – 20 minutes. Make 10 – 12 biscuits.

OATMEAL DROP BISCUITS

Sarah Ann Kaufman

1 C. all-purpose flour
1 C. quick oats
1/2 t. salt
1/2 C. shortening
1 beaten egg

1/3 C. milk
1 T. baking powder
2 T. honey

Stir thoroughly till mixture resembles coarse crumbs. Stir in oats, combine eggs, milk and honey add all at one time to the dry mixture. Drop by spoonfuls onto greased baking sheet. Bake for 8 – 10 minutes. This dough is also good for apple dumplings.

‏❧

Swallow your pride occasionally. It's not fattening!

BUTTERMILK OATMEAL MUFFINS

Sarah Ann Kaufman

1 C. rolled oats
1 C. whole wheat flour
1 C. buttermilk
$1/2$ t. soda

1 egg
$1/3$ C. oil
$1/4$ C. warm honey

Soak oats in buttermilk for $1/2$ hour, put egg into oat mixture add honey and mix well. Stir together flour, salt and soda. Stir into first mixture, add oil and mix until blended. Bake at 425° for 15 – 20 minutes.

CORNMEAL MUFFINS

Mrs. Reuben Miller

1 C. cornmeal
1 C. flour
4 t. baking powder
$1/2$ t. salt

2 T. brown sugar
2 beaten eggs
1 C. milk
$1/4$ C. oil

Mix dry ingredients. Make a well and add liquids. Stir just until smooth. Pour into greased muffin tins. Bake at 400°. Makes 16 muffins.

BRAN MUFFINS

Melva Schrock

2 C. All Bran
2 C. boiling water
1 C. shortening
$2^1/2$ C. white sugar
4 eggs
1 qt. buttermilk

2 t. soda
1 t. salt
5 C. flour
4 C. Bran Buds
1 lb. raisins
nuts, optional

Combine all ingredients. Can be stored in refrigerator for 2 – 3 weeks. They are better after dough has set for a few days. Bake at 350° for 20 minutes or until done.

APPLESAUCE RHUBARB MUFFINS

Mrs. Alfred Miller

2 C. flour
1 C. whole wheat flour
2 t. baking powder
2 t. cinnamon
$1/2$ t. soda
$1/2$ t. salt

2 eggs
$1^1/3$ C. brown sugar
  (packed)
$1^1/2$ C. applesauce
$1/2$ C. cooking oil
$1^1/2$ C. chopped rhubarb

Mix together. When ready to bake, squeeze 2 or 3 T. soft sweetened cream cheese into the middle of each muffin.

MORNING GLORY MUFFINS

Mrs. Alfred Miller

Combine:
2 C. flour
2 t. baking soda
1 1/4 C. sugar
2 t. cinnamon
1/2 t. salt

Add:
2 C. shredded carrots
1/2 C. raisins
1/2 C. coconut
1/2 C. pecans

Blend and add to other ingredients:
3 eggs
1 C. oil

2 t. vanilla

Stir in 1 grated apple. Spoon into muffin tin lined with cupcake liners. Bake at 350° for 15 – 18 minutes. Makes 18.

CHOCOLATE CHIP BANANA MUFFINS

Mrs. Alfred Miller

Mix together in small bowl and set aside:
2 1/2 C. flour
1 t. baking powder

1/2 t. soda
1/2 t. salt

In another bowl mix the following:
1 T. instant coffee granules

1 T. hot water

Dissolve then add:
3 mashed bananas

Cream the following till fluffy:
1 C. softened butter
1 1/4 C. sugar

1 egg

Add banana mixture to the butter/sugar mixture, add flour mixture and stir until well blended. Add 1 C. miniature chocolate chips. Bake in mini muffin pans at 350° until done.

BLUEBERRY MUFFINS

Mrs. Crist Miller

2 T. butter or margarine
2/3 C. sugar
1/2 C. milk
1 egg

1/8 t. salt
1 1/2 C. flour
1 t. baking powder
1 C. blueberries

Cream butter, sugar and egg, add milk, then add dry ingredients. Fold in blueberries. Sprinkle a little sugar on top. Bake at 350° for about 30 minutes. Use fresh or frozen blueberries.

BLUEBERRY SOUR CREAM STREUSEL MUFFINS

Mrs. Robert Miller

2 C. sifted all-purpose flour
2 t. baking powder
1/2 t. soda
1/2 t. salt
3 T. sugar
1 egg well beaten
1 C. sour cream
1/3 C. milk

1/4 C. vegetable oil
1 1/2 C. blueberries
1/2 C. brown sugar
  (firmly packed)
1/4 C. all-purpose flour
1 t. ground cinnamon
3 T. butter or margarine

Sift 2 C. flour with baking powder, soda, salt, and sugar. Beat egg with sour cream and milk. Stir in oil. Add liquids all at one time to dry ingredients. Stir only until blended. Carefully fold in blueberries. Spoon mixture into greased muffin pans. Mix brown sugar with 1/4 C. flour and cinnamon. Cut butter into mixture until crumbly. Sprinkle crumbs over top of muffins. Bake at 425° for 15 to 25 minutes or until topping is a deep brown. Remove and cool on a rack. Serve warm or cold. Yields 10 - 12 muffins.

BLUEBERRY-ORANGE MUFFINS

Larua K. Miller

1 C. oatmeal
1 C. orange juice
3 C. flour
4 t. baking powder
1 t. salt

1/2 t. baking soda
1 C. sugar
1 C. oil
3 beaten eggs
2 - 3 C. blueberries

Mix oatmeal and orange juice. Combine with the rest of the ingredients, add blueberries last. Sprinkle sugar and cinnamon on top and bake at 400° for 15 minutes or until done.

BUTTERHORNS

Maria Miller

1 T. yeast with 1 t. sugar
1 C. lukewarm water
1/2 t. salt
1/2 C. sugar

1 stick melted butter or oleo
3 beaten eggs
4 1/2 C. flour

Mix and let rise in refrigerator overnight, divide into 3 parts, roll out like a pie. Then cut into 8 pie shaped pieces, roll each piece from wide end to narrow end. Let rise and bake.

WHOLE WHEAT BUTTERHORNS

Mrs. Robert J. Yoder

2¾ C. all-purpose flour (divided)
2 T. dry yeast
1¾ C. water
⅓ C. packed brown sugar

½ C. butter or oleo (divided)
2 T. honey
2 t. salt
2 C. whole wheat flour

In a large mixing bowl, combine 1½ C. flour and yeast. Heat water, brown sugar, 3 T. butter, honey and salt to 120 - 130° add to flour mixture. Mix well. Stir in wheat flour and remaining all-purpose flour to form a soft dough. Turn out onto a lightly floured surface and knead until smooth and elastic, about 6 - 8 minutes. Place in greased bowl and let rise until double, about 1½ hours. Punch dough down and divide into thirds. Shape each into a ball and cover, let rest for 10 minutes. On lightly floured surface roll balls into 12" circles. Cut each circle into 6 - 8 wedges. Roll wedges into crescent shapes. Place on greased baking sheets. Let rise. Bake at 400° for 10 - 15 minutes or until golden brown. Brush with butter while still hot. Yields 18 - 24 rolls.

GOLDEN CRESCENTS

Mrs. Nathan Miller

2 T. active dry yeast
¾ C. warm water
½ C. sugar
1 t. salt

2 eggs
½ C. oleo or butter (soft)
3 - 4 C. flour

Dissolve yeast in warm water. Stir in sugar, salt, eggs, butter and 2 C. of flour till easy to handle. Knead. Cover and let rise until double, about 1½ hour. Divide dough into half, roll each into a 12" circle, spread with butter. Cut into 16 wedges. Roll up each wedge beginning at rounded end. Place on cookie sheet with pointed edge under cover. Cover and let rise till double. Bake at 350° for 12 - 15 minutes. Brush with butter. I also use this recipe for pizza dough.

BREAKFAST PUFFS

Twila Beachy

⅓ C. soft shortening
1 C. sugar
1 egg
1½ C. flour
1½ t. baking powder

½ t. salt
¼ t. nutmeg
½ C. milk
6 T. melted butter
1 T. cinnamon

Mix shortening, ½ C. sugar and egg. Sift flour, baking powder, salt and nutmeg together. Stir in shortening mixture alternately with milk. Fill greased muffin tins ⅔ full. Bake at 350° for 20 - 25 minutes or until golden brown. Immediately roll in butter, then in mixture of ½ C. sugar and 1 T. cinnamon. 12 servings.

PLUCKETS

Mrs. Mike Schrock

1 cake yeast dissolved in 1/4 C. lukewarm water
1 C. scalded milk   3 eggs well beaten
1/3 C. sugar   4 C. flour
1/3 C. melted butter   1/2 t. salt

Add sugar and salt to scalded milk. When lukewarm add dissolved yeast, eggs and flour. Beat thoroughly. Cover and let rise till double. Stir down and let rise again until double. Roll small ball the size of walnuts and dip them into 1/4 C. melted butter. Then roll balls into mixture of 3/4 C. white sugar, 1/2 C. nuts and 3 t. cinnamon. Pile balls loosely in ungreased angel food cake pan, and let rise 30 minutes. Bake at 400° for 10 minutes, then at 300° for 30 minutes. Remove from oven and turn pan upsidedown. Serve warm or hot.

SANDWICH BUNS

Mrs. Henry Beachy

1/2 C. white sugar   1/2 C. cooking oil
1 T. salt
Mix together then add:
2 beaten eggs   1 C. water
2 T. yeast   7 C. flour
1 C. warm milk   (Thesco or Robin Hood)

Mix yeast milk and water, let set for 10 minutes add first part, then add flour. Let rise once. Makes 2 1/4 doz. buns. Bake at 350° for 20 minutes.

DUTCH DINNER ROLLS

Mrs. Phillip Troyer

2 C. hot water   1/4 C. water
1/2 C. sugar   1 t. sugar
1/4 C. oleo   2 eggs beaten
1 T. salt   7 C. flour
2 T. yeast

Combine water, sugar, oleo and salt. Cool to lukewarm. Combine yeast, water and sugar, let rise. Add yeast and eggs to first mixture, add 4 C. flour, beat well. Add 3 more C. of flour. Let rise until double then punch down. Let rise again then shape into rolls. Let rise. Bake at 350° until golden brown.

OVERNIGHT CINNAMON ROLLS

Mrs. David Ray Yoder

2 eggs beaten
⅓ C. white sugar
½ t. salt
1 T. yeast, dissolved in ¼ C. warm water

1 C. milk, scalded
1 stick butter and oleo
   (melted)

Pour scalded milk over sugar, salt and butter in mixing bowl. Stir till butter is melted, add beaten eggs and dissolved yeast. Add 3½ C. Robin Hood flour. Mix well. Cover and refrigerate overnight. Roll out cold dough and spread with melted butter, sprinkle with cinnamon/sugar mixture. Roll up, slice and place in a greased baking pan, let rise. Bake at 325° for 15 - 20 minutes or until lightly brown. Ice with brown sugar icing before completely cool.

FRUIT FILLED BRAIDED ROLLS

Mrs. Roy Mast

Use standard roll recipe, using about 6 C. flour. Let rise and divide dough into half. Roll out each half into 8" x 16". Spread butter, cinnamon and brown sugar through the center third of each piece.Top with your favorite pie filling. Cut about 12 slits into dough along each side of filling. Making strips about 1" wide. Fold strips at an angle across filling, one side then the other. Let rise. Bake at 350°. Drizzle with icing.

CREAMSTICKS

Mrs. Henry Beachy

2 pkg. yeast
1 C. lukewarm water
1 C. milk
½ C. margarine or butter
⅔ C. sugar

2 eggs
½ t. salt
6 C. Robin Hood flour
1 t. vanilla

Dissolve yeast in warm water. Scald milk, then put your oleo in hot milk to melt. Put sugar into milk and butter mixture. When cooled enough, add yeast, well beaten eggs and vanilla. Add 6 C. flour. Set in warm place till double in bulk. Roll out and cut into pieces about 1½" wide and 3½" long. Let rise again.

Filling:
Cook 3 rounded t. flour in 1 C. milk, until thickened. Let cool. Cream 1 C. Crisco and 1 C. powdered sugar until creamy. Add to flour mixture when cooled. Add 1 t. vanilla and powdered sugar, cream well. Cut top of creamsticks open and fill. Frost with caramel frosting. (See page 195 for brown sugar or caramel frosting.)

ε❧

With every rising of the sun, think of your life as just begun.

DONUTS
Mrs. Henry Beachy

10 lbs. donut mix
10 C. warm water
$1/2$ C. yeast

$1/2$ C. white sugar
1 lb. bread flour

Mix water, yeast, sugar, let set for 10 minutes. Add donut mix and flour. Roll out and cut with donut cutter. Fry.

Glaze:
2 lb. powdered sugar
1 t. vanilla

2 T. cornstarch
enough water to mix

EASY CAKE MIX ROLLS
Mrs. Steve Engbretson

2 T. yeast
1 box yellow cake mix

$4^1/2$ C. flour
$2^1/2$ C. warm water

Soak yeast in warm water. Add cake mix and flour to this. Let rise. Roll out dough and spread with butter, cinnamon and brown sugar. Roll up and cut off pieces. Let rise. Bake at 350° until done.

PIZZA DOUGH
Mrs. Crist Beachy

1 T. dry yeast
1 C. warm water
3 C. flour

1 t. sugar
$1^1/2$ t. salt
$1/4$ C. oil

Dissolve yeast in water, add sugar, salt, oil. Add half of flour and beat, then add rest of flour. Knead 5 minutes. Pat dough in a greased cookie sheet. Add your favorite pizza toppings, and bake at 425° for 20 - 25 minutes.

FAST PIZZA DOUGH
Mrs. Henry Beachy

1 T. yeast
1 C. warm water
1 t. salt

1 t. sugar
2 T. vegetable oil
$2^1/2$ C. Thesco flour

Dissolve yeast and sugar in water. Stir in remaining ingredients and beat vigorously. Let rise 5 minutes. Roll out dough. Place in greased pizza pan, let set 30 minutes, add toppings. Bake at 375° for 20 minutes.

PIZZA DOUGH

Mrs. James Troyer

1 C. milk
1/4 C. sugar
4 T. butter
1 t. salt

1 beaten egg
1 T. yeast
approx. 3 1/2 C. flour

Heat the milk, then pour over butter, sugar and salt. When butter is all melted add beaten egg, yeast and enough flour so you can handle the dough. Let rise for 1 hour. Bake at 400° for 20 minutes.

PIZZA CRUST

Mrs. Wyman Wengerd

2 T. yeast
2 C. warm water
2 t. salt
1/2 C. oil

2 t. sugar
1 C. whole wheat flour
4 C. bread flour

Mix yeast and water until yeast is dissolved, then add remaining ingredients. Bake at 350° for 15 minutes or until golden brown. Makes 2 large crusts.

PIZZA CRUST

Mrs. Marvin Wengerd

1 C. warm water
1 T. yeast
1 t. sugar
1 t. salt

2 T. oil
1 1/4 C. white flour
3/4 C. graham flour
(or cornmeal)

Dissolve yeast in warm water, add sugar, salt and oil. Stir in white flour and graham flour or cornmeal. Let rise in warm place till double. Punch down. Grease one round 20" pizza pan. Spread dough with greased spatula, then top with sauce and toppings. Bake at 350° for 30 minutes or bake 20 minutes to freeze.

ITALIAN BREADSTICKS

Mrs. Marcus Mast

Combine, stirring until dissolved:
1 T. dry yeast
2/3 C. warm water
Add, mixing well:
1 t. salt
1/4 C. oil

1 T. white sugar

1 1/2 T. onion soup mix

Gradually add 2 C. bread flour, beating well. Knead slightly.

Sesame seeds to coat. Grease top and place in greased bowl. Cover and let rise till double. Roll out and cut into strips. Approximately 4" in length. Press in sesame seeds and place on greased baking sheet. Let set 15 minutes. Bake at 350° for about 12 minutes.

~ Just A Housewife ~

They call me "just a housewife"
    and I'm glad to bear the name,

You will never see me listed in the
    "Honor Roll of Fame";

Career women look with pity
    at my apron, broom and mop,

But I wouldn't trade them places
    for the things their money bought!

They call me "just a housewife",
    and I'm surely glad indeed

That God thought I would be useful
    in this work of love and need;

As I wash the floors and windows,
    stylish ladies pity me,

But I wouldn't trade them places,
    if their mansions were all free!

Some folks are quite successful,
    Kings of Finance so they say,

And they seem to find their glory,
    gathering gold along the way;

Let them have their golden moments,
    I'm not jealous of their life,

Tho' I may work hard at trying to be
    a more considerate wife.

Yes, they call me "just a housewife",
    but I'm more, much more you see,

I am a keeper of a household which is
    "Home, Sweet Home" to me;

I am rich in love and loved ones,
    I work hard in this old life.

I'm so glad God thought me useful,
    being "just a plain housewife!"

- Notes -

Soups, Salads
& Salad Dressings

BROCCOLI SOUP

Mrs. Willis Karen Miller

10 oz. frozen or
  1 bunch chopped cooked broccoli
6 T. butter
1 T. chopped onion
³/₄ t. salt

dash of pepper
5 heaping T. flour
2 C. milk
2 C. chicken broth or 1 T.
  chicken bouillon + 2 C. water

Mix and simmer, then add 1 can cream of celery or chicken soup and a few slices of Velveeta cheese. Can also add 1 C. cooked carrots and potatoes.

BROCCOLI SOUP

Twila Beachy

6 C. water
8 oz. narrow noodles (broken)
2 pkgs. chopped broccoli
1 large carrot, grated

2 large onions, chopped
5 chicken bouillon cubes
1 T. oil

Cook till vegetables are tender. Melt 1 lb. Velveeta cheese in milk, add remaining ingredients. Don't overcook.

BROCCOLI CHEESE SOUP

Mrs. Ella Miller

1 small can chicken broth
10 oz. broccoli
4 T. flour
¹/₂ t. salt and pepper
1 C. Velveeta cheese

2 bouillon cubes
3 med. chopped onions
3 T. oleo
2¹/₄ C. milk
1 C. mashed potatoes

Simmer broth, bouillon cubes and broccoli until tender. Use as much broccoli as desired. Simmer onions, flour, oleo, salt and pepper in large saucepan. Stir until thick. Add milk and Velveeta cheese. Add broth and broccoli to mixture then add mashed potatoes. (The more mashed potatoes you add the better.)

CHEESE SOUP

Mrs. Ivan Miller
Mrs. Robert Miller

1 qt. water + 4 bouillon cubes or
1 qt. chicken broth
1 med. onion, diced
1 C. celery

2¹/₂ C. potatoes
10 - 20 oz. mixed vegetables
2 cans cream of chicken soup
1 lb. Velveeta cheese

In saucepan cook together water or broth, onion and celery for 10 minutes. Add potatoes and cook until soft. Add soup and cheese. Thicken with water and clear jel if desired.

CHEESY CHICKEN CHOWDER

Mrs. Mark Hochstetler

3 C. chicken broth
2 C. diced peeled potatoes
1 C. diced carrots
1 C. diced celery
1/2 C. diced onion
1 1/2 t. salt

1/4 t. pepper
1/4 C. butter or margarine
1/3 C. all-purpose flour
2 C. milk
2 C. shredded Cheddar cheese
2 C. diced cooked chicken

In 4 qt. saucepan bring broth to a boil. Reduce heat, add potatoes, carrots, celery, onion, salt and pepper. Cover and simmer for 15 minutes or until vegetables are tender. Meanwhile melt butter in a medium saucepan add flour and mix well. Gradually stir in milk. Cook over low heat until slightly thickened. Stir in cheese and cook until melted. Add to broth along with chicken. Cook and stir over low heat until heated through.

CHICKEN CHOWDER

Mrs. Henry Schrock

2 C. chicken broth
2 C. chicken diced
1 C. milk
10 oz. mixed vegetables
1 sm. onion, chopped

1 t. chicken soup base
8 oz. Velveeta cheese
2 T. oleo
1/2 C. flour

Cook vegetables in broth, add soup base, chicken and milk. Heat to boiling. Sauté onion in oleo, add flour blend and add to soup. Simmer until thickened then add cheese, let melt and serve.

COUNTRY POTATO SOUP

Mrs. Dean Wengerd

3 C. diced, pared potatoes
1/2 C. carrots
1/2 C. onion
1 1/2 C. water
2 chicken bouillon cubes

1 t. chopped chives
1/2 t. salt
1 C. sour cream
2 T. flour
2 C. milk

Combine potatoes, carrots, onion, water, bouillon cubes and salt in large saucepan. Cover and cook for about 20 minutes or until potatoes are tender but not mushy. Add 1 C. milk, heat. Mix sour cream, flour, chives and remaining milk in medium bowl. Stir mixture into soup base gradually. Cook over low heat stirring constantly until thickened. Add a little Velveeta cheese for extra flavor.

CREAM OF MUSHROOM SOUP

Mrs. Henry Schrock

3 T. butter
2 T. flour
$\frac{1}{8}$ t. pepper
1 t. salt
2 C. half and half milk

2 C. chicken broth
1 C. finely chopped and
sautéed mushrooms
$\frac{1}{4}$ t. paprika
$\frac{1}{2}$ t. onion salt

Melt butter over low heat in heavy saucepan, blend in flour, pepper and salt. Remove from heat and stir in half and half milk and chicken broth. Bring to a boil and cook for 1 minute. Add mushrooms, paprika, onion salt and bring just to a boil. Serve.

HAM CHOWDER

Mrs. Jay Mark Martha Miller

$\frac{1}{4}$ C. butter
$\frac{1}{3}$ C. minced onion
$\frac{3}{4}$ C. diced ham
$\frac{1}{2}$ C. finely chopped celery
$1\frac{1}{2}$ C. diced raw potatoes

$1\frac{1}{2}$ t. salt
$\frac{1}{4}$ t. black pepper
3 T. flour
$4\frac{1}{2}$ C. milk

Add onion, ham and celery to melted butter. Sauté until vegetables are tender. Add potatoes and cook over low heat for 10 minutes or until potatoes are tender. Stir in flour, salt and pepper. Add milk and cook over low heat for 15 minutes.

HAM CHOWDER SOUP

Mrs. Dan J. Yoder

$\frac{1}{4}$ C. butter
$\frac{1}{2}$ C. onion
$\frac{3}{4}$ C. ham, diced
$\frac{1}{2}$ C. celery
$1\frac{1}{2}$ C. potatoes

$1\frac{1}{2}$ t. salt
$\frac{1}{4}$ t. pepper
$4\frac{1}{2}$ C. milk
3 T. flour

Cook onion, celery and potatoes until tender. Melt butter, blend in flour then add milk. Mix all together.

TOMATO SOUP

Mrs. Crist Miller

1 qt. tomato juice
1 qt. milk
1 C. flour
$\frac{1}{4}$ t. baking soda

1 T. sugar
1 t. Lawry's seasoning salt
$\frac{1}{4}$ t. red pepper

Bring tomato juice to a boil and mix milk, flour, soda, sugar and seasonings, until no lumps remain. Slowly stir into tomatoes keep stirring until mixture comes to a boil, remove from stove right away. Do not put lid on tight if you let it set. Serve with crackers.

TACO SOUP

Mrs. Jay Mark Martha Miller
Mrs. Crist Beachy
Mrs. Jr. Wagler

1 - 2 lbs. hamburger, seasoned and fried
1 qt. water
1 qt. pizza sauce

1 can hot chili beans
1 pkg. taco seasoning mix

Simmer for 15 minutes. Serve with cheddar cheese, sour cream and taco chips. Yummy!

TACO SOUP

Mrs. David Ray Yoder

1 lb. ground beef
15 oz. chili beans
1 sm. onion chopped
1 pkg. taco seasoning mix

1½ qt. tomato juice
1 pt. corn
⅓ C. sugar

Brown ground beef and onion. Add tomato juice, corn, beans and taco seasoning, bring to a boil, then simmer for 15 - 20 minutes. Serve over crushed corn chips. Sprinkle with grated Cheddar cheese, and top with sour cream.

SPLIT PEA SOUP

Mrs. Henry Schrock
Mrs. Marion Miller

16 oz. split peas
3 qts. water
1 sm. ham shank
1 lg. onion
1 bay leaf
2 T. chicken soup base

½ t. garlic powder
½ t. oregano
¼ - ½ t. pepper
1½ C. carrots, shredded
1 C. diced celery

In large pot combine peas, water, ham shank, onion, soup base and seasonings. Simmer for 1½ hour. Remove ham shank from pot, and debone meat, return meat to the soup. Stir in carrots and celery. Simmer 2 hours more or until soup reaches desired thickness. Makes 9 cups.

BROCCOLI SALAD

Mrs. Mark Hochstetler
Mrs. Matthias Mast

1 head broccoli, cut up
1 head cauliflower, cut up
1/2 lb. bacon, fried and crumbled
1 C. shredded Cheddar cheese

1 C. mayonnaise
1 C. sour cream
1/2 C. sugar
1/2 t. salt

Mix together mayonnaise, sour cream, sugar and salt. Add to broccoli, cauliflower, bacon and cheese. Reserve a small amount of cheese and bacon to sprinkle on top.

COLE SLAW

Mrs. Linus Troyer

1 head cabbage
1 C. sugar
1/2 C. oil
1/3 C. vinegar
salt
pepper

carrots
sunflower seeds
cucumbers
onions
green peppers
garlic salt

Use salt, pepper and garlic salt to taste.

COLE SLAW

Mrs. Noah J. Hostetler

1 sm. head cabbage, shredded
1 sm. onion, chopped fine
1 green pepper, chopped
salt, pepper and celery seed

1/2 C. salad oil
1/2 C. vinegar
1 C. granulated sugar

Arrange cabbage, onion and green peppers in layers in a large bowl. Sprinkle each layer with salt, pepper and celery seed. Combine oil, vinegar and sugar in saucepan, bring to a boil. Pour this over cabbage mixture. Refrigerate overnight. Do not stir until morning. This will keep for several days in the refrigerator.

MACARONI SALAD

Mrs. Eli B. Yoder

1 lb. spiral macaroni, cooked
1 lg. pepper, diced
1 jar black olives, optional

1 pt. Wishbone Italian dressing
4 T. Salad Supreme
tomatoes, if desired

Let set for 3 - 4 hours.

POTATO SALAD DRESSING

Mrs. Willis Priscilla Miller

2 C. sugar
1/4 C. flour
2 t. salt
2 T. dry mustard
1/2 t. turmeric

2 C. milk
1 C. vinegar
1 qt. salad dressing
1 t. celery seed, optional
6 eggs

I like to add 1/2 jar of Marzetti Slaw dressing. Mix dry ingredients. Add beaten eggs. It is important to beat eggs before adding. Add vinegar and milk. Mix thoroughly. Cook over medium heat, stirring constantly. It sticks easily. When thick, remove from heat. Cool. Add salad dressing, mix well. Makes a little more than 1/2 gallon. Also good for slaw, macaroni, or tossed salad. Keeps well in refrigerator for 2 or 3 months.

POTATO SALAD

Mrs. Allen Beachy
Mrs. Martha Sue Miller

3 qts. cooked, shredded potatoes
1/4 C. celery

12 hard boiled eggs
onions, optional

Dressing:
3 C. Miracle Whip
1/4 C. vinegar
6 T. mustard

2 t. salt
2 1/2 C. white sugar

Cook potatoes in jackets then peel and shred. Mix all ingredients. Makes 1 gallon.

POTATO SALAD

Mrs. Dean Wengerd
Mrs. Henry Hershberger

12 C. shredded potatoes
12 boiled, mashed eggs

chopped onion, optional
1 - 2 C. chopped celery

Dressing:
3 C. Miracle Whip
6 T. mustard
1/2 C. milk

2 - 2 1/2 C. sugar
1/4 C. vinegar
1 1/2 - 2 t. salt

Pour dressing over potato egg mixture. May be made 24 hours in advance.

ROMANIAN TOMATO SALAD

Orpha Peachey

6 C. chopped tomatoes
1 C. chopped cucumbers
1 C. red or green peppers

1 C. onions
1 clove garlic

Salt, pepper, oil and vinegar to taste, no sugar was used.

ITALIAN STYLE MARINATED TOMATOES

Mrs. Henry Beachy

20 large tomatoes
1 C. vegetable oil
$^1/_2$ C. red wine vinegar
2 t. salt

1 t. basil
2 t. oregano
$^1/_2$ t. pepper
1 clove garlic

Place oil and remaining ingredients in a shaker except for tomatoes and shake until well blended. Pour dressing over tomatoes, toss gently to mix well. Cover and refrigerate at least 2 hours.

VEGETABLE PIZZA

Mrs. David Ray Yoder

Crust:

$^1/_4$ C. oleo
2 T. sugar
$^1/_4$ C. boiling water
1 T. active dry yeast

$^1/_4$ C. warm water
1 egg, beaten
$1^1/_2$ C. all-purpose flour
1 t. salt

Dressing:

8 oz. cream cheese
1 pkg. dry Hidden Valley Ranch
   dressing mix

8 oz. sour cream
1 T. sugar

Combine oleo, sugar and boiling water in a mixing bowl. Stir until oleo is melted. Dissolve yeast in warm water then add yeast and beaten egg to butter mixture. Add flour, salt and mix well. Spread evenly on a well greased 10" x 15" pan. Fingers need to be well greased. Bake at 325° just till golden brown. Cool. Soften cream cheese to room temperature. Mix all ingredients and spread on cooled crust. Top with shredded carrots, green peppers, cut fine, chopped broccoli, cauliflower and onion. Top with shredded cheese. Cut into squares and serve. I prefer cutting it into squares before adding vegetable layer.

MILNOT DRESSING

Mrs. Martha Sue Miller

1 can Milnot
1 1/3 C. sugar
1/3 C. Sweet and Sour dressing
1/3 C. Catalina dressing

1 1/3 C. Miracle Whip
2 t. mustard
2/3 t. salt

Just mix with a spoon, you don't need a blender.

SWEET AND SOUR DRESSING

Mrs. David Schlabach

2 C. salad dressing
1 C. white sugar
2 T. vinegar

1/2 C. salad oil
2 T. mustard
celery seed

Recipe x 4 makes 1 gallon.

SWEET AND SOUR DRESSING

Mrs. Robert Yoder

3/4 C. oil
1/4 C. water
1/4 C. vinegar
1 C. white sugar
2 T. salad dressing

1 t. salt
2 t. mustard
1 t. celery seed
onion

Blend well.

FRENCH SALAD DRESSING

Mrs. Steve Engbretson

1 med. onion
3 T. water
1/4 C. vinegar
1 C. catsup
1/2 C. oil

1 1/2 t. salt
1 1/2 t. celery seed
1 1/2 t. paprika
2 C. sugar

Mix well with an egg beater.

ঽ▲

Keep a fair-sized cemetery in your backyard
to bury the faults of your friends.

FRESH APPLE SALAD

Mrs. Henry Schrock

8 C. unpeeled apples
1 can pineapple chunks, drained
   reserve juice

1 - 2 t. poppy seeds
1½ C. toasted pecans
2 C. seedless grapes

Dressing:
pineapple juice
¼ C. butter
¼ C. sugar
1 T. lemon juice

2 T. cornstarch
2 T. water
1 C. mayonnaise or
   ½ C. mayonnaise
   +½ C. yogurt

Make dressing first by combining juice, sugar, butter and lemon juice in sauce pan. Heat to boiling. Combine cornstarch and water, add to hot mixture. Cook until thick and smooth. Chill completely before stirring in mayonnaise. Combine apples, pineapples and grapes in a large glass bowl. Add chilled dressing. Refrigerate. Stir in pecans just before serving for crunchiness.

APPLE SALAD

Mrs. Eddie Miller
Mrs. Willis Wagler

1 C. water
1 t. vinegar
¼ t. salt
1 C. sugar

1 T. cornstarch or clear jel
¼ C. cream
1 t. vanilla

Mix sugar and cornstarch in a saucepan. Add all other ingredients. Bring to a boil and boil 1 minute. Cool and pour over mixed fruit.

Fruit:
8 raw diced apples
pineapple chunks
½ C. celery
½ C. raisins

½ C. peanuts or walnuts
1 C. grapes
marshmallows

FRUIT SALAD

Bena Beachy

8 oz. Cool Whip
1 can Eagle Brand milk
1 can cherry pie filling
1 can mandarin oranges

1 can pineapple tidbits
1 C. marshmallows
½ C. chopped nuts

Beat Cool Whip and Eagle Brand milk. Stir in remaining ingredients. Refrigerate 24 hours or less.

CREAM CHEESE SALAD

Mrs. Leroy Yoder

3 - 6 oz. lime jello
8 oz. cream cheese
1/2 C. drained crushed pineapple
1/2 C. chopped walnuts

2 C. unwhipped Rich's topping
1/2 C. white sugar
1 t. vanilla

Make 1 box jello according to directions. Pour into rectangle tupperware and chill until firmly set. Dissolve 1 box jello with 1 C. hot water, don't add any cold water. Set aside. Whip topping, cream cream cheese with sugar and vanilla. When jello is just starting to set, add jello, pineapples, nuts and cream cheese to whipped topping and stir gently. Pour this on top of chilled jello. Make 1 box jello according to directions. When starting to set, pour onto firmly set, middle layer.

CREAM CHEESE SALAD

Lois Mast

1 pkg. lemon jello
1/2 lb. marshmallows
1 can crushed pineapples
1 C. Miracle Whip
8 oz. cream cheese

1 C. whipped topping
1/2 C. chopped nuts
1 pkg. lime jello
1/2 C. maraschino cherries

Add enough water to juice drained from pineapples to make 2 C. Bring to a boil and pour over lemon jello, stir to dissolve, add marshmallows. Allow marshmallows to dissolve. Cool until partly set. Whip the cream and combine with cream cheese, Miracle Whip, pineapple and nuts, fold into lemon jello and pour into oblong dish. Allow to set. Prepare lime jello as directed when cooled add cherries and pour over lemon jello. Chill.

INDIANA SUMMER SALAD

Mrs. Jake Hershberger
Mrs. Allen Beachy

1st layer:
2 - 3 oz. lime jello, when partially set add:
20 oz. can crushed pineapple, drain and reserve

2nd layer:
8 oz. cream cheese
1/2 C. sugar

4 C. ready whipped topping

3rd layer:
Use drained pineapple juice and add water to make 1 1/2 C. Heat, then add.
3 T. clear jel
3 beaten egg yolks
pinch of salt

1/2 C. sugar
1/4 C. water, optional

Bring to a boil. Cool. Add 1 C. whipped topping and spread over 2nd layer.

CRUST SALAD   Mrs. Paul Mast

2 C. flour   ¹/₂ C. nuts
¹/₂ C. brown sugar   1 C. butter

Press in pan and bake at 350° for 15 - 20 minutes. Drain juice off of 1 can crushed pineapple. Heat the juice. Put in 1 pkg. lime jello, cool. Cream 8 oz. cream cheese and 1 C. white sugar. Blend in jello and add pineapple. Chill. Beat 1³/₄ C. Rich's topping. Mix all together. Pour on top of crust. Top with lime jello if desired.

COOL WHIP - COTTAGE CHEESE SALAD   Mrs. Eddie E. Miller

1 C. white sugar   1 C. cottage cheese
1 can crushed pineapple   1 C. nuts
6 T. cold water   1 lg. container Cool Whip
2 pkg. Knox gelatin   1¹/₂ C. Hellman's mayonnaise
2 lg. carrots, shredded   1 C. chopped celery

In large bowl mix white sugar and pineapple in saucepan. Soak gelatin in cold water then bring to a boil. Pour over sugar and pineapple, stir. Set in refrigerator and let set slightly. Add all other ingredients and mix together.

PINEAPPLE SALAD   Mrs. Linus Troyer

1 can pineapple chunks   1 C. whipping cream
¹/₂ C. sugar   2 T. flour
2 oranges   2 eggs
24 marshmallows   salt
1 C. nuts, optional

Drain juice from pineapple and heat in double boiler. When hot, beat sugar, flour, salt and eggs together and add to juice. Cook until thick. Cool then add whipped cream and pour over chunked fruit and cut up marshmallows (or use miniature marshmallows). Refrigerate for 1 hour before serving.

WALDORF SALAD   Mary Beth Mast

2 C. pineapple chunks, drained   6 diced apples
2 C. seedless grapes   nuts optional
¹/₂ C. chopped celery

Dressing: Bring to a boil 1 C. pineapple juice. Stir together ²/₃ C. sugar, 1 T. cornstarch, ¹/₂ t. salt. Add 1 egg and blend. Stir in 3 or 4 T. hot pineapple juice cook over low heat until thoroughly cooked, but do not overcook. Cool and add to fruit.

COTTAGE CHEESE SALAD
Mrs. Noah J. Hostetler

Stir together 1 box orange jello and 20 oz. can of crushed drained pineapple, 1 pt. cottage cheese, 1 pkg. Dream Whip, whipped or 1 can milnot. Stir and pour into pan and chill overnight.

BARLEY SALAD
Mrs. Eli B. Yoder

$\frac{1}{2}$ C. uncooked barley
  (2 C. cooked)
$\frac{1}{2}$ C. water chestnuts, drained and sliced
1 C. chopped celery

$\frac{1}{4}$ C. chopped pimento
$\frac{1}{4}$ C. sliced green onion
1 C. cubed, cooked ham
$\frac{1}{4}$ C. chopped green pepper

Dressing:
1 pkg. Italian dressing mix
$\frac{1}{3}$ C. sugar

$\frac{1}{4}$ C. oil
$\frac{1}{2}$ C. vinegar

ORANGE APRICOT SALAD
Mrs. Nathan Miller

6 oz. orange jello
2 C. boiling water
1 C. mixed juices
16 oz. can drained apricots, diced

1 C. cold water
20 oz. drained crushed
  pineapple

Topping:
1 egg beaten
$\frac{1}{2}$ C. sugar
2 T. flour
2 T. butter

1 C. juice, drained from fruit
  add water if not enough juice
1 C. Rich's topping

Dissolve jello in hot water add mixed juices and cold water, add pineapples and apricots once jello begins to set. Pour into oblong pan and refrigerate. Mix together 1st 3 ingredients for topping, add juice, cook until thick. Add 2 T. butter. Cool. Fold in whipped topping, spread on top of jello. Sometimes I use peaches instead of apricots.

TRIPLE ORANGE SALAD
Mrs. Mark Hochstetler

1 box orange jello
1 box instant vanilla pudding
1 box tapioca pudding

$2\frac{1}{2}$ C. water
1 can mandarin oranges
2 C. Cool Whip

Bring jello, vanilla pudding, tapioca and water to a boil, then take from heat, cool. Add Cool Whip and mandarin oranges.

CALORIE BURNING SALAD

Mrs. Henry Beachy

Slice and toss together:

$1/2$ cucumber
$1/2$ tomato
$1/2$ green pepper
$1/4$ onion
1 med. carrot

3 stalks celery
$1/2$ C. low calorie cottage cheese
$1/4$ C. low calorie dressing
top with unsalted croutons

ORANGE MANDARIN JELLO

Mrs. Crist Beachy

3 oz. orange jello
3 oz. vanilla tapioca pudding
3 C. water

Cook all together until it thickens slightly. Cool and add 8 oz. Cool Whip and drained mandarin oranges. Delicious!

PRETZEL SALAD

Joanna Miller

2 C. crushed pretzels
3 t. sugar
8 oz. cream cheese
6 oz. strawberry jello
2 - 10 oz. pkgs. frozen strawberries

$3/4$ C. margarine
8 oz. Cool Whip
1 C. powdered sugar
2 C. boiling water

Mix pretzels, margarine and sugar, spread in 9" x 13" pan. Bake at 400° for 8 minutes. Cool. Mix cream cheese, powdered sugar and Cool Whip, spread on top of pretzel mixture. Dissolve jello with boiling water, then add frozen strawberries. Chill and spread over cream cheese mixture. Chill overnight.

RIBBON SALAD

Mrs. Nathan Mast

1 box orange jello
1 box lime jello
1 C. crushed, drained pineapple

3 oz. cream cheese, softened
16 lg. marshmallows
1 C. Rich's topping, whipped

Mix orange jello as directed on box, pour $1/2$ of it into 9" x 13" pan. Let set. Mix lime jello with 2 C. water add marshmallows and cream cheese. Stir until melted. Let cool, add pineapples and Rich's topping, pour over, set jello. When set pour remaining orange jello on top.

MILLION DOLLAR RICE SALAD

Mrs. Roy Mast

8 oz. cream cheese, softened
2 T. sugar
2 C. cooked rice, cooled
12 maraschino cherries, cut up
10 oz. pkg. miniature marshmallows

20 oz. crushed pineapple,
   drained
12 oz. whipped toppping
1 C. chopped nuts, optional

Combine cream cheese and sugar until smooth. Add rice, cherries, pineapples and marshmallows. Mix well. Fold in whipped topping and nuts.

❧

A friend is: A push when you've stopped
A word when you're lonely
A guide when you're searching
A smile when you're sad
A song when you're glad.

- Notes -

Meats & Main Dishes

BREAKFAST PIZZA

Mrs. Martha Sue Miller

1 lb. bulk sausage
1 pkg. Crescent rolls
1 C. frozen hash brown potatoes
1 C. shredded Cheddar cheese
$^1/_8$ t. pepper

2 T. grated Parmesan cheese
5 eggs
$^1/_4$ C. milk
$^1/_2$ t. salt

In a skillet cook the sausage until browned. Drain off excess fat. Seperate and roll dough into 8 triangles. Place on ungreased 12" pizza pan. Points toward the center. Press over bottom and up sides to form crust. Seal perforation. Spoon sausage over crust. Sprinkle with potatoes, top with cheese. In a bowl, beat together eggs, milk, salt and pepper. Pour into crust. Sprinkle with Parmesan cheese and bake at 375° for 25 - 30 minutes. Makes 6 - 8 servings.

BREAKFAST BAKE

Mrs. Willis Wagler

1$^1/_2$ lb. sausage, browned and drained
9 eggs, beaten
3 C. milk

1 t. salt
4 slices cubed bread
1$^1/_2$ C. grated Cheddar cheese

Mix together and refrigerate overnight. Bake at 350° for 1 hour.

BREAKFAST CASSEROLE

Mrs. Nathan Miller

6 beaten eggs
2 C. milk
2 C. bread cubes
1 C. Velveeta cheese, cubed

$^1/_2$ t. salt
$^1/_8$ t. onion salt, optional
1 lb. bulk sausage,
    browned and chilled

Mix and pour into greased cake pan. Refrigerate overnight. Bake at 350°. When done top with Velveeta slices and leave in oven till cheese melts. Turn several times while baking. Serves 8.

BRUNCH CASSEROLE

Sarah Ann Kaufman

1 small onion
1 T. butter
2 C. chopped ham
3 lightly beaten eggs

1 C. shredded sharp cheese
$^2/_3$ C. crushed cracker crumbs
1$^1/_2$ C. milk

Sauté onion, butter and ham a little. Mix all ingredients together and put in buttered 8" x 8" casserole. Bake at 325° for 45 minutes or until knife comes out clean.

SUNRISE BURRITO

Mrs. Linus Troyer

1 lb. bulk sausage
chopped onions
chopped peppers
mushrooms
choice

8 eggs
4 T. water
8 - 10" flour tortillas
cheese, Velveeta or your

Brown sausage, onions and peppers, add mushrooms. Scramble eggs and add water. Add sausage mixture, do not overcook, eggs should be soft with no liquid remaining. Melt cheese on top. Heat tortilla on warm pan then fill with scrambled egg mixture.

SHEEPHERDER'S BREAKFAST

Mrs. Mark Hochstetler

$^{1}/_{2}$ lb. bacon
1 small onion
3 medium potatoes
5 eggs

salt and pepper to taste
1 C. shredded Cheddar cheese
chopped parsley

In a medium skillet, cook bacon and onions until bacon is crisp. Drain all but $^{1}/_{2}$ C. of drippings. Add potatoes cut as hash browns, I put them through the Salad Master. Brown. Add bacon and onions, again. Make 5 wells evenly spaced in the hash browns. Place one egg in each well. Sprinkle with salt and pepper. Sprinkle with cheese if desired. Cover and cook over low heat for about 10 minutes or until eggs are set. Garnish with parsley, serve immediately.

BAKED POTATOES

Mrs. John Mark Troyer

6 large potatoes
$^{1}/_{4}$ C. flour
$^{1}/_{4}$ C. Parmesan cheese
$^{1}/_{2}$ t. salt

$^{1}/_{2}$ t. seasoning salt
$^{1}/_{4}$ t. black pepper
$^{1}/_{4}$ C. melted margarine

Peel and chunk potatoes. Combine remaining ingredients in plastic bag except margarine. Moisten potatoes with water. Shake potatoes and mix in bag. Put a little salad oil in bottom of baking sheet. Dot potatoes with margarine. Bake at 375° for about 1 hour, turning once. Bake till golden brown. Serve with sour cream.

&

The best way to do good to ourselves,
is to do good to others.

CRUSTY BAKED POTATOES

Mrs. Mike Schrock

6 medium potatoes
4 T. melted butter

$^1/_2$ C. cracker crumbs
1 t. salt

Pare potatoes, wash and wipe dry. Cut in halves and roll in melted butter, then into crumbs in which salt has been added. Place in greased pan and bake at 350° for 1 hour.

STUFFED BAKED POTATOES

Mrs. Matthias Mast

2 lg. baking potatoes
2 T. butter
$^2/_3$ C. Cheddar cheese

1 T. chives, optional
salt and pepper to taste
3 bacon slices fried
   and crumbled

Bake potatoes until tender and skins are very crisp, about 1$^1/_4$ hours. Cut potatoes in $^1/_2$ lengthwise and scoop out centers into a bowl. Add butter and mash until smooth, fold in cheese, sour cream, chives, salt, pepper and bacon. Mound mixture back into potato shells and bake for another 15 minutes. Serves 4.

BROCCOLI/CHEESE TWICE-BAKED POTATOES

Melva Schrock

6 medium baked potatoes
$^1/_2$ C. sour cream
3 T. butter or margarine
dash of salt and pepper

2 onions thinly sliced
1$^1/_2$ C. cooked
   chopped broccoli
1 C. shredded Cheddar cheese

Bake potatoes at 425° until done. Cut potato lengthwise. Scoop out pulp and place in bowl. Mash potatoes, add sour cream, butter, salt, pepper, onions, broccoli and $^3/_4$ C. cheese. Refill potato shells, top with remaining cheese and sprinkle with paprika. Bake at 425° for 20 - 25 minutes or until thoroughly heated.

CAMPFIRE POTATOES

Mrs. Mark Hochstetler

5 medium potatoes, peeled and thinly sliced
1 medium onion, sliced
6 T. butter or margarine
$^1/_3$ C. shredded Cheddar cheese

2 T. minced parsley
1 T. Worcestershire sauce
$^1/_3$ C. chicken broth
salt and pepper to taste

Place potatoes and onion on large piece of heavy duty foil. (about 20" x 20") dot with butter. Combine the cheese, parsley, Worcestershire sauce, salt and pepper. Sprinkle over potatoes and add broth. Seal edges of foil well. Grill, covered over medium coals for 35 - 40 minutes or until potatoes are tender.

ITALIAN POTATOES   Mrs. David Ray Yoder

6 - 8 medium potatoes, peeled
1 1/2 lb. ground beef   1 t. basil
1 medium onion, chopped   1 t. oregano
1 1/2 t. salt   1 T. sugar
1 qt. spaghetti sauce   1/4 t. pepper
1/3 C. water   Mozzarella cheese

Slice potatoes and cook until slightly tender, drain. Brown ground beef and
chopped onion. Add spaghetti sauce, water, seasonings and sugar. Cook 2
minutes. In 9" x 13" baking dish evenly spoon 1/3 of meat mixture then arrange 1/2
of the cooked potatoes, sprinkle with 3/4 t. salt. Repeat layering ending with meat
mixture. Cover and bake at 375° for 1 hour. Sprinkle with Mozzarella cheese
and bake uncovered about 10 minutes or until cheese is melted. Mushrooms,
peppers and pepperoni may also be added.

NORWEGIAN PARSLEY POTATOES   Mrs. Ella Miller

Small red potatoes, boil till soft, peel strip around the center of each potato. Put
butter in skillet, stir potatoes till covered sprinkle with minced parsley and salt
to taste. A good way to use small red potatoes. And also nutritious.

POTATO STACKS   Mrs. Matthew Miller

baked potatoes   1 pkg. taco seasoning
1 can sour cream   1 can chili hot beans
2 lbs. browned hamburger   1 pkg. California blend
1/2 chopped, onion   vegetables
seasonings to taste   2 cans cheese sauce

Mix hamburger, onion, seasonings, taco seasoning and chili hot beans. Prepare
vegetables and cheese sauce as directed on package. Pass around in order
given everyone makes their own.

EVERYDAY POTATO CASSEROLE   Mrs. Robert Yoder

1 lb. ground beef   1 can cream of celery soup
1 sm. onion, chopped   American cheese to taste
4 - 5 medium potatoes, peeled and sliced   1 t. salt
1 lb. green beans   dash of pepper

Brown meat with onion, salt and pepper. Drain grease. Place meat into oblong
2 qt. casserole. Layer potatoes over meat. Add a layer of green beans. Heat
celery soup and cheese enough to melt cheese. Pour over top of casserole.
Cover and bake 1 - 1 1/2 hours at 350°.

POTATO HAMBURG CASSEROLE

Mrs. Eli B. Yoder

4 lbs. hamburger, fried with 2 onions
8 lbs. potatoes, cooked and diced
1 can cream of celery soup

3 cans cream of chicken soup
1 lb. Velveeta cheese
1/2 C. butter

Make a white sauce, about 2 qt. Add cheese and butter. When melted, add hamburger, potatoes and soups. Bake at 350° for 2 hours.

DRESSING

Mrs. Willis Priscilla Miller

3 loaves of bread
2 1/2 C. cubed potatoes (boiled)
3 C. diced celery
1 C. shredded carrots
8 eggs
3 pt. diced chicken
2 pt. chicken broth

1 can cream of celery soup
milk
butter
chicken base
salt
pepper

Cube bread and toast in butter. In large bowl, put toasted bread cubes, potatoes, celery, carrots, chicken broth and celery soup. Beat eggs with soup base, salt, pepper and add some milk. Pour over bread mixture and mix well. Add more milk until moist enough. Fry in butter.

MOCK TURKEY

Mrs. Joe Miller, Jr.

2 lbs. hamburger
2 cans cream of chicken soup
1 can cream of celery soup

4 C. milk
1 loaf of bread, toasted
salt and pepper to taste

Brown hamburger in butter. Mix all together and place in casserole. Bake at 350° for 45 minutes.

BARBEQUED CHICKEN

Mrs. Leroy Yoder

1 pt. vinegar
1 pt. water
1/4 lb. butter

1/2 C. oil
4 T. salt
1 T. Worcestershire sauce

This is enough sauce for 8 - 10 chickens. Heat chicken in sauce for 15 minutes. Remove from heat and let set another 15 minutes. Then barbeque to desired doneness, basting a few times.

ARIZONA CHICKEN
Mrs. Merle Hershberger

1 - 3 lb. fryer
1 stick oleo
1/2 C. flour

2 t. paprika
1 t. salt
pepper to taste

Melt oleo, cover bottom of cake pan or cookie sheet with tin foil. Pour oleo in pan. Mix rest of ingredients and roll chicken in it. Place chicken in pan. Bake at 425° for 30 minutes. Turn and bake 30 minutes longer. Crisp and delicious.

CHICKEN IN PIZZA SAUCE
Mrs. Henry Schrock

Pat dry cut up chicken and dip in your favorite pizza sauce. Place in loaf pan with skin side up, one layer only. Sprinkle with salt and pepper to taste. Bake 45 minutes - 1 hour or until chicken is tender. This is a simple and delicious way to prepare chicken.

CORNFLAKE CHICKEN
Mrs. Roy Mast
Mrs. Crist Beachy

1 chicken, cut up
1/2 C. melted butter
1 1/2 C. cornflake crumbs

1 t. salt
1/4 t. pepper
1/4 t. garlic or seasoning salt

Mix together cornflake crumbs, salts and pepper. Dip chicken in batter then roll in crumbs till well coated. Bake on foil lined baking pan, single layer, until well done, at 375°. No need to turn.

SMOKED TURKEY OR CHICKEN
Mrs. Paul Mast

1 C. Tenderquick
3 T. liquid smoke
8 - 10 C. water

Soak turkey or chicken in brine. Adjust recipe so it covers the bird. Drain and let stand overnight. Bake.

SMOKED TURKEY
Mrs. Wyman Wengerd
Mrs. Henry Beachy

1 C. Morton's Tenderquick
12 C. water

1 t. liquid smoke
6 - 7 lbs. turkey or chicken

No salt needed. Cover turkey or chicken with mixture. Refrigerate. Soak for 3 - 4 days. Place into roaster and bake for 1 1/2 - 2 hours at 375°.

69

BROCCOLI AND CHEESE CHICKEN

Melva Schrock

1 T. margarine
4 chicken breast halves
1 can broccoli cheese soup

⅓ C. water or milk
2 C. broccoli flowerets
dash of pepper

Brown chicken on both sides. Mix soup, water and a dash of pepper, heat to boiling. Add broccoli and reduce heat to low. Cover and simmer until broccoli is about done, pour over chicken breast in skillet and simmer 10 - 15 minutes. Do not overcook broccoli.

SUNDAY FRIED CHICKEN

Mrs. Reuben Miller

2 C. all-purpose flour
½ C. cornmeal
2 T. salt
2 T. dry mustard
2 T. paprika

1 T. celery salt
1 t. ground ginger
½ t. dried thyme
½ t. oregano

Combine all ingredients. Place about 1 C. of flour mixture in a bowl. Shake a few pieces of chicken in the bowl at a time, coating well. Fry chicken in butter and a little oil until brown. Remove to baking pan or roaster and bake until tender.

GROUND CHICKEN PATTIES

Mrs. Wyman Wengerd

5 lbs. ground chicken
1 bag Ritz crackers
1 T. salt

1 t. Lawry's seasoning salt
1 t. black pepper

Soak crackers in a little water, then add rest of the ingredients and mix well. Make patties, roll in chicken breading and fry in butter or oil.

CHICKEN POT PIE

Mrs. Crist Miller

2 C. chicken broth
2 C. water
2 C. boned chicken
½ C. diced carrots
1 C. diced potatoes

½ C. frozen, uncooked peas
1 sm. onion
1 T. chicken base
½ C. Velveeta cheese
½ C. flour

Cook carrots, onions and potatoes in chicken broth until tender. Make a paste with water and flour. Add to chicken broth and bring to a boil, turn off heat and add chicken, peas, Velveeta cheese and chicken base. Let cheese melt, then put in baking dish, top with biscuits. Bake until biscuits are browned.

CHICKEN POT PIE

Mrs. Fremon E. Miller

3 medium potatoes, diced
2 C. peas
3 C. diced chicken
¼ C. butter

3 sm. onions
2 C. chicken broth
1 t. salt
¼ t. pepper

Cook together until vegetables are tender. Pour into pan and top with the following crust.

1½ C. flour
½ t. salt

1½ C. shortening

Work as pie dough, mix with 5 T. water. Roll out and put on top. Make air holes. Bake at 425° for 35 minutes.

HAM OR CHICKEN POTPIE OR KNEPP

Mrs. Fremon E. Miller

1 C. flour
1 egg beaten

1 t. baking powder

Milk or water to make thick dough, drop into broth with meat and potatoes as desired. Cover and let stand 5 - 10 minutes before serving.

CHICKEN SUPREME

Mrs. Chuck Karn

2 C. cooked chicken or turkey
2 C. uncooked macaroni
2 cans cream of chicken soup
2 C. milk
½ med. onion chopped

½ t. salt
½ t. pepper
3 T. butter
1 C. grated cheese

Combine chicken, soup, milk, onion, salt, pepper, butter and cheese. Heat until cheese is melted. Add macaroni. Refrigerate overnight. Bake at 350° for 1½ hours. Bake longer for bigger recipes.

CHICKEN CASSEROLE

Mrs. Crist Beachy

15 slices bread, toasted
3 C. chicken
1 C. chicken broth
1 C. milk
4 eggs

¼ C. melted butter
1 t. salt
¼ C. salad dressing
2 cans cream of celery soup
Velveeta cheese

Combine milk and eggs, beat. Crumble bread into roaster. Pour chicken and broth over bread. Add milk and egg mixture, butter, salt and salad dressing. Put a layer of cheese on top, then add the celery soup. Bake at 350° for 1 hour.

CHICKEN LOAF

Mrs. Marvin Wengerd

Mix in order given:

3 C. ground chicken	2 T. minced green peppers
2 C. bread crumbs	1 1/2 C. chicken broth
2 C. cooked rice	1 1/2 C. milk
1/8 t. pepper	3 eggs, beaten
1 1/2 t. salt	2 T. chopped parsley

Shape into loaf, bake at 350° for 1 hour. Serve with fresh mushroom sauce.

Fresh Mushroom Sauce:

1/4 C. butter	1/4 C. cream
1/4 lb. fresh, sliced mushrooms	1 t. salt
6 T. flour	1 T. parsley
2 C. chicken broth	1/2 t. lemon juice

Sauté mushrooms in butter, blend in flour. Stir in then cook until thickened, add rest of the ingredients.

CHICKEN GUMBO

Melva Schrock

9 slices bread, lightly toasted and cut up
4 C. cooked, cut up chicken

Mix:

1/4 C. butter	1 C. milk
1/2 C. salad dressing	1 C. chicken broth
4 eggs, beaten	1 t. salt
2 cans celery soup	9 slices Velveeta cheese

Mix together, put in casserole with cheese on top and bread crumbs to cover. This can be fixed and refrigerated overnight. Bake at 350° for 1 1/4 hour.

CHICKEN CORDON BLEU

Twila Beachy

6 skinless chicken breast, cut up	1/4 lb. sliced Swiss or
2 bags saltine crackers or	Mozzarella cheese
Emma's breading mix	1/2 C. sour cream
4 eggs	1 can cream of mushroom
1/4 lb. thinly sliced ham	or chicken soup
1/2 C. white wine or a shot of lemon juice	

Dip chicken in beaten egg, then roll in crushed crackers, brown. Put in baking dish top with cheese and ham, Heat sauce for 5 minutes. Pour over chicken, ham and cheese. Bake at 375° for 30 - 45 minutes

CHICKEN FRIED STEAK

Mrs. Mark Hochstetler

1 lb. hamburger
1/2 C. flour
1 t. salt

1/4 t. pepper
crushed cracker crumbs
1 - 2 beaten eggs

Mix meat, flour, salt and pepper. Form into 1/4" thick steaks. Dip into beaten eggs then into cracker crumbs. Fry for 7 minutes. These can be fried immediately or frozen for later use.

MEXACALI CHICKEN

Mrs. Matthias Mast

3 cans biscuits
2 T. melted butter

Sauce:
1 can cream of chicken soup
1/2 C. sour cream

1 t. coriander

Chicken mixture:
1 C. cooked chopped chicken
1/2 C. chopped onion
1/2 C. chopped green pepper

1 small can chopped green
   chilies
2 C. Monterey Jack cheese

Place biscuits in 9" x 13" pan. Brush with melted butter. Make indentation in center of each biscuit. Mix chicken mixture with 1 C. cheese and 1/2 C. sauce. Place a scoop of filling in each biscuit. Bake at 375° for 20 minutes. Heat sauce. Drizzle with remaining sauce and cheese.

CHICKEN – N – RICE

Mrs. Henry Hershberger

1 C. rice
1 can mushroom soup
2 C. chicken broth or milk

1 pkg. onion seasoning mix
1/4 C. butter
1 chicken cut up or
   2 lbs. boneless chicken

Put rice, soup, broth or milk and onion seasoning mix into greased casserole dish. Dip chicken into melted butter and salt. Place on top and bake for 2 hours for raw chicken and 1 hour for cooked chicken. Or make on stovetop with your Lifetime cookware.

ফ

A clear conscience is a soft pillow.

CHICKEN PIZZA

Mrs. Linus Troyer

8 oz. pkg. Crescent dinner rolls
2 chicken breasts, cut into 1" pieces
1/4 C. vegetable oil
1 lg. onion, sliced in rings
1 lg. green pepper, sliced in rings
mushrooms
olives, optional

1 can pizza sauce
1 t. garlic salt
1 t. dried oregano
1/4 C. grated Parmesan cheese
2 C. Mozzarella cheese,
   shredded

Preheat oven to 425°. Separate Crescent rolls and press into lightly oiled 12" pizza pan, covering it completely. In large skillet heat oil over medium heat. Add chicken, onion, peppers, mushrooms and olives. Cook and stir about 5 minutes or until chicken is soft. Spread pizza sauce on dough, spoon chicken mixture evenly over sauce. Sprinkle with salt, oregano and Parmesan cheese. Top with Mozzarella cheese. Bake 20 minutes or until crust is golden brown.

CHICKEN ZUCCHINI BAKE

Mrs. Atlee Miller

2 1/2 C. 1/4" thick sliced zucchini
1 C. cream of chicken soup
2 T. milk
1/8 t. nutmeg
1 C. Bisquick

1/4 C. grated Cheddar cheese
1 egg
1 t. parsley flakes
1/4 C. melted margarine
2 C. cooked, cubed chicken

Arrange zucchini slices in 8" x 8" pan. Top with chicken. Mix soup, milk and nutmeg. Spread over chicken. Mix Bisquick, cheese and egg until crumbly. Sprinkle over soup mixture. Sprinkle with parsley and drizzle with margarine. Bake at 350° until golden brown about 25 - 30 minutes. I use 1 pt. of canned chicken and broth if I don't have soup.

ROAST CHICKEN

Mrs. Willis Karen Miller

1 broiler cut in pieces
Put in 9" x 13" pan and cover with
1/2 C. vinegar
1 stick melted oleo
Sprinkle with Lawry's seasoning salt.

Bake at 350° to 400° for 1 1/2 hours. Do not turn while it is in the oven. A very easy way to have good chicken.

CHICKEN FAJITAS

Mrs. Mark Hochstetler

¹/₄ C. lime juice
1 garlic clove, minced
1 t. chili powder
¹/₂ t. ground cumin
2 chicken breast, cut in strips
1 med. onion, cut into thin wedges

¹/₂ sweet red pepper
¹/₂ sweet yellow pepper
¹/₂ sweet green pepper
¹/₂ C. salsa
12 flour tortillas
1¹/₂ C. shredded
    Cheddar cheese

In a small bowl combine lime juice, garlic, chili powder and cumin. Add chicken, stir, marinate for 15 minutes. In a nonstick skillet, cook onion and chicken, marinate for 3 minutes or until chicken is no longer pink. Add peppers, cut into strips sauté for 3 - 5 minutes or until crisp and tender. Stir in salsa. Divide mixture among tortillas, top with cheese. Roll up and serve.

CHICKEN ENCHILADA CASSEROLE

Mrs. Paul Mast
Mrs. Ben Troyer, Jr.

2 chicken, cooked and diced
1 lb. Cheddar or Longhorn cheese
¹/₄ lb. Monterey Jack or Muenster cheese
2 cans cream of chicken soup
2 - 4 oz. cans green chilies
1 - 2 lg. onions

¹/₂ t. oregano
¹/₄ t. cumin
¹/₄ t. sage
¹/₄ t. chili powder
¹/₂ t. garlic powder
corn or flour tortillas

Cover bottom of casserole with tortillas. Layer half of chicken and half amount of green chilies, onions and grated cheese. Mix soup with small amount of chicken broth, and the rest of the cheese. Pour ¹/₂ of soup mixture over casserole. Cover with tortillas and repeat the previous layer. Top with more tortillas. Bake at 375° for 30 - 40 minutes. Can be served with lettuce, sour cream and salsa.

CHICKEN OR BEEF ENCHILADAS

JoAnne Schlabach

3 C. cooked chicken or
  2 lbs. fried ground beef
4 oz. green chilies, optional
1 can cream of chicken soup

1 C. sour cream
2 - 3 C. Mozzarella cheese
8 - 10 sm. flour tortillas

Mix all ingredients except cheese and tortillas. Spread 1 C. salsa, pizza, or enchilada sauce on bottom of cake pan. Spoon mixture down the center of each tortilla. Roll tortillas around in sauce and place in pan, seam down. Spread 1 C. sauce over top of enchiladas and cover with cheese. Bake at 350° for 15 - 20 minutes. Serve with lettuce and sour cream.

CHICKEN ENCHILADAS

Mrs. Willis Karen Miller

2 C. diced cooked chicken
2 C. shredded Monterey Jack cheese
2 t. dried parsley flakes
$1/2$ t. garlic powder
$1/2$ t. salt
$1/8$ t. pepper
6 - 8 flour tortillas

Sauce:
1 med. diced onion
$1/2$ diced green pepper
4 oz. chopped green chilies
15 oz. tomato sauce
2 t. chili powder
1 t. sugar
1 C. shredded Cheddar cheese

Combine first seven ingredients. Divide evenly among tortillas. Roll up and place seam side down in 9" x 13" pan. Sauté onion and green pepper in oil until tender. Add chilies, tomato sauce, chili powder, sugar and garlic powder. Mix well. Pour over tortillas and cover with foil. Bake at 350° for 30 minutes. Sprinkle with Cheddar cheese and return to oven for 10 minutes.

ENCHILADAS

Annalisa Miller

$1^1/2$ lb. hamburger, browned
1 pkg. enchilada sauce mix
1 qt. tomato juice

10 tortillas
cheese

Brown hamburger. Put tomato juice in pan, add enough enchilada sauce mix. Heat until boiling then simmer for 15 minutes. Add some of mixture to hamburger and roll up in tortillas. Put in cake pan, pour remaining enchilada sauce over top, top with cheese. Bake at 350° for 20 minutes. Serve with lettuce, tomatoes, sour cream and taco sauce.

MEXICAN CHICKEN ROLL UPS

Mrs. Mark Hochstetler

$2^1/2$ C. cubed fried chicken
$1^1/2$ C. sour cream
3 t. taco seasoning
1 C. cream of mushroom soup, undiluted
$1^1/2$ C. shredded Cheddar cheese
1 sm. onion chopped

$1/2$ C. salsa
10 - 7" flour tortillas
shredded lettuce
chopped tomatoes
additional salsa

In a bowl combine chicken, $1/2$ C. sour cream, $1^1/2$ t. taco seasoning, $1/2$ of the soup, 1 C. cheese, onion and salsa. Place $1/3$ C. of filling in each tortilla. Roll up and place seam side down in greased 9" x 13" baking dish. Combine remaining sour cream, taco seasoning and soup, pour over tortillas. Cover and bake at 350° for 30 minutes, or until heated through. Sprinkle with remaining cheese. Serve with shredded lettuce and chopped tomatoes. Top with additional salsa if desired.

BAKED BEANS

Mrs. Allen Beachy

1 can dark red kidney beans
1 can butter or lima beans
1 med. can pork and beans
Mix together don't drain juice.

1/2 lb. bacon, cut in strips
2 sm. onions chopped
1 C. brown sugar

1 C. catsup
1 t. prepared mustard

Start cooking bacon but don't brown. Leave grease on. Add onions, sugar, catsup and mustard. Heat. Pour over beans and mix well. Bake at 350° for at least 1 hour, uncovered.

BAKED BEANS AND HAMBURGER

Mrs. Noah J. Hostetler

1 lg. can pork and beans
1 lb. hamburger
1 pkg. dry onion soup mix

1/2 C. catsup
1 T. vinegar
1 T. mustard

Heat the beans while frying the meat. Add soup mix. After this is well blended add catsup, vinegar and mustard. A pinch of brown sugar may be added if desired. Mix all together and put in baking dish. Bake for 30 - 45 minutes.

CALICO BEANS

Mrs. Ivan Miller

1 1/2 lbs. ground beef or bacon
1 med. onion
1 C. catsup
1/2 C. brown sugar
1 T. mustard

1 med. can pork and beans
16 oz. kidney beans
2 - 16 oz. butter beans
salt and pepper to taste
1 t. Worcestershire sauce

Brown ground beef with onion, drain. Fry bacon, drain. In a saucepan heat catsup, sugar and mustard. Stir until well blended. Drain kidney beans, and butter beans. Add all the beans to the meat in baking dish. Stir in remaining ingredients. More catsup can be added as needed. Bake at least 1 hour at 325°. Makes 6 - 8 servings.

સ

Old Bible Recipes: If you have the blues, read the 27th Psalm.
If your pocketbook is empty, read 37th Psalm.
If you are discouraged about your work, read 126th Psalm.

CALICO BEAN CASSEROLE

Mrs. Jr. Kaufman

1 lg. can pork and beans
1 can kidney beans
1 can butter beans
1/4 lb. bacon, cut up
1 lb. ground beef

1 med. onion diced
1/2 C. firmly packed brown sugar
1/2 C. catsup
2 t. vinegar
1/2 t. salt

Drain kidney and butter beans. Keep liquid. Brown bacon, hamburger and onion in skillet. Combine all beans with meat and put in 9" x 13" baking dish. Combine sugar, catsup, vinegar and salt into sauce. Pour this mixture over beans and meat. If it looks dry add some of the liquid from the beans. Bake at 350° for 1 hour. Serves 12.

CAJUN RED BEANS, SAUSAGE AND RICE

Orpha Peachey

1 lb. dry red beans
1 1/2 C. chopped onion
1 1/2 C. chopped celery

1 C. chopped parsley
1 lb. sausage
14 oz. tomato sauce, seasoned
    with zatarains - cerole

Wash beans then let them soak in water overnight. Put beans in fresh water and add the rest of the ingredients in a large pot and cook until beans are done. Lay sausage on top, cover for 20 minutes. Serve over rice.

GROUND BEEF CASSEROLE

Sarah Ann Kaufman
Mrs. Roy Mast

1 lb. ground beef
1 lg. onion chopped
2 T. butter
2 T. flour

1 1/2 t. salt
1/4 t. pepper
1 lg. can evaporated milk
2 C. cooked peas

Brown onion in butter. Add beef and fry till brown. Blend in flour, salt and pepper. Stir in milk and peas. Heat but do not boil. Turn into 2 qt. baking dish. Arrange biscuits on top. Bake at 375° for 25 minutes or until biscuits are golden brown.

GROUND BEEF GRANDSTYLE

Mrs. Mark Hochstetler

1 1/2 lbs. hamburger
1/2 C. chopped onion
1 C. cream of chicken soup
8 oz. cream cheese

1/4 C. catsup
1 t. salt
1/4 C. milk
1 can oven-ready biscuits

Brown meat and onions. Add the rest of the ingredients, all but the biscuits. Bake 10 minutes, then add the biscuits and bake 15 - 20 minutes longer. Until golden brown.

GROUND BEEF STRAGANOFF

Mrs. Firman Miller

1 lb. ground beef
½ C. onion
4 oz. can undrained mushrooms
1 C. sour cream
2 T. Worcestershire sauce
½ t. salt

dash of pepper
2 T. flour
½ t. garlic salt
10¾ oz. cream of mushroom
  soup

Sauté onion in 1 T. butter. Add ground beef and brown. Add remaining ingredients, all but sour cream. Simmer until thickened and bubbly, then add sour cream. Serve with noodles cooked in salt water.

MASHED POTATO CASSEROLE

Mrs. Robert J. Yoder
Mrs. Robert Miller

3 lbs. potatoes, peeled, cooked
  and mashed
¼ C. butter
2 beaten eggs
salt to taste

½ C. milk
8 oz. cream cheese
½ C. sour cream
¼ C. chopped onion, optional

Put this in bottom of casserole then brown 2 lbs. hamburger, seasoned with salt and pepper. Remove from skillet and make a browned gravy, adding a can of mushroom soup to the gravy. Mix with hamburger and put on top of potatoes. Cheese may be put on top of this. Bake till heated through.

EASY TACO SKILLET MEAL

Mrs. Mike Schrock

1 lb. ground beef
1 pt. tomato juice
1 C. uncooked rice
1 C. shredded Cheddar cheese

¾ C. water
2 T. brown sugar
1 pkg. taco seasoning

Brown beef in large skillet with lid. Add tomato juice, water, seasonings and rice. Simmer for 20 minutes or until rice is tender, stirring several times. Top with cheese and let it melt. Serve with shredded lettuce, onions, sour cream and salsa.

≥▲

The happiest times we ever spend are
those we share with a special friend.

TACO RICE SKILLET

Mrs. Mark Hochstetler

1 lb. hamburger
1 pt. tomato juice
$1/2$ pkg. taco seasoning
2 T. brown sugar

1 C. cooked rice
1 C. Mozzarella cheese
lettuce
sour cream

Brown hamburger, add tomato juice, taco seasoning, brown sugar and rice. Simmer 20 minutes. Put cheese on top, melt. Serve with lettuce and sour cream.

HOT TACO SALAD

Mrs. Crist Miller

2 lbs. hamburger
2 sm. onions
1 t. hot sauce
$1/2$ t. salt
$1/2$ t. pepper
3 sm. cans tomato sauce
15 oz. hot chili beans

1 bag tortilla chips
1 C. sour cream
$1/2$ t. minced garlic
$1/2$ lb. shredded Cheddar cheese
$1/2$ head lettuce
tomatoes to garnish

Crush tortilla chips and put in bottom of 9" x 13" pan. Pour meat sauce over chips and top with cheese. Bake 30 minutes at 375°. Spread sour cream over top and let melt. Top with lettuce, shredded cheese and tomatoes. Serve with sour cream and taco sauce.

HOT TACO SALAD

Mrs. Martha Sue Miller

2 lbs. hamburger
$3/4$ qt. pizza sauce
$1/2$ jar Manwich sauce
$1/2$ pkg. taco seasoning

1 can chili hot beans
$1/2$ pt. sour cream
1 bag taco chips

Put taco chips in bottom of 9" x 13" pan. Brown hamburger with onion. Add pizza sauce, Manwich sauce, taco seasoning and chili hot beans. Spread sour cream over top and bake until bubbly. Put Mozzarella cheese on, when melted put on lettuce and top with tomato. Serve with taco sauce.

ॐ

There is no garden so complete. But roses make the place more sweet.
There is no life so rich and rare, but one more friend can enter there.

HOT TACO SALAD

Mrs. Levi Miller

2 lbs. hamburger
2 sm. onions
1/2 t. salt and pepper
1/2 t. garlic salt
1/2 pkg. taco seasoning
1 pt. pizza sauce

1 can chili hot beans
1 1/2 C. sour cream
1/2 lb. shredded Mozzarella
    cheese
1/2 head lettuce
6 flour tortillas

Break up flour tortillas and line 9" x 13" greased pan. Fry hamburger, add salt and taco seasoning, beans and pizza sauce. Pour meat mixture over tortillas. Add cheese. Bake at 375° until cheese is melted. Spread with sour cream and return to oven until sour cream is melted. Just before serving top with tomatoes and lettuce. Serve with hot sauce or salsa.

TACO PIE

Mrs. Duane Hershberger

1 lb. hamburger
2 - 8 oz. tomato sauce
1 pkg. taco seasoning
8 oz. Crescent rolls

1/2 lb. Mexican cheese
1 C. chopped lettuce
1/2 C. chopped tomatoes
sour cream

Preheat oven to 375°. Brown and drain meat. Stir in tomato sauce and seasoning. Simmer for 5 minutes. Unroll dough, press into sides and bottom of ungreased 12" pizza pan. Prick with fork. Bake 10 - 12 minutes or until golden brown. Cover crust with meat and top with cheese, continue baking until cheese begins to melt. Top with remaining ingredients. Serve with sour cream and taco sauce.

SPEEDY TACO BAKE

Mrs. Roy Mast

1 lb. ground beef
1/2 C. chopped onion
1 pkg. taco seasoning mix
1 pt. tomato sauce
1 can pork and beans

2 C. shredded Cheddar cheese
2 C. Bisquick mix
1 C. milk
2 eggs

Cook ground beef and onion until beef is browned. Drain. Spoon into ungreased 9" x 13" pan. Stir in taco seasoning mix, tomato sauce and beans. Sprinkle with cheese. Stir remaining ingredients until well blended. Pour over beef mixture. Bake 35 minutes or until light golden brown. Serve with sour cream, chopped tomatoes and shredded lettuce if desired.

MEXICAN HAT

Mrs. Reuben Miller

1 - 2 lbs. hamburger
chopped onion
salt to taste
1/2 t. chili powder

1 T. Worcestershire sauce
1 can cream of tomato soup
1 C. water

Brown hamburger and onions, add seasonings, soup and water. Bring to a boil, stirring occasionally. Pour into 8" x 8" pan.

Cornbread batter:
3/4 C. Bisquick mix
3/4 C. cornmeal

1/2 t. salt
3/4 C. milk

Combine ingredients and drop onto meat mixture. Bake in 450° for 20 - 30 minutes.

BURRITO CASSEROLE

Mrs. Martha Sue Miller
Mrs. Paul Mast

2 lbs. hamburger, browned with onions
2 sm. cans refried beans
1 pkg. taco seasoning
10 soft tortillas

1 1/2 - 2 cans cream of
   mushroom soup
2 C. sour cream

Mix first 3 ingredients and fill tortillas. Mix mushroom soup and sour cream. Spread a little on bottom of 9" x 13" pan. Place burritos in pan and add rest of soup mixture. Bake 1 hour at 350°. Put Cheddar cheese on top and put back in oven until melted. Serve with lettuce, tomatoes, sour cream and salsa sauce.

TORTILLA DOGS

Mrs. Mark Hochstetler

Velveeta cheese
flour tortillas
hot dogs
salsa

Place hot dogs on tortilla, top with 2 slices of cheese. Roll up, secure with toothpick. Bake at 350° until cheese is melted and hot dog is hot. Serve with salsa.

❧

Thanksgiving begins in the heart!

MEXICAN LASAGNA
Mrs. Crist Beachy

1 lb. hamburger, browned
16 oz. refried beans
12 - 15 uncooked lasagna noodles
2½ C. water

2½ C. pizza sauce
2 C. sour cream
1 C. shredded Mozzarella
   cheese

Combine hamburger and beans. Place 4 - 5 of the uncooked noodles in the bottom of 9" x 13" baking pan. Spread ½ of the beef mixture over the noodles and remaining beef mixture. Cover with remaining noodles. Combine water and pizza sauce. Pour over all. Cover tightly with foil, bake at 350° for 1½ hours or until noodles are tender. Spoon sour cream over casserole, top with cheese. Bake uncovered for 5 minutes or until cheese is melted.

MEXICAN LASAGNA
Mrs. Josiah Miller

1 lb. lean ground beef
1 can refried beans
2 t. dried oregano
¾ t. garlic powder
seasoning salt and pepper to taste
12 uncooked lasagna noodles

2½ C. water
2½ C. picante or salsa sauce
2 C. sour cream
1 C. shredded, Mozzarella
   cheese

Fry hamburger, add beans and seasonings. Place 4 uncooked lasagna noodles in the bottom of 9" x 13" baking pan. Spread ½ of the beef mixture over the noodles. Top with the 4 remaining noodles and remaining beef mixture. Cover with remaining noodles. Combine water and salsa and pour over all. Cover and bake at 350° for 1½ hours or until noodles are tender. Put sour cream and cheese on top and bake uncovered until cheese is melted.

MEXICAN LASAGNA
Mrs. Jr. Wagler

1 lb. lean ground beef mixed with 2 T. taco seasoning
½ C. chopped onion
½ C. chopped green pepper
2½ C. salsa
1 sm. can whole kernel corn, drained
1 t. chili powder

10 - 6" corn tortillas
3 C. cottage cheese
1 C. mild Cheddar cheese
2¼ oz. sliced, pitted ripe olives
1 t. ground cumin

Brown beef, onions and green peppers in large skillet, drain and add salsa, corn and seasonings. Layer ½ of meat sauce, ½ of tortillas and ½ of cottage cheese in 9" x 13" pan. Repeat layers ending with meat sauce. Sprinkle with cheese and olives. Bake at 375° for 30 minutes. Makes 8 - 10 servings.

NO FUSS LASAGNA

Mrs. Nathan Miller

1½ lb. hamburger, fried and seasoned with salt
2 t. oregano   ¾ t. garlic powder, optional

3 C. pizza sauce   ¼ C. milk
2½ C. water   ½ C. onion chopped fine
12 uncooked lasagna noodles   1 C. Mozzarella cheese
4 oz. cream cheese

Add 2½ C. pizza sauce to hamburger mixture. Layer noodles and meat mixture alternately in a cake pan, beginning and ending with 4 noodles. Put water over all then spread with ½ C. pizza sauce. Cover thickly with foil and bake at 350° for 1½ hour or until noodles are tender. Mix cream cheese, milk and onions and spread over top. Sprinkle cheese on top and return to oven till cheese is melted. 1 can refried or mild chili beans may be added to the hamburger mixture and 1 C. sour cream may be substituted for cream cheese and milk.

LASAGNA MEXICANA

Mrs. Ben Troyer, Jr.

2 lbs. hamburger   15 oz. Mexican or refried beans
½ C. chopped onion   4 oz. chopped green chilies
1 pkg. taco seasoning mix   6 - 8 flour tortillas
15 oz. tomato sauce   2 C. shredded Cheddar cheese

Brown hamburger and onion. Drain fat. Stir in seasoning mix, tomato sauce, beans and green chilies. Layer ½ of tortillas in bottom of baking dish. Spread half of mixture and cheese on top. Repeat layers. Bake at 350° for 30 minutes. May be served with lettuce, tomatoes, sour cream and salsa.

UNBELIEVABLE LASAGNA

Mrs. Matthew Troyer

4 - 5 C. spaghetti sauce   1 C. grated Parmesan cheese
8 oz. lasagna noodles   1 lb. cottage cheese
½ lb. Mozzarella cheese   1 lb. hamburger

Brown and drain hamburger and add to spaghetti sauce. Spread 1 C. sauce in 9" x 13" baking dish. Arrange uncooked lasagna noodles on top. Top with 1 C. sauce, ½ C. cottage cheese, ½ C. Mozzarella cheese, ½ C. Parmesan cheese and 1 C. sauce. Repeat layer, gently pressing noodles into cheese mixture. End with final layer of sauce. Make sure all noodles are covered with sauce. Lasagna will expand to the end of pan. Let set at least 2 hours before baking. Bake at 350° for 1 hour. Allow to stand 15 minutes after heat is turned off. Cut into squares and serve.

WESTERN CASSEROLE

Mrs. Josie Miller

1 lb. ground beef, browned
1 can whole kernel corn
1 can red kidney beans, drained
1 can cream of tomato soup

1 C. shredded Cheddar cheese
1 T. chopped onion
1/2 t. chili powder

Mix and bake for 20 - 30 minutes at 400°.

TACO FILLED PEPPERS

Mrs. Mark Hochstetler

1 lb. hamburger
1 pkg. taco seasoning mix
8 oz. kidney beans, rinsed and drained
1 C. salsa
4 med. green peppers

1 med. tomato chopped
1/2 C. shredded Cheddar
    cheese
1/2 C. sour cream

In large skillet, brown the hamburger, drain. Stir in the taco seasoning, kidney beans and salsa. Bring to a boil, reduce heat and simmer 5 minutes. Cut peppers in 1/2 lengthwise, remove and discard seeds and stems. Immerse peppers in boiling water for 3 minutes, drain. Spoon about 1/2 C. of meat mixture into each pepper. Place in an ungreased 9" x 13" baking dish. Cover and bake at 350° for 15 - 20 minutes, or until the peppers are crisp - tender and filling is heated through. Top each with tomato, cheese and a dallop of sour cream.

SARMALE - ROMANIAN CABBAGE ROLLS

Orpha Peachey

1 1/2 lbs. rice
5 chopped onions
8 lbs. hamburger
2 lbs. ground pork or turkey
1 T. salt
2 T. vegeta seasoning or
    crushed garlic clove

1 beaten egg
1 C. water
2 C. tomatoes
    chopped, fresh or canned
1 cabbage, scalded in
    boiling water
1 T. pepper

Simmer the rice and onions with oil for 2 - 3 minutes, cool in large bowl. Add the rest of the ingredients except cabbage, and knead 5 - 10 minutes. Let set for 1 hour. Shape in small rolls like pieces of sausage and wrap in the cabbage leaves. Try to shape like sausage with leaf ends tucked in. Put these in layers in stock pot with a few bay leaves. Cover with cabbage pieces. Cook slowly for 3 - 4 hours. More pieces of tomatoes, carrots, celery and peppers may be added for more flavor. This is typically a special dish for Romanian weddings, funerals and other ceremonies or celebrations.

QUICHE LORRAINE
Joanna Miller

½ lb. bacon
1 T. oleo
½ C. onions
3 eggs

1 t. salt
2 C. half and half
½ lb. Swiss cheese
season with pepper and nutmeg

Cook bacon until crisp. Crumble and put aside. Put oleo and onions in pan. Cook until onion is soft. Mix eggs, salt, half and half and season with pepper and nutmeg. Shred Swiss cheese and add to mixture. Add onion and pour into unbaked crust. Bake 10 minutes at 450°. Reduce to 325° and bake until firm, about 20 minutes. Cut in wedges and serve warm.

STIR FRY
Mrs. Leroy Yoder

2 C. cut up chicken
2 C. thinly sliced carrots
2 - 3 C. thinly sliced potatoes
1 sm. onion chopped
¼ C. soy sauce
2 - 3 T. Mazola oil
1 qt. chicken broth
½ C. celery

Optionals:
water chestnuts
mushrooms
garlic
cabbage

Heat oil in large saucepan. Sauté onions for a few minutes. Add carrots and stir fry till crispy tender. Repeat with celery and potatoes. Add chicken broth and soy sauce. Bring to a boil and add chicken. Cook this until chicken is tender, approximately 5 minutes. Do not overcook. Serve over rice or cooked noodles.

INDIANA STYLE CORN DOGS
Mrs. Willis Karen Miller

½ C. yellow cornmeal
1 C. all-purpose flour
1 T. baking powder
1 t. salt
1 T. sugar
1 C. evaporated milk

1 beaten egg
¼ t. paprika
½ t. dry mustard
dash of pepper
10 - 16 hot dogs
vegetable oil

In bowl mix cornmeal, flour, baking powder, salt, sugar, milk, egg, paprika, mustard and pepper. Pour mixture into tall glass. Skewer hot dogs with wooden skewers. Dip into mixture. Deep fry at 375° until golden brown, about 2 minutes. Drain on paper towels.

WEINER ROAST
Mrs. Duane Hershberger

10 oz. can tomato soup
1/2 C. chopped onion

2 T. Worcestershire sauce
1 C. sweet pickle relish

Cook all ingredients together. Serve warm with roasted hot dogs.

RUNZAS
Mrs. Martha Sue Miller

2 1/4 - 2 1/2 C. bread flour
3 T. sugar
1/2 t. salt
1 T. dry yeast

3/4 C. milk
1/4 C. water
1/4 C. shortening
1 egg

Measure flour into sifter. Add sugar and salt. Sift into large mixing bowl. Heat milk, water and shortening until warm 120° - 130°. Cool slightly. Add yeast and dissolve. Add beaten egg. Add liquid mixture to flour mixture. Blend with mixer, beat on medium speed for 2 minutes. Cover and let rise 1 hour or until double in bulk, then shape.

Filling:
1 lb. ground beef
1 chopped onion
3 C. chopped cabbage

1 t. salt
pepper to taste

Brown hamburger and onions, add salt, pepper and cabbage. Continue cooking on low heat until cabbage is wilted. Remove from heat and add several T. of water. Stir and set aside, cool while rolling dough. It is best if filling is cold. Roll dough very thin, in rectangles 18" x 24", cut into 6" or 7" squares. Place meat mixture in the center of each square. Bring together corners of dough and pinch edges together and place seam side down on greased baking sheet. Let rise, cover for about 30 minutes and bake at 375° for 15 - 20 minutes. Serve hot with mustard, ketchup or horseradish. Can also be frozen.

PENNY SAVERS
Sarah Ann Kaufman

6 weiners cut in pieces
4 med. potatoes, cooked and diced
2 t. minced onion
1/4 C. soft butter

1 C. cooked peas
1 can mushroom soup
1 can celery soup

Add salt and pepper to taste. Mix all ingredients and bake. You can add more vegetables and weiners.

CHOW MEIN DISH   Mrs. Jr. Kaufman

1 lb. hamburger
1 can cream of mushroom soup
1 can cream of chicken soup
3 C. water

1½ C. celery diced
½ C. rice
2 C. chow mein noodles

Brown hamburger then mix with the rest of the ingredients in a cake pan except for noodles. Put noodles on top after baking. Bake for 1½ hour at 350° uncovered.

CHOW MEIN   Mrs. Paul Mast

4 T. vegetable oil
2 C. thinly sliced onion strips
2½ C. diced celery
1 t. salt
2 t. sugar
1½ C. clear chicken stock

1 can bean sprouts
3 T. cornstarch
3 T. soy sauce
2 C. diced cooked chicken
1 - 2 cans chow mein noodles

Heat oil in 12" skillet over low heat. Mix in onions and celery. Sprinkle with salt and sugar. Add chicken stock. Cover and boil gently about 10 minutes. Drain bean sprouts. Mix cornstarch and soy sauce until smooth with ¼ C. liquid. Add to skillet. Cook and stir until thickened. Add bean sprouts and chicken. Mix and reheat. Serve over rice and top with chow mein noodles.

YUM YUM ONE DISH MEAL   Mrs. Matthew Troyer

1 lb. hamburger, browned with 1 chopped onion
1 can cream of mushroom soup   1 C. chopped celery, optional
1 can cream of chicken soup   4 T. soy sauce
½ C. uncooked rice   2 C. water

Mix all together and put in buttered casserole and bake 1 hour at 375°.

MEAT LOAF TATOR TOT CASSEROLE   Mrs. Henry Beachy

1 C. tomato juice
¾ C. oatmeal
1 beaten egg
¼ t. onion salt

1 t. salt
¼ t. pepper
2 lbs. hamburger
1 can cream of mushroom soup

Combine first 6 ingredients and mix well, add hamburger. Put in 9" x 13" baking pan. Add cream of mushroom soup and top with tator tots. Bake at 350° for 1 hour.

MEAT BALL AND VEGETABLE CASSEROLE

Mrs. Peter L. Miller

1 lb. ground beef
1/2 C. dry bread or cracker crumbs
1/3 C. milk
1 beaten egg
1/4 C. onion chopped fine
1 t. salt
1/4 t. dry mustard

2 T. butter or margarine
1 can cream of mushroom soup
1 1/2 C. shredded Cheddar
  cheese
1/2 t. sage
2 pkg. frozen mixed vegetables

In a bowl combine beef, crumbs, milk, egg, onion, salt and mustard. Mix lightly and shape into small balls about 1 1/4". In a large skillet melt butter, brown meat balls on all sides. Combine soup, cheese and sage. Meanwhile cook vegetables according to package directions. Drain, arrange meatballs around sides of shallow greased 1 1/2 qt. baking dish. Spoon soup mixture into center, place vegetables on top. Cover with foil. Bake in preheated oven at 350° for 30 minutes.

EL PASO CASSEROLE

Mrs. Peter L. Miller

1 3/4 lb. Velveeta cheese
2 lbs. ham, cut in small pieces
1 1/2 lb. noodles

1/2 lb. butter
1 C. flour
1/2 gal. milk

Cook noodles in water, drain and rinse with cold water so they won't stick together. Blend cheese and ham into white sauce. Pour over noodles in pan greased with oil and sprinkled with toasted bread crumbs. I put this batch in a stainless steel roaster. Bake at 350° for 25 minutes.

OVEN BAKED SAUSAGE CASSEROLE

Mrs. Marvin Wengerd

1 lb. bulk hot sausage
1 diced red pepper
1 diced green pepper
1 med. onion chopped
6 eggs

1/4 C. milk
1/2 t. garlic salt
1/2 t. white pepper
1 1/2 C. grated sharp Cheddar
  cheese

Crumble sausage, brown and drain. Sauté the vegetables and drain. Beat eggs, milk, garlic and salt until frothy. Layer sausage, vegetables and cheese in greased 1 1/2 qt. casserole. Top with egg mixture, bake at 350° until set, about 35 minutes. Yields 6 servings.

SAUERKRAUT WITH SAUSAGE

Twila Beachy

1 lb. bulk sausage
1 lg. can or bag sauerkraut
3 T. brown sugar

1 diced onion
1 C. ketchup

Mix all together. Bake at 275° for 4 - 5 hours. Stirring occasionally, may need to add a little water.

UNDERGROUND HAM CASSEROLE

Mrs. Ben Troyer, Jr.
Mrs. Paul Mast

4 C. diced ham
4 T. butter
1/2 C. onions
1 T. Worcestershire sauce
2 cans cream of mushroom soup

1 - 2 C. Velveeta cheese
1 C. milk
4 qt. mashed potatoes
1 pt. sour cream
browned crumbled bacon

Combine ham, butter, onions, Worcestershire sauce. Heat until onions are soft. Put in bottom of roaster. In saucepan heat soup, 1 C. milk and cheese, heat until cheese melts. Place over top of ham. Put in oven for 1 hour. Mash potatoes, add sour cream, milk, and salt. Put potatoes on top of ham mixture. Bake 20 minutes longer.

CHEESEBURGER PIE

Mary Ellen Schlabach

1 1/4 lb. hamburger
3/4 C. bread or cracker crumbs
3/4 C. spaghetti sauce

1/4 C. milk
3/4 lb. Velveeta cheese
1 beaten egg

Fry hamburger and then add bread or cracker crumbs and sauce. Put in unbaked pie crust. Bake till crust is browned. Heat milk and add Velveeta cheese. After cheese is melted add 1 beaten egg. Put on top of hamburger and bake until cheese turns a little brown.

PIGS IN A BLANKET

Mrs. Josiah Miller

1 lb. hamburger
3/4 C. tomato juice
1 sm. minced onion
1/2 t. Worcestershire sauce

1 t. salt
1/4 t. pepper
1 C. raw rice

Brown hamburger and onion together. Add rice and cook for a few minutes. Take a large cabbage leaf which has been steamed in boiling water. Put a few tablespoons of the meat mixture on the leaf, roll up and secure with toothpicks. Lay in greased casserole and top with tomato juice, tomato soup can also be used. Bake at 350° - 400° for 1 hour or until tender. I like to put these in a skillet and pour tomato juice and soup over them and simmer for 3/4 - 1 hour.

SHEPHERD'S PIE

Mrs. Henry Beachy

6 lb. hamburger
2½ C. oatmeal
3 eggs
1 t. pepper

4 t. salt
1 t. onion salt
3 C. milk

Mix together and bake in a large roaster at 350° for 1 hour. Cool. Cook 6 qt. peeled and cut up potatoes, when soft pour off water, mash and add the following:

4 oz. cream cheese
½ stick butter
4 t. salt

1 C. sour cream
1 t. onion salt

Add milk till it is creamy. Cool. When both are cold add 2 cans cream of mushroom soup on top of hamburger, and add mashed potatoes, top with Velveeta cheese. Refrigerate overnight. Put in oven at 250° for 3 hours.

CORNED BEEF AND CABBAGE CASSEROLE

Mrs. Robert W. Yoder

1 sm. head cabbage, cored and coarsley
   shredded about 4 C.
12 oz. flaked, corned beef

1 t. dry mustard
1 can cream of celery soup
1 med. onion chopped

Combine cabbage, corned beef, cream of celery soup, onion and mustard in medium sized bowl. Cook uncovered in a 10" skillet over low heat until cabbage is crisp - tender, about 20 minutes. This is very easy to make and delicious. Just make it in a skillet on top of the stove.

CABBAGE CASSEROLE

Mrs. Alfred Miller

1 lg. head cabbage, shredded
1 chopped onion
6 T. butter
1 can cream of mushroom soup

8 oz. American cheese, cubed
salt to taste
pepper
1 C. dry bread crumbs

Cook cabbage in boiling salt water till tender, drain well. Sauté onion and 5 T. butter in skillet until tender, add soup and mix well, add cheese, heat and stir until melted. Remove from heat stir in cabbage, salt and pepper. Pour into ungreased 2 qt. baking dish. Melt remaining butter, cook and stir in crumbs until lightly browned. Bake uncovered at 350° for 20 - 30 minutes.

BUBBLE PIZZA
Mrs. Fremon Miller

2 cans buttermilk biscuits
1 lb. hamburger or sausage, browned
1 qt. pizza sauce

mushrooms, optional
cut up peppers
cheese

Cut each biscuit into 4 pieces and toss into pan, add browned meat and pizza sauce. Add whatever pizza toppings you prefer. Mix together and pour into baking dish. Fill only to the depth of 3". Add shredded Mozzarella and Cheddar cheese. Bake at 275° for 1 hour.

DEEP DISH PIZZA
Mrs. Martha Sue Miller

1 lb. hamburger
onions
cheese
1 sm. chopped, green pepper
1 sm. can mushrooms
6 oz. pizza sauce

1 T. yeast
2 T. oil
1 t. sugar
1 t. salt
2½ C. flour

Dissolve yeast in 1 C. warm water. Stir in sugar, salt, oil and flour, beat vigorously. Let rest for 5 minutes. Press dough evenly on bottom and halfway up sides of greased 9" x 13" pan. Brown hamburger and drain. Mix pizza sauce with hamburger. Place mixture on dough and top with mushrooms and your favorite kind of cheese. Bake at 375° for 20 - 25 minutes.

POUR PIZZA
Mrs. Matthias Mast

1 lb. ground beef
1 chopped onion
1 t. salt
⅛ t. pepper
1 C. flour
2 eggs

⅔ C. milk
⅛ t. oregano
1 can pizza sauce
2 C. grated cheese
pepperoni
mushrooms

Brown hamburger and onion, season with salt and pepper. Combine flour, oregano, eggs and milk, to make a soft batter. Pour into greased 9" x 13" pan. Sprinkle meat, mushrooms and pepperoni over batter and bake at 400° for 15 - 20 minutes. Remove from oven spread with pizza sauce and sprinkle with cheese. Return to oven for 15 minutes.

ે&

Kindness is becoming at any age.

QUICK SOUTHWESTERN PIZZA

Mrs. Mark Hochstetler

1½ C. Bisquick mix
⅓ C. very hot water
2 C. cooked, cut up chicken
½ C. salsa

2 C. shredded Mozzarella
  cheese
¼ C. onion, chopped
½ pepper, cut into rings

Grease 12" pizza pan. Mix Bisquick mix and water, beat vigorously, 20 strokes. Turn onto floured surface. Knead about 60 times or until no longer sticky. Press into pizza pan. Mix chicken and salsa. Sprinkle crust with 1 C. of cheese, top with onions, chicken mixture and pepper. Sprinkle with remaining cheese. Bake at 450° for 12 - 15 minutes, or until crust is brown and cheese is bubbly.

UPSIDE DOWN PIZZA

Mrs. Henry Beachy

2 lbs. hamburger or sausage
2 C. pizza sauce
pepperoni
peppers

16 oz. sour cream
Mozzarella cheese
1 tube Crescent rolls
mushrooms

Brown meat, add salt and pepper to taste. Add pizza sauce. Put in bottom of 9" x 13" pan. Layer with pepperoni, mushrooms and peppers. Bake at 350° for 15 - 20 minutes. Remove from oven and cover with sour cream and Mozzarella cheese. Top with unrolled Crescent rolls. Bake until Crescent rolls are browned.

RICE AND CURRY

Mrs. Chuck Karn

1 lb. hamburger
2 lg. diced onions
1½ t. curry powder
2 C. tomato juice or sauce
salt and pepper to taste

1 bowl cooked rice
1 qt. frozen peas, prepared
1 bowl salad with lettuce,
  tomatoes, chopped peppers
  and onions, any dressing

Fry hamburger and onions, add tomato sauce, curry powder, salt and pepper. Simmer. To serve make stacks on plate as for haystacks in this order – rice, peas, hamburger mixture and salad.

SAUSAGE OR HAM CASSEROLE

Lois Mast

1 lb. lean ground sausage, browned. Place 8 slices of cubed bread into bottom of 9" x 13" greased pan. Drain sausage and sprinkle over bread. Whip 6 eggs. Add ¾ t. dry mustard and 2½ C. milk. Mix well and pour over bread and sausage. Grate 2 C. cheese on top. Can be refrigerated overnight. When ready to bake, mix 1 can cream of mushroom soup and 2½ cans milk and pour over top of casserole. Bake at 350° for 45 minutes.

SWEET AND SOUR PORK WITH RICE

Mrs. Mike Schrock

2 T. cooking oil
1 lb. boneless pork, cut up in 1" cubes
15¼ oz. can pineapple chunks or
    just the juice from pineapple
½ C. light corn syrup
¼ C. vinegar

2 T. soy sauce
2 T. cornstarch
½ C. red and green peppers
    sliced
1 T. Worcestershire sauce
1 T. barbeque sauce

Heat cooking oil in skillet. Brown pork, add next 4 ingredients. Bring to a boil. Simmer 10 minutes or until done. Add Worcestershire sauce and barbeque sauce. Mix cornstarch and 2 T. water. Add to pork to thicken. Boil 2 minutes, stirring constantly. Just before serving add peppers. Serve over rice.

CALICO RICE

Mrs. Willis Karen Miller

1 med. green pepper, diced
1 med. yellow pepper, diced
1 med. sweet red pepper, diced
1 med. onion, diced
2 T. butter or margarine
1½ C. uncooked long grain rice
1 pkg. dry onion soup mix

2 T. picante sauce or salsa
1 T. ground cumin
4 garlic cloves, minced
½ t. salt
3 C. water
sour cream, optional

Sauté peppers and onions with butter in skillet for 3 minutes. Stir in rice, soup mix, picante sauce or salsa, cumin, garlic, salt and water. Bring to a boil. Reduce heat, cover and simmer for 20 - 25 minutes, or until rice is tender. Garnish with sour cream if desired.

SPANISH RICE

Mrs. Mark Hochstetler

¼ C. butter
2 C. uncooked instant rice
14½ oz. cut up tomatoes with liquid
1 C. boiling water
2 beef bouillon cubes
1 med. onion chopped

1 minced garlic clove
1 bay leaf
1 t. sugar
1 t. salt
¼ t. pepper

In sauce pan over medium heat, melt butter. Add rice and stir until browned. Add remaining ingredients. Bring to a boil, reduce heat, cover and simmer 10 - 15 minutes or until liquid is absorbed and rice is tender. Remove bay leaf before serving. This tastes great with taco filled peppers.

QUICK TUNA CASSEROLE   Bena Beachy

1 can cream of mushroom soup
1/3 C. milk
7 oz. tuna, drained and flaked

1 1/4 C. crushed potato chips
1 C. cooked or canned peas

Combine soup and milk in casserole. Add tuna, 1 C. chips and peas. Blend. Sprinkle remaining chips on top. Bake at 350° for 25 minutes.

MACARONI CASSEROLE   Mrs. Willis Wagler

4 lbs. chicken
2 C. uncooked macaroni
1/2 lb. Velveeta cheese
1/2 C. cream

1/2 C. flour
4 C. broth
4 C. bread crumbs
2 T. butter

Cook chicken, season and cut into cubes. Cook macaroni and drain. Thicken broth with flour, mix chicken, macaroni and cheese with broth. Put in greased roaster. Brown bread crumbs in butter, add cream and mix with bread crumbs. Put on top of chicken mixture. Bake at 325° for 30 minutes.

ZUCCHINI PATTIES   Mrs. Ben Troyer, Jr.

2/3 C. Bisquick mix
1/4 C. Parmesan cheese
2 eggs

2 C. grated zucchini
1 sm. chopped onion
salt and pepper

Combine the above ingredients and drop by spoonful into heavy skillet containing a thin layer of hot oil or butter. Spread out and flatten as you turn them with a spatula. Fry until golden brown on both sides.

FRENCH FRIED ONIONS   Mrs. Nathan Mast

1/2 C. flour
1/4 t. salt
1/2 t. baking powder

1 egg slightly beaten
2 t. vegetable oil
1/4 C. milk

Mix all ingredients together. Slice and separate 3 - 4 large onions, dip in batter and deep fry in vegetable oil.

❧

Many people are like sign posts. They spend their lives pointing in the right direction, but never go that way themselves.

CUBE STEAK POTATO CASSEROLE

Mrs. Mark Hochstetler

1/3 C. oleo
6 cube steak
3 med. onions
1 can sliced mushrooms
1 can cream of mushroom soup
1 C. buttermilk

3 T. chopped parsley
1 t. salt
1/4 t. dry mustard
6 med. sliced potatoes
5 med. sliced carrots

In skillet melt oleo, brown meat slowly. Remove meat and sauté onions till tender, remove. Use drippings and add the next six ingredients. Heat through. Arrange in layers in greased casserole, 1/2 of potatoes and carrots, 3 cube steaks, onions and 1/2 of the sauce. Repeat layers. Bake slowly at 325° for 3 hours covered. Uncover and bake 1/2 hour longer.

PEPPER STEAK

Mrs. Henry Schrock

2 lb. steak cut in 1/4" strips
1 T. paprika, tossed with meat strips
4 T. butter or oleo
1/4 t. garlic salt
1/2 C. onions, sliced thin
1 green pepper sliced thin

1 1/2 C. beef broth
2 T. cornstarch
1/4 C. water
1 T. soy sauce
1 can bean sprouts
rice

Brown meat in butter, sprinkle with garlic salt. Remove meat and add peppers and onions. Cook 2 minutes and add beef broth. Cool 1 minute and add soy sauce with water and cornstarch. Cook 1 minute longer, then add meat and bean sprouts. Cover and simmer for 30 minutes or until meat is tender. Can also be baked 30 - 45 minutes. Serve over cooked rice. Serves 8 people.

POOR MAN'S FILET MIGNON

Mrs. Jay Miller

2 lbs. extra lean ground beef
4 slices bread crumbled
2 eggs beaten
1/2 C. milk
2 t. salt
12 slices uncooked bacon

1 T. minced onion
2 t. dried celery flakes
1/2 t. chili powder
18 oz. smoke flavored
    barbeque sauce

Combine first 8 ingredients and 2 T. barbeque sauce. Form into 12 thick patties. Wrap a bacon slice around the sides of each patty and secure with a toothpick. Bake on a rack at 350° for 50 - 60 minutes or until desired doneness. Baste frequently with remaining barbeque sauce the last 30 minutes. Yields 12 servings.

MEAT LOAF

Mrs. Mark Hochstetler

2 lbs. hamburger
2 eggs
1 pkg. onion soup mix

1 bag crackers
2 med. onions
salt and pepper

Mix together. Put in a baking dish. Top with ³/₄ C. ketchup, ¹/₂ C. brown sugar and a little mustard mixed together. Bake 45 minutes or until done.

MEAT LOAF

Mrs. Allen Beachy

1¹/₂ lbs. ground beef
³/₄ C. oatmeal
2 eggs beaten
¹/₄ C. chopped onion

2 t. salt
¹/₄ t. pepper
1 C. tomato juice

Sauce:
¹/₂ C. catsup
1 T. mustard

2 T. brown sugar

Combine ingredients thoroughly and pack firmly into loaf pan or 9" x 9" pan. Top with sauce. Bake at 350° for 1 hour. Let stand 5 minutes before slicing.

MEAT LOAF

Mrs. Marvin Wengerd

1 egg
³/₄ C. quick oats
1 C. tomato juice
¹/₂ onion, minced

1 t. salt
¹/₄ t. pepper
1¹/₂ lb. ground beef
1 T. soy sauce

Beat egg. Add remaining ingredients and mix well. Form into loaf and bake at 350° for 1 hour. Just before serving put a few slices of cheese on top and sprinkle with parsley for an attractive look.

SAVORY MEAT LOAF

Mrs. Nathan Miller

2 lbs. hamburger
¹/₄ C. onion, minced
1 C. oatmeal or crackers
2¹/₂ t. salt

1 beaten egg
¹/₄ t. pepper
1 t. mustard
¹/₄ C. catsup

Glaze:
¹/₂ C. brown sugar
1¹/₂ t. prepared mustard

1 T. Worcestershire sauce
¹/₄ C. catsup

Mix and form into loaf. Bake at 350° for 1 hour. After baked for ¹/₂ hour spread glaze on top and bake till done.

BREADED PORK CHOPS

Mrs. Duane Hershberger

1/2 C. milk
1 egg lightly beaten
1 1/2 C. crushed saltine crackers

1/4 C. cooking oil
6 pork chops, 1" thick

In a shallow pan, combine milk and egg. Dip each pork chop in this mixture, then coat with cracker crumbs, patting to make a thick coating. Heat oil in large skillet. Cook pork chops, uncovered, for about 8 - 10 minutes per side or until browned and no pink remains inside.

SAUCY MEATBALLS

Mrs. Firman Miller
Mrs. Dean Wengerd
Mrs. John Mark Troyer

1 lb. hamburger
1/2 C. dry bread or cracker crumbs
1/4 C. milk
2 T. finely chopped onion

1/4 t. salt
1/2 t. Worcestershire sauce
1 egg

Sauce:
10 3/4 oz. can cream of chicken soup
1/3 C. milk

1/8 t. ground nutmeg
1/2 C. dairy sour cream

Mix ingredients for meatballs. Shape into 20 - 1 1/2" balls. Brown both sides in skillet. Combine sauce ingredients, all but sour cream. Pour sauce over meatballs. Cover and simmer for 20 - 30 minutes. Add sour cream. Heat another 10 minutes, or bake in ungreased pan at 400° for 20 minutes or until light brown. Mix sauce all but sour cream and add to meatballs. Then bake at 350° for 30 minutes. Stir in sour cream and bake another 10 minutes. We like these with mashed potatoes.

SWEDISH MEATBALLS

Mrs. Henry Schrock

1 lb. ground beef
1 t. salt
1/8 t. garlic salt
1/2 C. water

1/8 t. pepper
1/8 T. celery salt
1/2 C. dry bread or cornflake
   crumbs

Sauce:
1 chopped onion
1 can mushroom soup

1/2 C. water
1 t. Worcestershire sauce

Mix together and form into balls. Brown or grill and place in casserole in layers with sauce. Bake 1 1/2 hours or until gravy is nicely browned. This is enough sauce for 2 batches of meatballs.

PORCUPINE MEATBALLS IN BBQ SAUCE   Mrs. David Ray Yoder

1 1/2 lb. hamburger
3 slices bread, diced
1 egg, beaten
3/4 C. milk

1/4 C. minute rice
1 t. salt
1/4 t. pepper
1/2 onion

Barbeque Sauce:
1 C. tomato juice
1/2 t. Worcestershire sauce
1/2 t. chili powder

1/2 C. catsup
1/4 C. brown sugar

Soak bread in milk, add beaten egg, mix with hamburger and remaining ingredients. Shape into balls and place in a single layer in baking dish. Mix sauce ingredients and pour over meatballs. Bake at 400° for 35 minutes, uncovered, cover and bake 35 minutes longer at 350°.

SOPHISTICATED MEATBALLS   Mrs. Jay Miller

1 lb. hamburger
1 can cream of mushroom soup
8 oz. cream cheese

1/4 C. milk
noodles

Mix hamburger like for meatloaf, make balls. Brown and drain grease. Melt cream cheese, soup and milk. Mix until smooth. Add meatballs and simmer. Cook noodles in salt water. Pour sauce over noodles and serve.

SAUSAGE BALLS   Orpha Peachey

1 lb. uncooked sausage
4 oz. Cheddar cheese

3 C. buttermilk Bisquick mix

Mix and roll into 1" balls. Bake at 350° or until done. Can prepare the day before the party. Makes 70 - 75 balls.

HOT HAM SANDWICHES   Mrs. Henry Beachy

1 doz. buns
2 lbs. chipped ham

12 slices hot pepper cheese

Make sandwiches, wrap in foil and put in oven. Bake at 425° for 12 - 15 minutes.

DELICIOUS HAM LOAF WITHOUT HAM   Mrs. Willis Karen Miller

1 lb. hamburger
1/2 lb. ground hot dogs or bologna
1 C. cracker crumbs
Mix together and add 1/2 of the following glaze:
3/4 C. brown sugar
1/2 t. dry mustard

1 egg
1 t. salt

1 T. vinegar
1/2 C. water

Shape in loaf form and baste with remaining glaze. Bake at 350° for 1 - 1 1/2
hours.

MOCK HAM LOAF   Mrs. Crist Miller

2 lbs. hamburger
1 lb. ground Trail bologna
2 eggs
pepper to taste

1/2 C. oatmeal or cracker
   crumbs
Lawry's seasoning salt to taste

Glaze:
1/2 C. ketchup
1 T. mustard

1/4 C. brown sugar

Mix hamburger, Trail bologna, eggs, quick oats, salt and pepper. Add a little milk
if it seems too solid. Form into pan. Mix ketchup, mustard and brown sugar for
glaze. Put glaze on top of meat and bake at 350° for 1 hour.

MOCK HAM LOAF   Mrs. Roy Mast

2 lbs. ground beef
1 lb. wieners, ground
2 C. cracker crumbs

2 eggs
2 t. salt

Glaze:
1 1/2 C. brown sugar
1 t. dry mustard

2 T. vinegar
1 C. water

Mix beef and wieners with crackers and eggs. Add 1/2 of the glaze. Make a loaf
shape and pour the rest of the glaze over the loaf. Bake at 350° for 1 1/2 hours.
Or you can use only 1/2 of the glaze recipe, adding it all to the meat mixture
then baste the top and sides of the loaf with 1 C. catsup, 1 T. mustard and 2
T. brown sugar.

MOCK HAM LOAF

Mrs. Philip Troyer

2 lbs. hamburger
1 lb. ground wieners
2 C. cracker crumbs
2 eggs
1 T. vinegar

2 t. salt
3/4 C. brown sugar
1/2 C. water
1/2 t. dry mustard

Barbeque Sauce:
1 C. catsup
1/4 C. brown sugar

1 T. Worcestershire sauce
1/4 t. mustard

Mix all ingredients together. Bake at 350° for 1 hour. Baste with barbeque sauce. Bake another 1/2 hour.

BURGER BUNDLES

Mrs. Alfred Miller

2 lbs. hamburger
1 pkg. onion soup mix
1 egg
1/2 t. pepper

2 T. water
1/3 C. dry bread crumbs
3/4 lb. Velveeta cheese

Mix all together, except cheese. Press into bottom of 10" x 15" baking pan, prick meat with fork. Bake 15 minutes or until desired doneness. Drain. Place cheese slices over meat. Bake 1 minute more until cheese is melted. Cut into 24 squares and serve on buns topped with a pickle slice.

BARBEQUED BEEF

Rosanna Miller

1 qt. chunk beef, cut up
1 onion, diced
1/2 C. catsup
2 T. brown sugar

2 T. vinegar
2 t. prepared mustard
1 t. Worcestershire sauce
1 t. salt

Heat chunk beef and drain juice, add rest of ingredients.

BARBEQUED HAMBURGERS

Mrs. Matthias Mast

1 lb. ground beef
1/2 C. milk
1 t. salt

1/2 C. cracker crumbs
1 sm. onion
1/4 t. pepper

Mix together and bake with barbeque sauce.

BARBEQUES

Mrs. Mark Hochstetler

1½ lbs. hamburger
¾ C. quick oats
½ C. milk
1 T. onion flakes
1½ t. salt
½ t. pepper

1 T. Worcestershire sauce
2 T. brown sugar
3 T. vinegar
1 C. catsup
½ C. water
6 T. chopped onion

Mix the first six ingredients. Form patties and brown. Mix the next six ingredients and pour over the hamburgers. Bake at 350° for 1 hour. Seven batches makes approximately 100 patties. This hamburger mixture is also delicious made on the grill with butter and regular barbeque sauce.

SLOPPY JOE

Mrs. Mark Hochstetler

1 lb. hamburger
¼ C. quick oats
onion
2 - 3 T. flour
1 t. salt
⅛ t. pepper

¾ C. water
½ t. Worcestershire sauce
¾ C. catsup
1½ T. mustard
4 T. brown sugar
salsa, optional

Mix hamburger, quick oats, onions, salt and pepper. Brown. Sprinkle with flour and stir. Add water and simmer. Then add catsup, Worcestershire sauce, mustard, brown sugar and salsa.

SLOPPY JOES

Mrs. Willis Wagler

2 lbs. hamburger, browned with onions
¾ C. water
3 T. white sugar
1 T. salt
2 T. vinegar

1 C. ketchup
1 C. chopped celery
¾ C. oatmeal
1 C. milk

Bake 1½ hour at 200°.

PIZZA BURGERS

Mrs. Mark Hochstetler

2 lbs. hamburger, browned and drained
1 lb. ground bologna
¼ lb. ground pepperoni
1 lb. Cheddar cheese
  ½ sharp and ½ mild

1 pt. pizza sauce
1 T. oregano
1 t. salt
½ t. pepper

Mix together and spread on ½ of bun. Open face. Bake at 325°. Yields approximately 3 doz.

PIZZA BURGERS   Mrs. Nathan Mast

1 lb. hamburger, browned and drained   2¹/₂ t. oregano
10 oz. Velveeta cheese   ¹/₂ t. salt
¹/₂ lb. bologna   ¹/₈ t. pepper
¹/₄ lb. pepperoni   Mozzarella cheese
1¹/₂ C. pizza sauce

Grind first 4 ingredients. Add remaining 4 ingredients. Mix well. Put on half buns top with Mozzarella cheese. Bake at 375° until cheese melts. This freezes well.

BARBEQUE SAUCE FOR CHICKEN   Mrs. Firman Miller
                                       Mrs. Merle Hershberger

1 pt. vinegar   5 T. Worcestershire sauce
1 pt. water   ¹/₂ t. garlic salt
¹/₂ lb. butter   ¹/₂ t. pepper
¹/₂ C. salt

Marinate chicken for 20 - 22 hours then barbeque. This is very good. 6 recipes for 26 halves.

BARBEQUE SAUCE FOR RIBS   Mrs. Willis Karen Miller

3 pt. ketchup   ¹/₂ C. barbeque sauce
1¹/₄ T. salt   ¹/₂ C. Worcestershire sauce
1¹/₄ T. onion salt   1¹/₂ C. water
dash of black pepper   6 C. brown sugar
1 t. mustard

Pour over meat and bake 2 hours.

STEAK BARBEQUE SAUCE   Barbara Schrock

1 sm onion, minced   2 T. Worcestershire sauce
2 T. cooking oil   2 T. vinegar
1 T. mustard   1 can tomato paste
2 T. sugar   ¹/₄ C. catsup
a few drops of Tabasco sauce

Brush this on steak as you barbeque it. This sauce is good on spare ribs and other pork.

PINEAPPLE SAUCE FOR HAM

Mrs. Marvin Wengerd
Mrs. Willis Karen Miller

1/4 C. water
1 1/2 C. brown sugar
1 1/2 T. ketchup
1 1/2 T. soy sauce
1/2 C. water

1 1/2 t. dry mustard
1 1/2 C. crushed pineapple
  with juice
2 1/4 T. cornstarch

Combine water, sugar, ketchup, soy sauce, mustard and pineapple in sauce-pan. Bring to a boil, simmer 10 minutes. Dissolve cornstarch in 1/2 C. water, add to sauce, cook stirring until clear. Serve over ham slices. Yield, about 4 C. sauce.

MARINADING SAUCE

Mrs. Crist Beachy

1 C. ketchup
1 C. barbeque sauce
1/4 C. Worcestershire sauce

1 squirt lemon juice
1/4 C. cooking wine
1/4 C. A-1 steak sauce

Combine everything. Soak meat overnight, then barbeque. Use this as your barbeque sauce also.

STEAK MARINADE

Anna Fern Troyer

1 C. Regina red wine vinegar
1 t. salt

3 dashes pepper
1/2 C. butter flavored oil or
  Wesson oil

Marinade for at least 3 hours before grilling.

SHAKE AND BAKE

Mrs. Willis Wagler

1 C. flour
dash of pepper
1/2 t. salt

2 t. paprika
1 t. baking powder

Mix thoroughly. Place in a plastic bag and put chicken pieces in the bag and shake. In pan melt 1/4 lb. butter place chicken pieces in pan. Bake at 350° for 1 1/2 or 2 hours until tender.

TOMATO GRAVY   Mrs. Henry Beachy

1 C. tomato juice   1 t. salt
$^1/_2$ C. water $^1/_3$ C. flour
$^1/_2$ C. brown sugar   1 C. milk

Heat juice, water, sugar and salt. Mix flour and milk, add to juice and cook until thick. If it gets curdly, keep on stirring and it will disappear. Serve on home fries or buttered bread.

- Notes -

Large Quantity Recipes

POTATO AND HAM SOUP

Mrs. Eddie Miller

1½ C. butter
2½ C. flour
1 large onion chopped
6 qts. shredded potatoes

6 qts. milk
10 lbs. ham, chunked
2 lb. box Velveeta cheese

Put butter in canner and brown. Add flour to make a paste. Add onion. Put potatoes in another kettle and add enough water to cover, heat till boiling then add to browned mixture, water and all. Add milk and ham. Last add cheese, salt, and pepper to taste. Don't let boil after adding milk and ham. This almost fills a 20 qt. canner.

COOKED NOODLES

Mrs. Henry Beachy

1 stick butter
¼ C. chicken base
2 qt. chicken broth
1 qt. water

3 - 8 oz. pkg. noodles
1 can cream of chicken soup
salt

In 6 qt. kettle heat butter until brown, add water, broth, chicken base and salt. Bring to a boil then add noodles. Cook on low heat about 15 minutes. Add soup, heat and turn off, cover and let set for a while.

LARGE BATCH SLOPPY JOES

Mrs. Eddie Miller

1 lb. oleo
1½ C. flour
5 lb. hamburger
3 onions

3 C. ketchup
¼ C. mustard
1 C. brown sugar

Brown flour and butter, add hamburger stirring constantly till hamburger is browned. Then add the rest and simmer for 10 - 15 minutes.

BBQ HAM SANDWICHES FOR CHURCH

Mrs. Roy Mast

50 lbs. chipped ham
6 onions
20 C. ketchup

2½ C. vinegar
7½ C. brown sugar

Combine chopped onion, ketchup, vinegar and brown sugar. Pour over ham. Alternate layers. Bake uncovered in roasters at 300°. Stir a few times.

BBQ SAUCE

Mrs. Henry Beachy

3 gal. ketchup
9 T. salt
9 T. onion salt
3 T. pepper
4 T. mustard

2$\frac{1}{4}$ C. Mom's BBQ sauce
2$\frac{1}{4}$ C. Worcestershire sauce
12 C. water
28 C. brown sugar

Mix all ingredients well. This make a 21 qt. canner full. Put sauce between layers of meat. This is enough sauce for 170 lbs. ham. You can buy Mom's brand BBQ sauce at Der Dutchman's Bakery.

POT LUCK POTATOES

Mrs. Henry Beachy

18 - 20 lbs. potatoes, cooked and diced
Mix:
1 lb. melted butter
5 C. sour cream
3 lbs. Velveeta cheese, melted
2 - 10 oz. cans cream of chicken soup
$\frac{1}{4}$ t. garlic salt

4 C. crushed cornflakes
$\frac{1}{2}$ C. melted butter

Pour over potatoes and stir, add some milk. Top with 4 C. crushed cornflakes mixed with $\frac{1}{2}$ C. melted butter. Bake at 350° for 1$\frac{1}{2}$ hours.

POTATO AND HAMBURG CASSEROLE

Mrs. Roy Mast

6 lb. hamburger
3 onions
6 cans cream of celery soup or
  cream of mushroom soup

6 cans cream of chicken soup
$\frac{1}{2}$ box Velveeta cheese
12 lbs. potatoes
  (diced and cooked)

Fry hamburger with onions. Add potatoes, soups and cheese. Bake until thoroughly heated. Makes large roaster full.

CORN MADE IN OVEN

Mrs. Henry Beachy

7 qt. frozen corn
7 t. salt

1 lb. butter

Put $\frac{1}{2}$ lb. butter in roaster and add corn, top with salt and $\frac{1}{2}$ lb. butter. Cover and bake at 300° for 3 hours.

DRESSING
Mrs. Henry Beachy

2 loaves white bread, toasted and cubed
2 loaves brown bread, toasted and cubed
2 qt. deboned chicken
2 C. diced celery
2 C. diced carrots
4 C. diced potatoes

Mix:
12 beaten eggs
1 qt. chicken broth
1 C. parsley
1 T. Lawry's seasoning salt
1 t. pepper
2 T. salt
¼ t. onion salt
1½ T. chicken soup base
3 qt. milk

Cook vegetables until tender. Take a 13 qt. mixing bowl and fill ¾ full with bread cubes, add vegetables and chicken, then combine and mix all ingredients. Fry with butter in skillet until well done. Place in slow cooker to keep warm until served.

GRAVY (1 GALLON)
Mrs. Henry Beachy

1 gallon chicken broth
9 egg yolks
13 T. Cally Lilly flour

1 T. chicken base
salt

Heat 3 qt. broth. Take remaining 1 qt. broth and add egg yolks, water, and flour to make a paste. Add to heated broth.

POTATO SALAD
Leona Yoder

12 C. potatoes - cooked, peeled and diced
12 hard boiled eggs, diced

½ C. chopped celery
½ C. chopped onion

Sauce:
3 C. Miracle Whip
2¼ C. white sugar
¼ C. vinegar

¼ C. mustard
¼ C. milk
4 t. salt

CUCUMBER SALAD
Twila Beachy

3 C. sour cream
2 C. Miracle Whip
2 T. vinegar

2½ C. white sugar
2 gal. sliced cucumbers

Slice cucumbers, soak in 2 T. salt for 1 - 2 hours. Drain, mix Miracle Whip, vinegar, sour cream and white sugar and add to cucumbers.

SWEET AND SOUR DRESSING   Twila Beachy

8 C. Miracle Whip   2 C. salad oil
4 C. white sugar $1/2$ C. mustard
$1/2$ C. vinegar   2 T. celery seed

Blend well.

FRUIT SLUSH   Mrs. Nathan Miller

$6^1/2$ C. white sugar
9 C. boiling water
Dissolve then add:
3 - 12 oz. frozen orange juice   4 qt. pineapple tidbits
54 oz. 7-Up   10 - 12 qt. peaches,
10 lbs. bananas, sliced thin   chunks, or slices
5 lbs. grapes, cut in half   3 C. blueberries

Mix all together. Put in containers and freeze. Yield 25 qts.

CREAM WAFER COOKIES   Mrs. Henry Beachy

2 C. oleo   6 t. soda
4 C. brown sugar   2 t. salt
8 eggs beaten   2 t. baking powder
4 t. vanilla   11 C. Gold Medal flour
8 T. cream

Mix together in order given. Don't refrigerate. Put in cookie press. Bake at
350°. Do not cut strips of cookie until you put frosting on them. Make frosting
and use cookie press to spread, this works very good. For chocolate wafers
put 8 squares of chocolate in dough. A batch chocolate and a batch vanilla
makes approximately 14 doz. Put chocolate wafer on one side and vanilla on
the other.

Frosting:
2 sticks butter, melted   4 t. vanilla
add $1/2$ C. milk   9 C. powdered sugar

CROUTONS   Mrs. Henry Beachy

1 loaf white bread
Put bread in refrigerator overnight. Oleo at room temperature. Spread oleo
on one side of bread. Put bread side by side and season with celery salt and
Lawry's seasoning salt. Stack slices and cut in $1/2$" squares. Put on cookie sheet
and bake at 250° for 1 hour.

SERVES 100 PEOPLE

This may vary as to what the rest of your meal consists of
and how many children there are.

Baked Beans	5 gal.	Meat Loaf	24 lbs.
Beef	40 lbs.	Milk	6 gal.
Beets	30 lbs.	Nuts	3 lbs.
Bread	10 loaves	Olives	$1^3/_4$ lbs.
Butter	3 lbs.	Pickles	2 qts.
Cakes	8	Pies	18
Carrots	3 lbs.	Potatoes	35 lbs.
Cheese	3 lbs.	Potato Salad	12 qts.
Chicken Pot Pie	40 lbs.	Roast Pork	40 lbs.
Coffee	3 lbs.	Rolls	150
Cream	3 qt.	Salad Dressing	3 qts.
Fruit Cocktail	21/2 gal.	Scalloped Potatoes	5 gal.
Fruit Juice	4 - 10 lb. cans	Soup	5 gal.
Fruit Salad	12 qt.	Tomato Juice	4 - 1 lb.cans
Ham	40 lbs.	Vegetables	4 - 10 lb. cans
Hamburger	30 - 36 lbs.	Wieners	25 lbs.
Ice Cream	4 gal.	Vegetable Salad	20 qt.
Lettuce	20 heads	Whipping Cream	4 qt.

ಇ

Thank God for dirty dishes,

They have a tale to tell;

While others may go hungry,

We're eating very well.

With Home, Health and Happiness,

I shouldn't want to fuss;

By the stack of evidence

God's been very good to us.

ಇ

If there's not enough left to save,
And a little to much to dump.
Then there's nothing to do but eat it,
That's what makes the housewife plump.

- Notes -

Desserts

YOGURT

Mrs. Matthew Troyer

Heat 1 quart milk to 150°. Add ½ t. plain gelatin soaked in a little cold water. Cool this down to 115°. Add 2 T. plain yogurt and beat well. Put in jar with lid on and put in oven with pilot light on. Keep in oven until it starts to thicken. (6 - 10 hours) Then refrigerate.

YOGURT

Mrs. Aaron Coblentz

2 qts. milk
1 T. Knox gelatin

2 T. active yogurt
½ C. sugar

Heat milk to 180°. Remove from heat and cool to 130°. Soak gelatin in a small amount of cold water. Add sugar, yogurt and gelatin to warm milk and mix well, stirring briskly for a few minutes. Put in containers and keep in warm place for about 12 hours. Cool. Good with red raspberry pie filling mixed in, or any other flavor.

YOGURT

Mrs. Eddie Miller

2 qts. milk
2 T. active yogurt
1 C. sugar

1 T. gelatin
⅓ C. cold water

Heat milk in saucepan to 190°. Remove and let cool to 130°. Meanwhile soak gelatin in cold water. Add to 130° milk. Mix sugar and yogurt, also add to milk mixing well. Put mixture in pint or quart jars. Cover with lids but not rings. Place in warm place for 8 hours or overnight. Screw on rings and chill. Serve plain or mix with dry jello.

YOGURT (1 GALLON)

Mrs. Alfred Miller

1 gallon milk
3 C. Carnation dry milk
5 t. gelatin

½ C. plain yogurt
1¼ C. sugar

Heat 1 gallon milk to 150°. Mix together 3 C. Carnation dry milk and 5 t. gelatin add to 150° milk stirring constantly and heating till it reaches 180°. Remove from heat and set in cold water, till temperature reaches 118° - 120°. Add ½ C. plain yogurt. Stir well, strain into bowl. Set bowl in hot water and keep at 115° for 8 hours. Do not stir. Leave thermometer in to check temperature. After 8 hours skim off top and add sugar and flavoring.

YOGURT

Mrs. Ivan Miller

1 gallon milk
2 T. unflavored gelatin
pie filling

1/2 C. plain yogurt
1 - 2 C. sugar

Heat milk to 180°. Let cool, soak gelatin in 1/2 C. cold water. Add plain yogurt and sugar. Beat all together and set in oven over pilot light for 8 hours. Skim off skin on top and beat well. Add pie filling to taste. Be sure to beat well before chilling and each time before you serve. Delicious and very smooth. Add more sugar and vanilla if plain yogurt is desired.

APPLE DUMPLINGS

JoAnne Schlabach

2 C. pastry flour
1/4 C. milk
2 t. baking powder

1/3 C. sugar
1/2 C. butter Crisco
1/2 t. salt

Syrup:
3/4 C. brown sugar
1/4 C. oleo
1 1/3 C. water

3 T. clear jel
cinnamon to taste

Knead dough gently like pie dough. Bake at 350° approximately 45 minutes or until done. Make 6 - 8 dumplings. Remove from oven and top with syrup.

APPLE DUMPLINGS

Mrs. Henry Beachy

10 - 12 lg. cooking apples
2 C. flour
2 1/2 t. baking powder

1/2 t. salt
2/3 C. Crisco
1/2 C. milk

Sauce:
1/2 C. brown sugar
1 C. sugar
1 T. flour

1/2 t. salt
1 T. butter
1 C. hot water

Mix dumpling ingredients and roll out. Slice apples and put on pastry with a dash of cinnamon on top. Roll like a pinwheel and slice about 2" thick. Arrange in 9" x 13" baking pan. Make sauce and pour on top. Bake at 350° for 30 - 40 minutes until apples are tender.

ॐ

Wisdom is knowing what to do next, virtue is doing it.

APPLE DUMPLINGS
Mrs. Nathan Mast

4 C. pastry flour   1 egg
$^1/_2$ C. white sugar   milk
1 C. Crisco $^1/_2$ t. salt

Mix first 3 ingredients like pie dough, put egg in 1 C. and fill with milk. Beat slightly and pour most of this into flour mixture, till right consistency. Roll dough out into $^3/_8$" thick and cut in squares. Place half of and apple in center of dough. Fill apple center with 1 t. of sugar cinnamon mixture. Moisten edges of dough and pinch shut. Place in cake pans. Pour caramel sauce over top and bake at 400°, till apples are tender.

Cinnamon Mixture:
1 C. white sugar   2 t. cinnamon

Caramel Sauce:
1 C. water $^1/_4$ t. cinnamon
1 C. brown sugar   2 T. butter
Bring to a boil and simmer 10 minutes.

OLD FASHIONED APPLE DUMPLINGS
Maria Miller

6 medium sized apples $^1/_2$ t. salt
2 C. flour $^2/_3$ C. shortening
$2^1/_2$ t. baking powder $^1/_2$ C. milk

Sauce:
2 C. brown sugar $^1/_4$ C. butter
2 C. water $^1/_4$ t. cinnamon

Pare and core apples. Cut into halves. Sift flour, baking powder and salt together. Cut in shortening until particles are the size of a pea. Sprinkle milk over mixture and press together lightly working dough only enough to hold together. Roll dough as for pastry and cut into six squares and place apples on each. Fill cavity of apple with sugar and cinnamon. Pat dough around apples to cover it completely. Fasten edges securely on top of apple. Place dumplings 1" apart in a greased baking pan. Pour the sauce over the dumplings. Which has been cooked together for 5 minutes. Bake at 375° for 35 - 40 minutes.

❧

A friend is a person who goes around saying
nice things about you, behind your back.

CHERRY - PEACH DUMPLINGS

Mrs. Robert W. Yoder

$^1/_2$ C. water
2 T. lemon juice
$^1/_2$ t. cinnamon
$^1/_8$ t. cloves
1 can cherry pie filling

1 can peaches, drained
milk
1 egg beaten
1$^1/_2$ C. Bisquick mix

In a 10" skillet mix water, lemon juice, cinnamon and cloves into pie filling. Add peaches and bring to a boil. Add milk to beaten egg to make $^1/_2$ C. Stir in Bisquick mix. Drop dough by tablespoon on top of boiling fruit. Cook over low heat for 10 minutes. Cover and cook 10 minutes more. Serve warm with milk and ice cream.

CARAMEL DUMPLINGS

Mrs. Duane Hershberger

Sauce:
2 T. butter
1$^1/_2$ C. packed brown sugar
1$^1/_2$ C. water

Dumplings:
1$^1/_4$ C. flour
$^1/_2$ C. sugar
2 t. baking powder
$^1/_2$ t. salt
$^1/_2$ C. milk

2 T. butter
2 t. vanilla
$^1/_2$ C. coarsely chopped peeled
    apple, optional

In a skillet heat the butter, brown sugar and water to boiling. Reduce heat to simmer. Meanwhile mix together all dumpling ingredients. Drop by tablespoons into the simmering sauce. Cover tightly and simmer 20 minutes. Do not lift lid. Serve warm with ice cream.

APPLE GOODIE

Mrs. Eli B. Yoder

$^3/_4$ C. white sugar
$^1/_2$ t. cinnamon
1 T. flour

$^1/_8$ t. salt
2 C. sliced apples

Topping:
$^1/_2$ C. oatmeal
$^1/_2$ C. brown sugar
$^1/_2$ C. flour

$^1/_4$ C. butter
$^1/_8$ t. soda
$^1/_8$ t. baking powder

Sift together sugar, flour, salt and cinnamon, combine with sliced apples. Mix well and place in the bottom of a greased casserole. To make topping, combine dry ingredients and cut in butter to make crumbs. Put crumbs on top of apple mixture. Bake at 375° for 35 - 40 minutes. Serve hot or cold with milk.

WARM APPLE PUDDING
Mrs. Jake Hershberger

4 T. melted butter   2 t. cinnamon
6 C. sliced apples   2 C. water
1 C. white sugar

Melt butter in 9" x 13" pan. Add apples, cinnamon and sugar. Pour water over mixture. Put the following on top of batter:

1 C. white sugar   2 t. baking powder
1/2 C. oleo   1 t. vanilla
2 eggs beaten   2 C. flour
1 t. salt   1 C. milk

Bake at 425° for 45 - 50 minutes. Serve with milk.

MINI APPLE CRISPS
Mrs. Mark Hochstetler

2 medium apples   2 T. butter or margarine
2 T. all-purpose flour   4 T. quick oats
4 T. brown sugar   1/4 t. cinnamon

Place apple slices in a small greased baking dish. In a small bowl combine flour and brown sugar. Cut in butter until mixture resembles coarse crumbs. Add oats and cinnamon. Sprinkle over apple slices. Bake uncovered at 350° for 35 - 40 minutes, or until tender. Serve with ice cream if desired. Just right for two!

APPLE ROLL
Mrs. Roy Mast

2 C. flour   3/8 C. milk
1/2 t. salt   4 chopped apples
3 t. baking powder   4 t. brown sugar
2 T. white sugar   butter
3 T. butter   cinnamon
1 egg

Syrup:
1 1/2 C. brown sugar   3/4 C. hot water
1 t. butter

Combine flour, salt, baking powder and 2 T. white sugar. Blend in 3 T. butter and egg. Add milk. Roll out and spread with apples. Sprinkle with 4 t. sugar. Dot with cinnamon and butter. Roll as jelly roll. Slice 1 1/2" thick. Lay in syrup in oblong pan and bake at 350°.

APPLE ROLL

Mrs. David Ray Yoder

2 C. flour
1/4 t. salt
4 t. baking powder
3 T. shortening

1/2 C. milk
4 peeled and shredded apples
2 T. sugar
1 egg, beaten

Sift together dry ingredients, add shortening and mix to form coarse crumbs. Add egg and milk. Roll out on floured board 1/2" thick, spread with apples and sprinkle with cinnamon. Roll up and slice. Place slices in 9" x 13" pan in a syrup made of 1 1/2 C. brown sugar and 2 C. hot water. Bake at 350° for 40 - 45 minutes. Serve warm with milk or ice cream.

APPLE FRITTERS

Maria Miller

1 C. finely chopped or grated unpeeled cored apples
1 beaten egg
3/4 C. milk
1/4 C. sugar
1/4 t. salt
1 t. grated orange peel
confectioners sugar

3 T. orange juice
1/2 t. vanilla
2 C. all-purpose flour
1 T. baking powder
oil for frying

In mixing bowl, combine beaten egg, milk, chopped apple, sugar, salt, orange peel, juice and vanilla. Stir together flour and baking powder, fold into egg mixture, stirring only until flour is moistened. Drop batter by rounded teaspoons into hot oil, 350°. Fry until deep golden brown about 3 - 4 minutes, turning once. Drain fritters thoroughly on paper towels. Roll in sugar and sift sugar over tops. Are also good glazed. Yield: about 40 fritters.

JELLY ROLL

Mrs. Paul Mast

4 eggs separated
3/4 C. sugar
1 t. vanilla

3/4 C. sifted cake flour
3/4 t. baking powder
1/4 t. salt

Beat egg yolks until light and lemon colored. Slowly add sugar, beating until creamy. Add vanilla, beat and sift together flour and baking powder. Gradually add to sugar mixture. Beat only until smooth. Beat egg whites with salt until stiff but not dry. Fold into flour mixture. Spread batter on a greased 10" x 15" jelly roll pan, lined with heavily greased wax paper. Bake at 375° for 15 minutes. Invert onto clean towel sprinkled with powdered sugar. Roll up in towel. Remove and fill with favorite filling.

CHOCOLATE CREAM ROLL

Mrs. David Ray Yoder

³/₄ C. flour
¹/₄ C. cocoa
1 t. baking powder
¹/₄ t. salt

1 C. white sugar
5 T. water
1 t. vanilla
3 large eggs separated

Sift dry ingredients and set aside. Beat the egg yolks until light, gradually add
³/₄ C. of the sugar beating thoroughly until thick and creamy. Beat in water and vanilla. Beat the egg whites until frothy, gradually beat in remaining ¹/₄ C. sugar and beat until the whites are stiff. Gently fold whites into the egg yolk mixture. Gradually fold in the sifted dry ingredients. Pour into 10" x 15" baking sheet which has been lined with wax paper. Bake at 325° for 20 minutes. When done quickly invert onto a towel dusted with powdered sugar. Carefully remove wax paper. Roll in towel and cool well before filling.

Cream Roll Filling:
2 T. flour
¹/₂ C. milk
¹/₄ C. butter
¹/₄ C. Crisco

pinch of salt
¹/₂ t. vanilla
¹/₂ C. white sugar

Mix flour and milk until smooth. Cook over low heat until thick, stirring constantly. Remove from heat and cool completely. Pour into mixing bowl and add butter and shortening. Blend on low speed. Add the salt, beat, until smooth and fluffy, at high speed. Add vanilla and sugar. Beat one more minute at high speed. Spread on cooled roll, reroll and chill before serving. Freezes well. I also use this filling for twinkies or ho ho cake.

APPLE CRISP

Mrs. Willis Priscilla Miller

8 C. shredded apples
2 C. water
2 C. sugar

4 T. clear jel
2 T. butter
cinnamon

Topping:
3 C. quick oats
1 C. flour
1¹/₂ C. brown sugar

3 t. cinnamon
³/₄ C. melted butter
1¹/₂ t. salt

Mix water, sugar, clear jel and butter. Cook until thick. Stir in apples and cinnamon. Put in pan. Mix together topping ingredients and spread over apples. Bake at 350° for about ¹/₂ hour or until lightly browned.

PEACH CRISP

Mrs. Jay Mark Martha Miller

1 C. oatmeal
$1/2$ C. brown sugar
$1/3$ C. melted butter
$1/3$ C. flour

$1/4$ t. nutmeg
$1/2$ t. cinnamon
5 C. peaches, fresh or canned

Place peaches in 9" baking dish. Combine remaining ingredients and spread on top of peaches. (When using fresh peaches sprinkle with sugar.) Bake at 375° for 30 minutes or until peaches are tender. Serve warm with milk or ice cream.

PEACH CRUMBLES

Mrs. Robert W. Yoder

8 peaches sliced
1 t. lemon juice
1 C. sifted flour

1 C. brown sugar
$1/8$ t. salt
$1/4$ C. butter

Arrange sliced peaches in buttered 8" baking dish. Sprinkle with lemon juice. Blend flour, sugar and salt together. Cut in butter. Sprinkle over peaches. Bake at 375° for 30 minutes. Serve with ice cream or whipped topping. 6 servings.

PUMPKIN TORTE

Mary Ellen Schlabach
Mrs. Roy Mast

Mix and press into 9" x 13" pan:
24 graham crackers, crushed
$1/3$ C. sugar

$1/2$ C. butter

Mix and pour over crust. Bake 20 minutes at 350°:
2 beaten eggs
$3/4$ C. sugar

8 oz. cream cheese

2 C. pumpkin
3 eggs separated
$1/2$ C. sugar
1 T. gelatin
$1/4$ C. cold water

$1/2$ C. milk
$1/2$ t. salt
1 T. cinnamon
8 oz. whipped topping

Cook pumpkin, egg yolks, $1/2$ C. sugar, milk, salt and cinnamon until mixture thickens. Remove from heat and add gelatin dissolved in cold water. Cool. Beat egg whites and $1/4$ C. sugar, fold into pumpkin mixture. Add 1 C. whipped topping. Pour over cooled crust. Top with rest of whipped topping.

PUMPKIN TRIFLE

Mrs. Mark Hoschtetler

2 - 3 C. leftover crumbled, unfrosted spice cake, muffins or gingerbread
16 oz. can pumpkin
1 t. ground cinnamon
1/4 t. ground nutmeg
1/4 t. ground ginger
2 C. whipping cream

1/4 t. ground allspice
2 1/2 C. cold milk
4 pkgs. instant butterscotch
pudding mix (3.4 oz.)
maraschino cherries

Set aside 1/4 C. of cake crumbs for top. Divide remaining crumbs into four equal portions. Sprinkle one portion into the bottom of a trifle bowl or 3 qt. serving bowl. Combine pumpkin, spices, milk and pudding mixes, mix until smooth. Spoon half into the serving bowl. Sprinkle with second portion of crumbs. Whip cream until stiff. Spoon half into bowl. Sprinkle with third portion of crumbs. Top with remaining pumpkin mixture, then last portion of crumbs and remaining whipped cream. Sprinkle the remaining crumbs on top around the edge of the bowl. Place cherries in center if desired. Cover and chill at least 2 hours before serving.

ALMOND DELIGHT

Mrs. Jay Mark Martha Miller
Ruby Beachy

12 oz. chocolate chips
2/3 C. peanut butter

6 C. Almond Delight cereal
1 gal. vanilla ice cream

Melt chocolate chips and peanut butter over low heat, stir in cereal and cool. Reserve 1 C. coated cereal for topping. Mix the rest of coated cereal with ice cream. Pour into 9" x 13" pan. Freeze.

UPSIDE DOWN DATE PUDDING

Mrs. John Troyer
Mrs. Nathan Miller

1 C. dates, cut up
Blend with 1 C. boiling water and cool.
1 1/2 C. flour
1/2 C. brown sugar
1/2 t. baking powder
1 egg
1/2 - 1 t. salt

2 T. butter
1 t. soda
1 C. nuts, chopped
1/2 C. granulated sugar

Blend sugar, eggs and butter. Add dry ingredients to sugar mixture. Stir in nuts and cooled date mixture. Pour into large cookie pan. Top with the following sugar sauce.

1 1/2 C. brown sugar
1 T. butter

1 1/2 C. boiling water

Bake at 375° for 30 - 40 minutes. Cut into squares invert on plate and serve with bananas and whipped cream.

DATE PUDDING

Mrs. Matthias Mast
Mrs. Wyman Wengerd

1 C. dates, cut fine
1 t. soda
1 C. hot water
1 C. brown sugar

1 T. butter
1 C. flour
1 egg
1/2 C. nuts

Boil water, dates and soda, until dates are tender. Add remaining ingredients and pour onto greased cookie sheet. Bake at 350° for 20 - 30 minutes.

Sauce:
2 T. butter
1 C. brown sugar
Boil 10 minutes then add.
2 t. vanilla
2 T. pancake syrup

1 1/2 C. water
3 T. clear jel

1 1/2 t. maple flavoring

Cut up date cake alternate layer of cake, whip, sauce and bananas to fill bowl.

TAPIOCA

Debra Kay Miller
Mrs. Willis Karen Miller

4 1/2 C. water
1 C. tapioca

1/2 t. salt
1 1/4 C. sugar

Bring water and salt to boiling in saucepan. Add tapioca and bring to a boil, stirring constantly. Cover and simmer over low heat for 25 minutes. Remove from heat and add sugar and a 3 oz. box of any flavor jello. When cool add pineapples, bananas, and whipped topping.

GRAPE TAPIOCA PUDDING

Mrs. David Ray Yoder

2 1/2 C. grape juice
4 T. granulated tapioca
1/2 C. sugar

pinch of salt
whipped cream

Mix together the juice, tapioca, sugar and salt. Bring to a full boil, stirring constantly. Take from heat and chill thoroughly without stirring. Add desired amount of sweetened whipped cream and fold in until mixed together.

ORANGE TAPIOCA PUDDING

Mrs. Phillip Troyer

3 C. water
3 oz. orange jello
3 oz. vanilla pudding

3 oz. tapioca pudding
3 1/2 C. Cool Whip
1 can mandarine oranges

Bring water to boiling point. Add jello and puddings, cool. Add Cool Whip and oranges.

TAPIOCA CREAM
Mrs. Henry Hershberger

3/4 C. pearl tapioca
3 C. milk
3 egg yolks

1/2 t. salt
3/4 C. sugar

Soak tapioca in water overnight. Scald milk in double boiler. Stir in drained tapioca. When transparent, add beaten egg yolks, salt and sugar, stir till thick. Cool, and add Cool Whip, vanilla and bananas.

ORANGE JELLO MOLD
Mrs. Dan J. Yoder

6 oz. orange jello
1 can crushed pineapples (with juice)
1 C. boiling water
Heat and let set, then add:
2 C. whipped topping
8 oz. cream cheese

1/2 C. sugar
1 pkg. miniature marshmallows

1/4 C. celery
1/4 C. nuts

Pour into jello mold and serve with cottage cheese.

DELICIOUS CUSTARD
Mrs. Henry Hershberger

12 eggs, beat well
1 C. white sugar
1 C. brown sugar

1 heaping T. flour
1/2 gal. milk
1 t. vanilla

Beat eggs, then heat milk to a rolling boil and add remaining ingredients. Pour custard into stainless steel pan. Bake at 475° for 3 minutes. Turn oven off, leave set in oven until cool. Remove and chill.

VERNA'S CUSTARD
Mrs. Ray Troyer

1/2 gal. scalded milk
1 C. white sugar
1 C. brown sugar

1 T. flour
12 eggs
sprinkle with cinnamon

Beat eggs till light in color, add rest of ingredients and beat till smooth. Bake in 10" x 15" stainless steel pan at 475° for 3 minutes. Do not remove from oven until cooled.

વ્

It costs nothing to say something nice to someone.

FROSTY STRAWBERRY FLUFF

Twila Beachy

2 C. flour
1/2 C. brown sugar
3/4 C. butter
4 egg whites

1 T. ReaLemon or lemon juice
2 C. cream
4 C. strawberries
2 C. sugar

Cream brown sugar, butter and flour together. Press lightly into 9" x 13" pan. Bake at 350° for 20 minutes. Let cool. Beat egg whites, add 1/2 C. sugar. Beat cream, add 1 1/2 C. sugar. Fold egg whites, and cream together, add strawberries. Pour on top of cooled crust and freeze.

FRESH STRAWBERRY PUDDING

Mrs. Marion Miller

Crust:
1 1/2 C. flour
2 T. white sugar

1/2 C. softened butter

Blend with pastry blender and press into 9" x 13" pan and bake at 425° until lightly browned and cool.

Filling:
2 - 3 oz. boxes strawberry jello
1/2 C. clear jel
1 1/2 C. white sugar

1/2 t. salt
4 C. cold water

Cook until thickened, cool, add fresh strawberries. Pour filling over crust and top with whipped topping.

STRAWBERRY YUM YUM

Mrs. Martha Sue Miller

1 C. flour
1/2 C. butter
1/4 C. brown sugar
1/2 C. chopped nuts

2 egg whites
1 C. sugar
2 t. lemon juice
10 oz. frozen strawberries
1 pkg. Dream Whip

Mix the first 4 ingredients until crumbly and press into 8" x 8" pan. Bake at 350° for 20 - 25 minutes. Cool and break into crumbs. Place crumbs in 9" x 13" pan. Set aside, combine the egg whites, lemon juice, sugar and strawberries. Beat at medium speed for 15 - 20 minutes. Spread strawberry mixture over crumbs and freeze. Serve frozen.

GRAHAM CRACKER FLUFF

Mrs. Ella Miller

2 egg yolks
$1/2$ C. milk
Graham Cracker Crust:
20 graham crackers crushed fine
3 T. butter

1 scant C. sugar

3 T. brown sugar

Dissolve 1 pkg. gelatin in $1/4$ C. cold water. Mix milk and sugar, add beaten egg yolks. Bring to a boil. Remove from heat and add gelatin. Let mixture cool until slightly thickened. Add beaten egg whites and 2 C. whipped cream. Pour over graham cracker crust. Enjoy!

BLUEBERRY COBBLER

Mrs. Wally Detweiler

3 C. blueberries
$1/2$ C. sugar
$1 1/2$ t. lemon juice
1 C. water
$1/4$ C. shortening

$3/4$ C. sugar
$1 1/4$ C. flour
3 t. baking powder
$1/4$ t. salt
$1/2$ C. milk

Mix together blueberries, sugar, lemon juice and water. Bring to boil and simmer for 5 minutes. Cream together sugar and shortening add rest of ingredients for dough. Mix until smooth. Pour batter into 10" x 15" baking pan. Spoon your blueberry mixture on top and bake at 350° for 45 minutes.

LAYERED BLUEBERRY DELIGHT

Mrs. Merle Hershberger

14 whole graham crackers
6 oz. pkg. instant vanilla pudding

1 C. Cool Whip
21 oz. can blueberry or
cherry pie filling

Line 9" square pan with whole graham crackers, breaking crackers if necessary. Prepare pudding mix as directed on package. Let stand 5 minutes, then blend in Cool Whip. Spread half of pudding mixture over crackers. Add another layer of crackers, top with remaining pudding mixture and remaining crackers. Spread pie filling over top layer of crackers. Chill 3 hours.

❧

*Lord, you know how busy I will be today, if I forget you,
please do not forget me!*

BLUEBERRY CHEESECAKE
Mrs. Matthew Miller

1 C. graham cracker crumbs with small amount of brown sugar and melted butter.

2 - 8 oz. cream cheese

2 eggs

1/2 C. white sugar

1 t. vanilla

2 T. ReaLemon juice

Cream together cream cheese and sugar. Beat in eggs, vanilla and ReaLemon. Prepare crust in 9" pie pan, only enough filling for 1 pie. Bake at 375° for 10 minutes. Cool, top with blueberry pie filling. Best when refrigerated for a few hours.

BLUEBERRY BUCKLE
Mrs. Nathan Mast
Mrs. Josie Miller

1/4 C. butter

3/4 C. sugar

1 egg

1/2 C. milk

2 C. cake flour

2 t. baking powder

1/4 t. salt

2 C. blueberries

Topping:

1/3 C. flour

2/3 C. sugar

1 t. cinnamon

3 T. melted butter

Cream butter and sugar. Add egg and milk. Beat well. Add dry ingredients and fold in blueberries. Mix topping ingredients together and put on top. Bake in 9" x 13" pan for 20 - 25 minutes at 350°.

FROZEN CHEESECAKE
Mrs. Willis Priscilla Miller

Crust:

2 pkgs. graham crackers, crushed

3/4 C. melted butter

6 T. brown sugar

Filling:

2 - 8 oz. cream cheese

1 C. white sugar

1 C. Rich's topping, whipped

4 eggs, well beaten

1 t. vanilla

Mix crust and press into bottom of pan. Mix together rest of ingredients and pour over graham cracker crust and freeze. Remove from freezer 15 - 30 minutes before serving. Serve with any thickened fruit. (Strawberrries, raspberries, cherries, peaches, etc.)

CREAMY BAKED CHEESECAKE

Mrs. Joe Miller Jr.

1/4 C. butter, melted
1 C. graham cracker crumbs
1/4 C. sugar
2 - 8 oz. cream cheese
14 oz. Eagle Brand milk

3 eggs
1/4 t. salt
1/4 C. lemon juice
8 oz. sour cream

Preheat oven to 300°. Combine butter, crumbs and sugar. Pat firmly on bottom of buttered 9" spring form pan. Beat cream cheese until fluffy. Beat in Eagle Brand milk, eggs and salt until smooth. Stir in lemon juice. Bake 50 - 55 minutes or until cake springs back when lightly touched. Cool to room temperature. Chill. Spread sour cream on cheesecake. Refrigerate leftovers.

FROZEN CHEESECAKE

Mrs. Fremon Miller
Mrs. Willis Karen Milller

2 pkg. graham crackers, crushed
1 C. butter
6 T. brown sugar
2 - 8 oz. cream cheese

1 C. white sugar
1 T. vanilla
1 C. Rich's topping, whipped
4 eggs beaten

Crush crackers and add sugar and melted butter. Mix and press into 9" x 9" pan. Cream together cream cheese and sugar, add beaten eggs, vanilla and whipped topping. Pour over top of crackers. Freeze. When ready to serve top with your favorite pie filling.

CHEERY CHERRY CHEESECAKE

Mrs. Mike Schrock

2 - 8 oz. cream cheese
2/3 C. white sugar

3 eggs
1 t. vanilla

Preheat oven to 350°. In a bowl combine all ingredients in order given. Beat on medium speed for 5 minutes. Bake 25 - 30 minutes. Chill. Top with cherry pie filling.

CHERRY CRUNCH

Twila Beachy

1 can cherry pie filling
1 can dark sweet cherries
    drained and pitted
3/4 C. Bisquick mix

1/4 C. brown sugar
1/2 t. cinnamon
1/4 C. oleo
1/2 C. chopped nuts

Mix pie filling and cherries in ungreased 8" x 8" baking dish. Spread evenly. Mix Bisquick mix, nuts, sugar and cinnamon. Cut in oleo until crumbly. Sprinkle over cherry mixture. Bake at 375° for 25 minutes, or until golden brown. Serve warm with ice cream.

CHERRY BERRY ON A CLOUD

Mrs. Ben Troyer, Jr.

3 egg whites
3/4 C. sugar

1/4 t. cream of tartar

Filling:
3 oz. cream cheese
1 C. whipped topping
1 C. miniature marshmallows

1/2 t. vanilla
1/2 C. sugar

Beat egg whites with cream of tartar until foamy. Then beat in 3/4 C. sugar, 1 T. at a time. Beat until very stiff and glossy. Bake on a brown paper (cut to fit the size of dish or tupperware you want to put it in) for 1 1/2 hour at 275°. Turn oven off and leave in for another hour. Finish cooling away from draft. Mix filling ingredients, put on crust and chill. Top with cherries or pie filling of your choice.

BUTTERFINGER DESSERT

Mrs. Karen Miller
Mrs. Roy Mast

1 1/2 pkg. graham crackers
30 soda crackers

1 1/2 sticks oleo

2 - 3 oz. boxes vanilla instant pudding
2 C. milk
8 oz. Cool Whip, optional

1 qt. vanilla ice cream, softened
3 Butterfinger candy bars

Crush crackers and add melted butter. Mix and press 3/4 of it in 9" x 13" pan. Beat pudding and milk together, then add softened ice cream. Put on top of crackers. Top with Cool Whip if desired. Crush candy bars and mix with the rest of the crumbs. Sprinkle on top. It is best to fix in the morning and keep in refrigerator till ready to serve.

ICE CREAM PUDDING

Mrs. Jr. Kaufman

1 box vanilla instant pudding
1/2 box butterscotch pudding
1 1/2 C. milk
Mix well and pour over crust made of:
60 Ritz crackers
1 stick oleo

8 oz. Cool Whip
1/2 gal. vanilla ice cream

1/2 C. nuts

OREO ICE CREAM PUDDING

Mrs. Crist Beachy

40 Oreo cookies, crushed
3 qt. vanilla ice cream

12 oz. Cool Whip

Mix and freeze. Very simple and delicious!

RHUBARB CAKE DESSERT

Mrs. Martha Sue Miller
Mrs. Mike Schrock

Crumble together:
1 C. butter	2 T. sugar
2 C. flour	

Press into cake pan.

Mix:
5 C. rhubarb, chopped fine	4 T. flour
6 egg yolks	1 C. cream
1½ - 2 C. sugar	¼ t. salt

Pour on top of crumb mixture and bake at 350° for 40 - 45 minutes.

Meringue:
6 egg whites (beaten)	2 T. vanilla
¾ C. sugar	pinch of salt

Put this on top of baked filling that is not quite done. Bake till golden brown.

RHUBARB COBBLER

Deborah Troyer

4 C. rhubarb, cut in small pieces	2½ C. water
1 C. sugar	1½ T. butter
2 T. cornstarch	2 T. strawberry jello

Mix the sugar and cornstarch together and stir into the rhubarb. Add 1 C. water and bring to a boil, stirring constantly. Cook for 5 minutes. Stir in the rest of the water and pour into a baking dish. Dot with butter.

1 C. flour	¼ C. butter
2 T. sugar	¼ C. milk
1½ t. baking powder	1 egg, slightly beaten
¼ t. salt	

Sift dry ingredients together and cut in the butter until the mixture forms coarse crumbs. Mix the egg and milk together. Add to dry ingredients. Stir just enough to mix. Drop by spoonfuls over fruit mixture and bake at 400° for about 20 minutes, or until nicely browned.

ప

If we noticed little pleasures
As we noticed little pains,
If we quite forgot our losses
And remembered all our gains
If we looked for people's virtues
And their faults refused to see
What a comfortable, happy, cheerful
Place this world would be!

RHUBARB CRUNCH

Debra Kay Miller

1¼ C. flour
1¼ C. oatmeal
1 C. brown sugar
½ C. melted butter
1 t. cinnamon

3 C. rhubarb, diced
1 C. sugar
1 C. water
2 T. cornstarch
1 t. vanilla

Mix flour, oatmeal, brown sugar, melted butter and cinnamon until crumbly. Press half of the crumbs into 9" x 9" pan. Put rhubarb on top of crumbs. Combine sugar, water, cornstarch and vanilla. Bring to a boil, stirring well. Pour over rhubarb. Top with remaining crumbs. Bake approximately 1 hour at 350°.

ANGEL FOOD TRIFLE

Melva Schrock

5 C. cubed angel food cake
½ C. confectioners sugar
3 oz. cream cheese
fruit pie filling

8 oz. whipped topping
½ C. toasted chopped pecans,
    optional

Combine sugar and cream cheese (room temperature) until well blended. Fold in whipped topping. Mix pecans with cake cubes and put in layers with fruit pie filling. 8 - 10 servings.

CHOCOLATE ANGEL DESSERT

Mrs. David Ray Yoder

1 - 10" angel food cake
6 oz. chocolate chips
2 T. milk
½ C. sugar

salt
2 egg whites
2 C. whipped cream
2 egg yolks

Melt chocolate chips in double boiler. Beat egg yolks, add milk, sugar and salt. Add to melted chocolate chips, and heat. Cool. Beat egg whites till stiff. Whip cream and fold into beaten egg whites, add to cooled chocolate mixture and blend well. Break up angel food cake and put in layers in a serving dish. Refrigerate 24 hours. To serve, garnish with whipped cream and chopped M & M's or chocolate crunch bar pieces.

FRUIT SLUSH

Laura K. Miller

2 C. sugar
3 C. boiling water
12 oz. frozen orange juice

6 - 8 bananas, sliced
20 oz. crushed pineapple
8 oz. 7-Up

Dissolve sugar in boiling water, add orange juice, bananas and pineapple, stirring until orange juice is thawed. Stir in 7-Up, then pour into large container or several small containers and freeze. Thaw approximately 1 hour or until slushy, before serving.

FROZEN FRUIT SLUSH

Mrs. Roy Mast

12 oz. frozen orange juice
6 oz. frozen lemonade
2 C. sugar
3 C. water

12 oz. 7-Up
20 oz. crushed pineapple
8 - 10 bananas
1 qt. fresh or frozen peach slices

Mix and freeze. When partly frozen, stir to blend. Thaw to slush consistency to serve.

FRUIT SLUSH

Mrs. James Troyer

1³/₄ C. sugar
3 C. water
12 oz. frozen orange juice

1 can crushed pineapple
6 sliced bananas

Mix together and freeze. Remove from freezer 30 minutes before serving.

FRUIT PIZZA

Mrs. Josie Miller

Crust:
¹/₂ C. butter
¹/₂ C. white sugar
1 egg

1¹/₃ C. flour
1 t. baking powder
pinch of salt

Filling:
8 oz. cream cheese
¹/₂ C. powdered sugar

¹/₂ t. vanilla
1¹/₂ C. whipped topping

Glaze:
2 C. pineapple juice or other fruit juice
¹/₂ C. sugar

1 heaping T. clear jel
2 T. lemon or pineapple jello

Cream together butter, sugar and egg. Add flour, baking powder and salt. Press into greased pizza pan. Bake at 375° for 10 minutes or until light brown. Cream filling ingredients together and spread over cooled crust. Cook glaze ingredients together until clear. Cool. Arrange fruit on filling and top with pie glaze.

FRUIT SALAD

Mrs. Martha Sue Miller

2 C. water
¹/₂ C. honey

1 C. mint leaves

Cook to a boil. Simmer for 10 minutes. Strain, add small frozen lemon juice. Pour over fresh fruit. At least 10 C.

FRUIT PIZZA

Mrs. James Troyer

Dough:
3/4 C. margarine
1 rounded C. sugar
2 small eggs
2 C. flour
Cream cheese mixture:
8 oz. cream cheese
1 C. whipped topping

1 1/2 t. baking powder
3/8 t. salt
3/4 t. vanilla

1/2 C. sugar
1/2 t. vanilla

Blend margarine and sugar, add beaten eggs. Stir in baking powder, salt, vanilla and flour. Spread on cookie sheet and bake at 375° for 12 minutes. Cool crust, and top with cream cheese mixture. Then top with your favorite fruits.

CANDY PIZZA

Regina Miller

1/2 C. butter
3/4 C. brown sugar, packed firmly
1 egg
1 1/4 C. flour

1/2 t. baking soda
mini marshmallows
M & M's
chocolate chips

Preheat oven to 350°. Grease pan. Cream together butter, sugar and egg. Stir in flour and baking soda. Bake 10 minutes, remove from oven and arrange candy on top. Bake 5 more minutes.

SAUCE FOR FRUIT OR WALDORF SALAD

Mrs. Henry Beachy
Mrs. Mark Hochstetler
Mrs. Fremon E. Miller

2 cans pineapple juice
3 C. water
1 1/2 C. sugar
1/4 C. ReaLemon juice

1/3 C. lemon jello
pinch of salt
1/2 C. clear jel
3/4 C. water

Mix and heat pineapple juice, water, ReaLemon, jello and salt. Thicken with clear jel and water. When cool, add peaches, grapes, pineapples, apples, etc.

DANISH FRUIT DESSERT SAUCE

Mrs. Ivan Miller

1 1/2 T. clear jel
1 1/2 C. pineapple juice and water
1/4 t. salt

1/4 C. any flavor jello
1/3 C. sugar

Heat 1 C. liquid. Combine jello, sugar and clear jel. Make a paste of it with remaining liquid. Stir into boiling juice and let cook until thick and clear. Cool and pour over drained frozen or canned fruit.

CRANBERRY SALAD
Laura K. Miller

1 box red raspberry jello
1 box strawberry jello
1 C. cranberries

1 orange, peeled
5 unpeeled apples
1 C. sugar, scant

Put the cranberries, apples and orange through grinder and add sugar. Prepare jello according to directions on package. Chill until jello starts to thicken, then add fruit mixture.

PINEAPPLE CHERRY CRISP
Mrs. Mark Hochstetler

1 can pineapple rings
1 can cherry pie filling
1 yellow or white cake mix

1 stick butter
³/₄ C. pecans

Spread pineapple rings evenly in bottom of 9" x 13" pan. Pour cherry pie filling over pineapples. Sprinkle dry cake mix on top. Cut butter in slivers and dot on top of cake mix. Top with pecans. Bake at 350° for 45 minutes. Can be served warm or cold with ice cream.

ORANGE SHERBET DESSERT
Mrs. Willis Karen Miller

6 oz. orange jello
2 C. boiling water
1 pt. orange sherbet ice cream

1 can mandarin oranges
1 can crushed pineapples

Drain pineapple juice into saucepan and thicken with clear jel. Cool, then add whipped topping and mix together, put on top of chilled jello. This is a very refreshing dessert.

CREAMY PINEAPPLE DESSERT
Mrs. Robert Miller

20 oz. pineapple tidbits
1 pkg. vanilla pudding
1 pkg. lemon jello

4 oz. whipped topping
2 C. vanilla cookie crumbs
¹/₄ C. melted butter

Drain pineapple, reserve juice. Add water to juice to make 2 C. of liquid. Combine pudding mix, jello and measured liquid in medium saucepan. Cook over medium heat stirring until mixture comes to a boil. Pour into bowl and chill until thickened. Fold thawed topping into pudding mixture. Meanwhile, combine cookie crumbs and melted butter. Press into 9" square pan. Bake at 375° for 8 minutes. Cool, top with pudding and pineapples. Chill.

PINEAPPLE COTTAGE CHEESE SALAD
Anna Fern Troyer

20 oz. crushed pineapple
8 oz. cream cheese
20 large marshmallows

8 oz. small curd cottage cheese
2 C. whipped topping

Combine first 3 ingredients in saucepan and heat until marshmallows and cream cheese are melted. Chill. Stir in cottage cheese and mixed nuts. Garnish with nuts.

HAWAIIAN PINEAPPLE PUDDING
Regina Miller

1 box Jiffy cake mix (yellow or white)
8 oz. cream cheese
20 oz. pineapple, drained
9 oz. Cool Whip

1 box French vanilla
  instant pudding
2 C. milk
3/4 C. coconut

Bake cake in 9" x 13" pan and let cool. Soften cream cheese with a little pineapple juice. Blend pudding with milk. Beat cream cheese and pudding together. Spread on cake. Put pineapple over pudding then cool. Top with Cool Whip and coconut.

LEMON HEAVEN
Mrs. Matthew Troyer

2 - 3 oz. lemon jello
2 C. hot water
2 C. cold water

1 C. crushed, drained pineapple
4 C. diced apples
2 C. small marshmallows

Let set, then put on topping. Mix 1/2 C. white sugar with 2 T. flour. Add 1 C. pineapple juice and 1 egg, slightly beaten. Cook over low heat stirring constantly until smooth and thick. Add 2 T. butter and cool. Then fold in 1 C. whipped cream.

CREAM PUFFS
Mary Ellen Schlabach

1 C. Robin Hood flour
1/4 t. salt
1/2 C. shortening

1 C. water
4 eggs

Mix flour and salt. Mix shortening and water and bring to a boil. Add dry ingredients quickly. Beat constantly until mixture pulls away from sides of pan and forms a ball. Remove from heat and let cool. Add eggs one at a time, beating until smooth after each addition. Drop by tablespoons onto ungreased cookie sheet. Bake at 400° for 40 - 45 minutes. Fill with instant puddings of your choice.

CINNAMON PUDDING

Mrs. Marvin Wengerd

Syrup:
2 C. brown sugar
1½ C. water
Bring to a boil, remove from heat.

2 T. butter

Pudding:
1 C. white sugar
2 T. butter
2 t. cinnamon
2 rounded t. baking powder

2 C. flour
1 C. milk
1 t. vanilla
pinch of salt

Cream sugar and butter, add rest of ingredients and beat until batter is light. Pour in greased 9" x 9" pan. Cover with warm syrup. Bake at 350° for 35 - 40 minutes. Delicious warm, with ice cream or cold with whipped topping. A good dessert, or make if your out of eggs!

HEATH BAR DELIGHT

Mrs. Ben Troyer, Jr.

1 pkg. Lorna Doon cookies, crumbled
1 stick oleo or butter, melted
Mix and press in bottom of dish.

2 pkg. instant vanilla pudding
2 C. milk

1 qt. softened Heath bar
ice cream or other brand

Mix pudding, milk and ice cream, pour over crumb mixture. Refrigerate 6 hours or overnight. Top with small carton Cool Whip. Crush 6 heath bars, sprinkle over top.

BLACK MAGIC DESSERT

Mrs. Paul Mast

6 oz. chocolate chips
2 T. sugar
4 egg yolks

Beat 4 egg yolks well. Stir in chocolate chips and sugar gradually. Let cool to room temperature. Beat 4 egg whites, add ¼ of egg whites to chocolate mixture. Blend. Fold in remaining egg whites. Whip 1 C. heavy cream or Rich's topping and fold in chocolate mixture. Tear angel food cake into bite size pieces and fold into chocolate and whip mixture. Chill 24 hours. Use double recipe for one angel food cake.

CHOCOLATE CREAM CHEESE PUDDING   Mrs. Willis Karen Miller

6 oz. milk chocolate chips
8 oz. cream cheese
3/4 C. brown sugar
1/2 t. salt

1 t. vanilla
2 eggs, separated
2 C. heavy cream, whipped
graham cracker crust

Melt chocolate over hot, not boiling, water, cool 10 minutes. Blend cheese, 1/2 C. sugar, salt and vanilla. Beat egg whites until stiff, not dry. Slowly beat in 1/4 C. sugar. Beat till very stiff. Fold chocolate mixture into beaten egg whites and fold in whipped cream. Pour into crust and chill overnight. Very Good!!!

FUDGE SUNDAE DESSERT   Mrs. Josiah Miller

1/2 C. Karo
4 T. brown sugar
6 T. margarine
5 C. Rice Krispies

1/2 C. peanut butter
1/2 C. fudge sauce
6 T. Karo
2 qt. ice cream

Mix first 3 ingredients and cook over low heat till it boils. Remove from heat and add Rice Krispies until well coated. Press into 9" x 13" dish. Stir together peanut butter, fudge sauce and 6 T. Karo. Pour 1/2 on Rice Krispies and freeze until firm. Spoon ice cream over mixture and drizzle remaining peanut butter mixture over top.

DIRT PUDDING   Janice Schlabach

1 large pkg. Oreo cookies
1/2 C. margarine, melted
8 oz. cream cheese
3 C. milk

1/2 C. white sugar
1 C. powdered sugar
2 boxes instant pudding

Crumble cookies, mix sugar and margarine. Press into a 9" x 13" pan. Save some for the top. Cream together cream cheese and powdered sugar. Beat instant pudding and milk. Add to cream cheese mixture. Add 1 C. Cool Whip and pour over Oreo cookies. Sprinkle with remaining cookies.

EAGLE BRAND MILK AND PINEAPPLE RINGS   Mrs. Mark Hochstetler

Remove labels from Eagle Brand milk cans. Set 4 cans in 4 qt. stainless steel kettle. Fill with cold water. Turn on medium high heat till it cooks, then turn down to medium. Keep adding warm water. Do not let the water evaporate or the cans will explode. Boil for 3 hours. Cool. Drain cooled pineapple rings and arrange on plate. (One can of Eagle Brand milk should be just right for one can of pineapples.) Open both ends of the milk cans. Remove one end and press the other end so that about 1/4" sticks out of the end. Slice along the can with a sharp wet knife, slide onto pineapple ring. Top with cool whip and a cherry.

CHOCOLATE ECLAIR DESSERT

Mrs. David Schlabach

1 box graham crackers
9 oz. Cool Whip

2 C. vanilla instant pudding mix
5 C. milk

Prepare pudding, heat milk to almost boiling, cool. Then add pudding mix. Fold in Cool Whip. Line bottom of 9" x 13" pan with whole graham crackers. Put ½ of pudding mixture over crackers. Cover with another layer of crackers. Add remaining pudding. Cover with another layer of crackers.

Topping:
1 C. chocolate chips
3 T. margarine
3 T. milk

2 T. corn syrup
1 T. vanilla
1½ C. powdered sugar

Melt chocolate chips and margarine, add remaining ingredients, putting powdered sugar in last. Stir well and spread over crackers. Refrigerate at least 1 day before serving.

MOCHA CREAM TORTE

Mrs. Willis Priscilla Miller

Crunch layer:
1½ C. graham cracker crumbs
¾ C. brown sugar

½ C. finely chopped nuts
1 T. instant mocha coffee mix

Cake:
Devil's Food cake mix, mix as directed on package.

Frosting:
8 oz. whipped topping or
1½ C. Rich's topping, beaten stiff
8 oz. cream cheese

mocha coffee mix to taste
6 t. sugar

Place crunch layer in 3 - 8" or 9" pans. Divide cake mixture evenly over crunch layer. Bake at 350° until toothpick comes out clean. Beat frosting ingredients and place between and on top of cooled cake.

BUTTERSCOTCH SAUCE

Mrs. Robert Miller

1 egg yolk
¼ C. water
⅓ C. corn syrup

1 T. flour
½ C. brown sugar
¼ C. butter

Cook until thickened, stirring constantly.

DELICIOUS ICE CREAM FOR 1½ GALLON
Mrs. Willis Karen Miller

½ C. brown sugar
1⅔ C. white sugar
3 T. cornstarch

1½ qt. milk
4 egg yolks

Cook together and cool. When cooled add:

1 C. white sugar
4 beaten egg whites
2 t. vanilla

1 C. Pet milk
1 can Eagle Brand milk
1 qt. milk

Mix all together and freeze in ice cream freezer.

HOMEMADE ICE CREAM
Mrs. Eddie Miller

4 eggs
3 C. sugar
pinch of salt
3 t. vanilla
1 can evaporated milk

3 pkg. Knox gelatin
¾ C. cold water
1½ C. boiling water
2 boxes vanilla
   instant pudding

Beat eggs, dissolve gelatin in cold water. Add boiling water. Stir well and add beaten eggs. Add sugar, salt and vanilla. Beat well. Add evaporated milk and pudding. Add enough milk to make freezer ⅔ full. Freeze in ice cream freezer and enjoy.

HOMEMADE ICE CREAM
Mrs. Jr. Wagler

1 pt. whipping cream, whipped
¾ C. white sugar
1 t. vanilla
2 - 3 oz. boxes instant pudding, desired flavor

1 can Eagle Brand milk
3 eggs, separated

Mix in order given, mix pudding as directed on box. Blend into whip, sugar and vanilla mixture. Stir in Eagle Brand milk, then add beaten egg yolks and beaten egg whites last. Blend well. Freeze in ice cream freezer.

HOMEMADE ICE CREAM
Mrs. Atlee Miller

1 qt. whole milk
3 T. cornstarch
6 slightly beaten eggs
2 C. white sugar

½ t. salt
3 T. vanilla
1 pt. half and half
1 pt. whipping cream

Mix cornstarch with small amount of milk. Combine with remaining milk. Cook until mixture thickens. Pour over beaten eggs. Add sugar, salt, vanilla and strain into 1 gallon freezer can. Fill can to 4" from the top with cream. I use evaporated milk instead of half and half.

ICE CREAM FOR 2 GALLON FREEZER

Mrs. Moses S. Miller

4 C. white sugar
4 egg yolks
3 T. unflavored gelatin
11½ C. milk

3 C. cream, whipped
¼ t. salt
2 t. vanilla

Dissolve gelatin in additional 1½ C. milk. Scald 11½ C. milk. Remove from heat and stir in gelatin mixture. Stir till dissolved. Add sugar and stir. Chill till slightly thickened. Blend egg yolks into whipped cream and add to milk mixture. Add salt and vanilla. Freeze in ice cream freezer.

ORANGE PINEAPPLE ICE CREAM

Mrs. Ray N. Troyer

8 eggs, well beaten
3 C. white sugar
1 pkg. orange Kool-Aid
1 box instant vanilla pudding

13 oz. crushed pineapple
2 cans evaporated milk or
2 C. cream
1½ - 2 qt. milk

Beat eggs and sugar thoroughly. Add pudding, Kool-Aid and crushed pineapple. Add milk. Freeze in ice cream freezer and enjoy. This is enough for a 6 qt. freezer.

SOFT CUSTARD ICE CREAM

Mrs. Jay Miller

3 T. gelatin
¾ C. water
6 C. milk
3 C. sugar

4½ C. cream
3 t. vanilla
½ t. salt

Soften gelatin in water while you heat the milk to scalding. Add gelatin and sugar to hot milk. Stir to dissolve. Add vanilla and salt. Cool, then add cream and chill before freezing. Makes 1½ gallons. Freeze in ice cream freezer.

STRAWBERRY ICE CREAM - 2 GALLON

Mrs. Henry Beachy

3 boxes vanilla instant pudding
6 C. milk
8 eggs
3 C. sugar

1 qt. cream
⅓ C. strawberry jello
1 qt. crushed strawberries
    fresh or frozen

Mix milk, jello and 2 C. sugar and instant pudding. Beat eggs, add 1 C. sugar, whip cream. Mix all together, put in freezer can. Add 1 qt. strawberries and enough milk to fill can ⅔ full. For chocolate ice cream use 2 chocolate and 1 instant vanilla pudding.

LEMON SPONGETTES

Mrs. Moses S. Miller

2 T. butter
1 C. white sugar
4 T. flour
$\frac{1}{8}$ t. salt

3 beaten egg yolks
$1\frac{1}{2}$ C. milk
3 stiffly beaten egg whites
grated rind and juice of 1 lemon

Cream butter and sugar until soft. Stir in flour, salt, lemon rind, and juice. Add egg yolks mixed with milk. Mix thoroughly, fold in egg whites. Pour into custard cups or flat round baking dish and set in pan of water. Bake at 325° - 350° for about 45 minutes. May be served warm or cold.

- Notes -

Cookies

CHOCOLATE CHIP COOKIES

Mrs. Josie Miller
Melva Schrock

¹/₄ C. white sugar
³/₄ C. brown sugar
1 C. butter or margarine
4 oz. pkg. instant vanilla pudding
1 t. vanilla

2 eggs
2¹/₄ C. flour
1 t. baking soda
12 oz. chocolate
nuts optional

Melt butter and mix with sugar, instant pudding and vanilla. Beat and add eggs, then add remaining ingredients. Bake on ungreased cookie sheet at 350°.

CHOCOLATE CHIP COOKIES

Mrs. Mark Hochstetler

1 C. white sugar
¹/₂ C. brown sugar
¹/₂ C. oleo, softened
¹/₂ C. shortening
2 eggs
2 t. vanilla

1 t. salt
1 t. baking soda
2¹/₂ C. sifted flour
  (Gold Medal)
12 oz. chocolate chips
1 C. chopped nuts
  (optional)

Combine first five ingredients. Stirring well after adding each one. This makes it nice and creamy. Add the rest of the ingredients in order given. Milk chocolate chips make these extra delicious! Bake at 350°. Do not overbake.

CHOCOLATE CHIP COOKIES

Mary Miller

1 C. margarine, melted
1 C. white sugar
1 C. brown sugar
2 eggs beaten
3 C. flour (heaping)
1 t. soda

¹/₂ t. salt
1 t. vanilla
1 t. water
1 C. chocolate chips
³/₄ C. nuts

Mix in order given. Bake at 350° for 10 - 12 minutes. Do not overbake.

CHOCOLATE CHIP PUDDING COOKIES

Mrs. Josiah Miller

3¹/₂ C. Gold Medal flour
1¹/₂ t. soda
1 C. butter, softened
1 C. brown sugar
2 C. chocolate chips

1¹/₂ t. vanilla
3 eggs
6 oz. instant vanilla
  (pudding)

Combine butter, sugar and pudding mix. Beat eggs until creamy. Gradually stir in mixture then stir in flour and soda. Add chips last. Bake at 350° until lightly browned.

SOFTBATCH CHOCOLATE CHIP COOKIES   Mrs. Matthias Mast

1³/₄ C. flour
1 t. baking soda with one drop water
1 C. brown sugar
¹/₂ C. oleo

1 t. vanilla
1 egg
8 oz. chocolate chips
4 oz. nuts (optional)

In large bowl cream sugar and oleo until smooth. In another bowl beat egg, add baking soda with one drop water and vanilla. Add to sugar and oleo. Gradually stir in flour. Fold in chocolate chips. Bake on greased cookie sheet at 350°. Don't overbake and they will be very soft.

NEIMAN'S $250 CHOCOLATE CHIP COOKIES   Mrs. Roy Mast

2 C. butter
4 eggs
2 C. brown sugar
2 C. white sugar
2 t. baking powder
2 t. baking soda
2 t. vanilla

1 t. salt
5 C. oatmeal (ground fine)
4 C. flour
24 oz. chocolate chips
1 C. nuts
2 - 8 oz. chocolate bars
   (grated)

Cream butter, sugar and eggs. Add remaining dry ingredients. Stir in chocolate chips, nuts and chocolate bar. Roll in walnut size balls. Bake at 375° for 10 minutes, or until they are lightly browned.

MRS. FIELDS COOKIES   Mrs. Henry Schrock

2 C. butter
2 C. white sugar
2 C. brown sugar
4 eggs for crisp cookies or
5 eggs for soft cookies
4 C. flour
5 C. oatmeal (powdered in blender)

1 t. salt
2 t. baking powder
2 t. soda
24 oz. chocolate chips
8 oz. Hershey Bar (grated)
3 C. chopped nuts

Cream together butter and sugars. Add eggs. Mix together flour, oatmeal, salt, baking powder and soda. Combine the 2 mixtures then add chocolates and nuts. Drop on ungreased cookie sheets. Bake at 375° for 6 - 8 minutes. Makes about 9 dozen cookies.

OATMEAL CHIP COOKIES

Mrs. Robert J. Yoder

1½ C. margarine
2 C. white sugar
2 C. brown sugar
4 eggs
2 t. vanilla

6 C. quick oats
4 C. all-purpose flour
2 t. baking soda
1 t. salt
2 C. chocolate chips

In a bowl cream butter, sugars, eggs and vanilla. Combine oats, flour, soda and salt. Stir into creamed mixture then add chocolate chips, mix well. Drop cookies in greased cookie sheet. Bake at 350° for 11 - 13 minutes or until lightly browned. Yields 7 dozen.

OATMEAL CHEWIES

Mrs. Dan J. Yoder

1 C. oleo
2 C. brown sugar
1 t. baking powder
½ t. salt
1 t. soda

1½ C. flour
2 eggs
1 t. vanilla
3 C. oatmeal
chocolate chips or raisins

Chill dough then make balls and roll in powdered sugar. Bake at 350°.

DROP OATMEAL COOKIES (DEBBIE)

Mrs. Allen Beachy

4½ C. brown sugar
2½ C. oleo
6 eggs
6 C. quick oats
5 C. flour

2¼ t. soda
1½ t. salt
3 t. cinnamon
3 t. vanilla

Bake at 350°.

Filling:
4 C. powdered sugar
2 t. vanilla

1½ C. Crisco

Mix these 3 together then fold in 4 beaten egg whites.

≈▲

The unheard and often unuttered cry in the heart of a teenager is as important to answer as the cry of a baby still in mother's lap.

OATMEAL WHITE CHIPPERS

Mrs. Alfred Miller

1 C. flour
1 t. baking soda
³/₄ C. oleo
¹/₂ C. white sugar
¹/₂ C. brown sugar

2¹/₂ C. oatmeal
1¹/₂ C. coarsely chopped
   white chocolate
¹/₂ C. nuts.
1 egg

Mix all together add chocolate, oatmeal and nuts last. Drop by rounded table-spoon on ungreased cookie sheet. Flatten cookie slightly before baking. Bake at 375° until done, cool on wire racks.

ROLLED OATS COOKIES

Mrs. Willis Karen Miller

2 C. brown sugar
1 C. shortening
3 eggs
1 C. sour milk or buttermilk
2 C. rolled oats
3 C. flour

¹/₂ t. salt
1 t. cinnamon
1 t. baking powder
2 C. raisins
1 C. chopped nuts
1 t. baking soda

Blend all ingredients and drop by spoon onto ungreased cookie sheet. Bake at 350° for 12 to 15 minutes.

DATE OATMEAL COOKIES

Mrs. Ella Miller

1¹/₂ C. shortening
1 C. white sugar
¹/₂ C. water
3 C. flour
1 t. soda
1 t. cinnamon
1 C. chopped nuts

2 C. brown sugar
2 eggs
2 t. vanilla
2 t. salt
4 C. Quick Mother's oats
¹/₂ t. nutmeg
¹/₂ lb. dates

Put dates in pan, add 1 C. water. Heat and cook until dates are tender. Cream together in bowl - shortening, sugar, eggs, water and vanilla. Add dry ingredients, and blend into the above mixture to which the cooled dates have been added. Drop by teaspoons on a greased cookie sheet. Bake at 400° for 10 to 15 minutes. Makes 8 dozen.

&.

Joy is not the absence of trouble but the presence of God.

DATE ORANGE SAUCIES

Mrs. Henry Schrock

8 oz. chopped dates
1/2 C. brown sugar
1/2 C. butter or oleo
1/2 C. orange juice
1 t. orange rind
2 eggs

1 1/4 C. flour
1 t. salt
3/4 t. soda
6 oz. butterscotch chips
1 C. chopped nuts

Cook first five ingredients until slightly thickened. Let cool completely then add eggs. Sift flour, soda and salt add to mixture. Stir in chips and nuts. Drop by spoonful on cookie sheets or spread evenly in a jelly roll pan. Bake at 375°. 10 minutes for drop cookies or 20 to 25 minutes for bars. Ice with orange flavored icing or put butterscotch chips on top as soon as they are finished, spread evenly. Sprinkle with nuts.

DATE PINWHEEL COOKIES

Mrs. John Shetler

1/2 C. lard
2 C. brown sugar
2 eggs well beaten
4 C. flour

1/2 t. soda
1/2 t. salt
1 t. vanilla
1/2 t. cream of tartar

Cream sugar and lard, add eggs and rest of ingredients. Roll out and spread with filling. Roll up as a jelly roll. Keep in cold place overnight. Slice and bake.

Filling:
1/2 lb. dates cut up
1/2 C. nuts
Heat till well mixed.

1/3 C. water
1/4 C. white sugar

PEANUT BUTTER COOKIES

Mrs. Josiah Miller

1 C. oleo
1 C. brown sugar
1 C. peanut butter
2 t. soda
2 eggs

1 t. vanilla
1/2 t. salt
1 C. white sugar
3 C. flour

Mix together oleo and sugar, beat eggs and gradually add rest of ingredients.

Filling:
1/2 C. peanut butter
4 T. milk

1 C. powdered sugar
1/2 t. vanilla

CHOCOLATE PEANUT BUTTER CHIP COOKIES

Lois Mast

1 C. butter or margarine
1¹/₂ C. sugar
2 eggs
2 t. vanilla
2 C. flour (scant)

²/₃ C. Hershey's cocoa
³/₄ t. baking soda
¹/₂ t. salt
2 C. Reese's Peanut
   Butter Chips

Cream butter or margarine and sugar. Add eggs and vanilla. Combine flour, cocoa, soda and salt add to creamed mixture. Stir in peanut butter chips. Drop by teaspoonful onto ungreased cookie sheet and flatten. Or chill until firm enough to handle, then shape small amounts of dough into 1" balls. Place on ungreased cookie sheet and flatten slightly with fork. Bake at 350° for 8 - 10 minutes. Cool 1 minute before removing from cookie sheet onto wire rack.

SOFT PEANUT BUTTER COOKIES

Mrs. Steve Engbretson

1 C. white sugar
1 C. brown sugar
1 C. shortening
2 beaten eggs
1 t. vanilla

1 C. peanut butter
3 C. flour
¹/₂ t. salt
1 t. soda

Cream sugar and shortening, add eggs, peanut butter and vanilla. Mix well. Add dry ingredients. Drop by teaspoonful onto cookie sheet. Bake at 325° for 10 minutes only.

PEANUT BUTTER TEMPTATIONS

Mary Miller
Mary Beth Mast

¹/₂ C. peanut butter
¹/₂ C. oleo
¹/₂ C. sugar
¹/₂ C. brown sugar
1 egg

¹/₂ t. vanilla
1¹/₄ C. flour
³/₄ t. soda
¹/₂ t. salt
48 Reese's Peanut Butter Cups

Cream oleo, peanut butter and sugars. Add egg and vanilla, beat until creamy. Stir in dry ingredients till well blended. Chill. Roll into balls 1" thick. Press in small muffin tin. Bake at 350° for 12 minutes. Remove from oven and immediately press one peanut butter cup into each hot cookie. Cool.

PEANUT BUTTER COOKIES

Mrs. Josie Miller

14 oz. sweetened condensed milk
³/₄ C. peanut butter

1 egg
2 C. Bisquick mix

Cream together milk, peanut butter, and egg. Add Bisquick mix. Chill dough for one hour. Roll into 1" balls then roll into sugar. Press with fork. Bake at 350° for 6 - 8 mintues.

PEANUT BUTTER CUP COOKIES

Mrs. Crist Beachy

³/₄ C. peanut butter
¹/₂ C. shortening
¹/₃ C. white sugar
¹/₃ C. brown sugar
1 egg

2 T. milk
1 t. vanilla
1²/₃ C. flour
1 t. baking soda
peanut butter cups

Cream peanut butter, shortening and sugars. Add egg, milk and vanilla. Beat well. Gradually add flour and baking soda to creamed mixture, blend thoroughly. Shape dough into balls, roll in sugar. Place on ungreased cookie sheet and bake at 350° for 10 - 12 minutes. Remove from oven and immediately press peanut butter cups in the middle. Cool slightly before removing from cookie sheet.

PEANUT BUTTER BLOSSOMS

Mrs. Mark Hochstetler

2 C. white sugar
2 C. brown sugar
2 C. butter
2 C. peanut butter
4 eggs

¹/₂ C. milk
4 t. vanilla
7 C. Gold Medal flour
4 t. soda
2 t. salt

Cream sugars, butter and peanut butter together. Beat eggs, milk and vanilla. Sift flour, soda and salt, stir in with the batter. Chill thoroughly. Shape into balls the size of a walnut, then roll in additional sugar. Bake on ungreased cookie sheet at 350°. Press chocolate Hershey's Kisses in the center while still hot.

PEANUT BUTTER FINGERS

Mrs. Paul Mast
Maria Miller

1 C. white sugar
1 C. brown sugar
1 C. shortening
2 C. flour
2 C. oatmeal

3 eggs
2 t. salt
1 t. soda
1 t. vanilla
³/₄ C. peanut butter

Put in jelly roll pan to bake. Bake at 350° for 35 minutes. When done cover with miniature marshmallows. Put back in oven for 5 minutes. Melt 1 C. chocolate chips and ¹/₂ C. peanut butter together, melt in saucepan over low heat. Then add 2 C. powdered sugar and 4 T. milk. Spread over top. Then cut into bars.

❧

Anyone can count the seeds in an apple, but
only God can count the apples in a seed.

PEANUT BUTTER DREAM BARS

Annalisa Miller

2 C. quick oats
1½ C. flour
1 C. peanuts (optional)
1 C. brown sugar
⅓ C. peanut butter

1 t. soda
¾ t. salt
1 C. oleo (melted)
1 can Eagle Brand milk
1 C. M&M's

Combine oats, flour, peanuts, sugar, soda and salt. Mix well. Add oleo. Mix until dry ingredients are thoroughly moistened and resemble coarse crumbs. Reserve 1½ C. crumbs. Press mixture into bottom of 15" x 10" pan. Bake at 375° for 12 minutes. Combine milk and peanut butter, spread over partially baked crust to within ¼" from edge. Combine reserved crumbs and M&M's. Sprinkle evenly over milk mixture, pressing in lightly. Bake for another 20 minutes. Cool and cut into bars.

MOLASSES CRINKLE COOKIES

Annalisa Miller

4 C. oleo
8 C. brown sugar
1 C. Brer Rabbit Molasses (light)
8 eggs
1 C. sour cream
16 C. flour

1 t. ginger
8 t. cinnamon
2 t. salt
12 t. soda
4 t. baking powder

Mix and refrigerate overnight. Roll into balls, then roll them in white sugar. Fill with filling recipe.

Filling:
1 C. milk
2 T. cornstarch
1 t. vanilla

1 C. sugar
½ C. Crisco
½ C. oleo

MOLASSES COOKIES

Mrs. Eli A. Mast

2½ C. sugar
1⅛ C. shortening
⅔ C. dark molasses
1 C. sour milk
6½ C. flour
2 C. oatmeal

1 C. raisins
¾ C. nuts
3 eggs
2 T. baking powder
2 T. soda
1½ t. nutmeg

Drop by teaspoonful onto cookie sheet and bake at 350°.

MOLASSES SUGAR COOKIES

Mrs. Eli B. Yoder

3³/₄ C. shortening
5 C. sugar
1¹/₂ C. sorghum molasses
5 eggs
6 T. soda

12¹/₂ C. sifted flour
1 t. cloves
2¹/₂ t. ginger
2¹/₂ t. cinnamon
2¹/₂ t. salt

Have shortening at room temperature. Add sugar, eggs and molasses. Beat well. Sift together flour, soda, spices and salt. Add to the first mixture. Mix well, chill and form into balls. Roll into granulated sugar. Bake at 375° for 8 - 10 minutes.

SORGHUM COOKIES

Mrs. Allen Beachy
Mrs. Alfred Miller
Mrs. Fremon Miller

2¹/₂ C. white sugar
2¹/₂ C. brown sugar
3 C. shortening
4 eggs
8 t. soda, dissolved in
　1 C. buttermilk or sour milk

1 C. sorghum or cane molasses
2 t. baking powder
4 t. cinnamon
1 t. salt
9¹/₂ C. flour

Chill. Roll into small balls then in white sugar, do not flatten. Bake at 350°. When cool spread filling between two cookies. For a delicious treat spread with ice cream and freeze. You can also use Ho-Ho cake filling on page 181.

Filling:
4 C. powdered sugar
2 t. vanilla
Mix together then fold in 4 beaten egg whites.

1¹/₂ C. Crisco

DEBBIE COOKIES

Joanna Miller

4¹/₂ C. brown sugar
2¹/₂ C. oleo
6 beaten eggs
6 C. quick oats
5 C. flour
Mix together and bake at 350°.

2¹/₄ t. soda
3 t. cinnamon
1¹/₂ t. salt
3 t. vanilla

Filling:
4 beaten egg whites
2 t. vanilla

4 C. powdered sugar
1¹/₂ C. Crisco

MONSTER COOKIES
Joanne Schlabach

$^1/_2$ C. Crisco
1 C. brown sugar
1 C. white sugar
3 eggs
$^3/_4$ t. vanilla
$^3/_4$ t. corn syrup

2 t. soda
1$^3/_4$ C. peanut butter
$^3/_4$ C. flour
4 C. oatmeal
$^3/_4$ C. chocolate chips
$^3/_4$ C. M&M's

Mix in order given and chill. Form into balls and roll in powdered sugar. Bake at 350° for 15 minutes.

SUNSET BUTTER COOKIES
Mrs. John Mark Troyer

1 lb. oleo
$^3/_4$ C. white sugar
red and green decorating sugar

2$^1/_2$ t. vanilla
4$^1/_2$ C. flour

Shape dough into 8 logs approx. 5" long. Roll logs in sugar. Chill overnight (can be frozen). Slice dough in $^1/_8$" slices. Bake at 350° for 15 minutes. Makes 9 dozen.

MEXICAN MOCHA BALLS
Twila Beachy

1 C. butter
$^1/_2$ C. sugar
2 t. vanilla extract
1$^3/_4$ C. flour
$^1/_4$ C. unsweetened cocoa
powdered sugar

1 T. instant coffee
$^1/_4$ t. salt
1 C. finely chopped nuts
$^1/_2$ C. chopped maraschino
   cherries

Cream butter. Gradually add sugar and vanilla, continue beating. In separate bowl, combine flour, cocoa, coffee and salt. Gradually add to creamed mixture. Blend in nuts and cherries. Chill dough. Preheat oven at 325°. Shape dough into 1" balls. Place in ungreased cookie sheet. Bake for 20 minutes. Remove from pan onto wire rack, dust with confectioners sugar.

SCOTCHAROOS
Mrs. Firman Miller

1 C. sugar
1 C. light Karo
1 C. peanut butter

6 C. Rice Krispies
1 C. chocolate chips
1 C. butterscotch chips

Bring sugar and Karo to a boil. Add peanut butter and stir until smooth. Pour mixture over Rice Krispies. Mix well, pour into 9" x 13" pan. Melt chips over very low heat. Spread over Rice Krispies. When cool, cut into squares and store in covered container.

MAPLE LEAF COOKIES
Mrs. Henry Beachy

1 lb. butter
4 C. brown sugar
8 beaten eggs
10$\frac{1}{2}$ C. Gold Medal flour

6 t. soda
1 t. salt
$\frac{3}{4}$ C. heavy cream
4 t. maple flavoring

Mix in order given, refrigerate dough several hours. Roll out and cut with maple leaf cutter. Bake at 350° for 5 - 7 minutes.

TWINKIES
Mrs. Henry Beachy

1 white cake mix
1 box instant vanilla pudding
$\frac{3}{4}$ C. Crisco oil

4 eggs
$\frac{3}{4}$ cup water

Mix everything together and put into two well greased 10" x 15" pans. Bake at 350° for 20 minutes. Switch pans at 10 minutes. When done put one pan on a wet towel and flip that one on the one with filling.

Filling:
2 egg whites beaten
1 t. vanilla

3 C. powdered sugar
1 C. Crisco

TRIPLE TREAT COOKIES
Ruby Beachy

1 C. brown sugar
1 C. white sugar
1 C. oleo
1 C. peanut butter
2 eggs

2 t. baking soda
1 t. salt
3 C. flour
1 C. chocolate chips

Make balls and bake at 350°. Do not overbake.

Filling:
$\frac{1}{2}$ C. peanut butter
1 t. vanilla
$\frac{1}{3}$ C. milk

2 - 3 C. powdered sugar
2 T. soft oleo

Spread between 2 cookies to make sandwich.

OREO COOKIES

Mrs. Josiah Miller
Mrs. Fremon Miller
Mrs. Nathan Mast

18 oz. chocolate cake mix
2 eggs + 2 T. water

2 T. cooking oil
1/2 C. cocoa

Blend well until you can shape dough into balls. Let stand 20 minutes. Form dough into 1/2" balls, place on greased cookie sheet. Flatten each with the smooth bottom of a glass greased once or dipped into Nestle's Quick with each cookie. Bake at 300° - 350°, remove cookies and flatten immediately.

Cookie filling:
1 envelope Knox gelatin
1/4 C. cold water
1 t. vanilla

1 C. Crisco
1 lb. + 1 C. powdered sugar

Soften gelatin in cold water, beat Crisco until light and fluffy adding sugar and vanilla. Beat well about 10 minutes add gelatin and beat some more. Spread 1 T. filling between 2 cookies and press gently so that filling pushes out to the edge like the original Oreo cookies. These cookies freeze well.

BANANA WHOOPIE PIES

Mrs. David Ray Yoder

1 1/2 C. brown sugar
1 C. shortening
2 eggs
2 C. mashed bananas
1 t. soda

1 t. vanilla
3 1/2 C. flour
1 t. salt
1 t. baking powder
1 t. cinnamon

Mix all together, then drop by teaspoonful onto cookie sheet. Bake at 350° for 10 minutes. When cool, sandwich together with the following icing:

Icing:
1 beaten egg white
2 T. flour
1 T. milk
1 C. powdered sugar

1 t. vanilla
1/2 C. Crisco
1 C. powdered sugar

Cream together first 5 ingredients, then add shortening and the additional powdered sugar.

❧

"O weary mother mixing dough
Don't you wish that food would grow?
A smile would come, I know to see,
A cookie bush or doughnut tree."

157

PUMPKIN WHOOPIE PIES

Mrs. David Ray Yoder

1¾ C. brown sugar
1 C. vegetable oil
1½ C. pumpkin
2 eggs
3 C. flour

1 t. baking powder
1 t. soda
1 t. vanilla
1½ t. cinnamon
1 t. salt

Cream sugar and oil, add eggs, pumpkin and vanilla. Blend well. Add sifted dry ingredients and mix well. Drop by teaspoonfuls onto cookie sheet and flatten slightly. Bake at 350° for 10 - 12 minutes. Yields 3 doz.

Filling:
3 oz. cream cheese
¼ C. oleo

½ t. vanilla
3 C. powdered sugar

DOUBLE CRUNCHES

Mrs. Martha Sue Miller

1 C. flour
½ t. soda
¼ t. salt
½ C. shortening
½ C. white sugar
1 C. corn flakes

½ C. brown sugar
1 egg
½ t. vanilla
1 C. quick oatmeal
½ C. coconut

Combine flour, soda and set aside. Cream shortening, sugar, eggs and vanilla. Beat gradually until fluffy, stir in flour mixture, corn flakes, oats, and coconut. Bake at 350° for 8 - 10 minutes. Cool.

Filling:
1 C. chocolate chips
½ C. powdered sugar

1 T. water
3 oz. cream cheese

Melt chocolate chips, sugar and water, blend in cream cheese until smooth. Cool, then spread between cookies.

SPELLBINDERS

Mrs. Mike Schrock

3 C. flour
2 t. soda
1½ C. oleo
2 C. quick oats

1 t. baking powder
2 eggs
2 C. brown sugar

Roll dough into balls and roll into crushed cornflake crumbs. Do not flatten balls. Bake at 350°.

Icing: Melt 4 T. oleo in a saucepan, add 2 C. powdered sugar, 2 T. hot water, and 2 t. vanilla. Thin with a little water if necessary. Drizzle over cookies.

CHOCOLATE SANDWICHES

Rosanna Miller

1 C. soft butter
2 C. sugar
2 eggs
2 t. vanilla
2 C. milk

4 C. flour
1 t. baking powder
3 t. baking soda
1 t. salt
1 C. cocoa

Mix all ingredients together in order given. Beat until smooth. Drop by rounded teaspoon onto buttered cookie sheet. Bake at 400° for 7 minutes. Cool and make sandwiches using the following filling.

Marshmallow Filling:
1 C. white shortening
4 C. powdered sugar
6 - 8 t. milk

2 C. marshmallow creme
2 t. vanilla

Cream shortening and sugar together and beat in other ingredients. Spread between cookies.

CHEWY DUNKING SNAPS

Mrs. Jay Mark Miller

1½ C. margarine
2 eggs
2 C. sugar
⅔ C. Brer Rabbit molasses (mild)
4⅔ C. flour

2 t. cinnamon
4 t. baking soda
1 t. cloves
½ t. salt
1 t. ginger

Mix margarine, sugar, eggs and molasses. Add flour, spices, soda and salt. Mix well, shape into balls and roll in sugar. Bake on ungreased cookie sheet at 375° for 10 - 12 minutes.

ALMA SCHROCK COOKIES

Mrs. Ben Troyer, Jr.

3 C. brown sugar
¾ C. butter
1 C. cream
4 eggs

2 t. baking powder
2 t. soda
1 t. vanilla
5 C. flour

Beat eggs, add butter and sugar. Mix well. Add rest of ingredients. Frost with caramel frosting on page 195.

BUTTERSCOTCH CRUNCH COOKIES

Mrs. Eli B. Yoder

2 C. shortening
2 C. brown sugar
2 C. white sugar
2 t. vanilla
4 eggs (1 at a time)

3 C. flour
2 t. salt
2 t. soda
6 C. oatmeal

Mix well and bake at 400° for 10 minutes. Do not bake too hard. Ice with brown sugar frosting on page 195 if desired.

GRAHAM CRACKER COOKIES

Mrs. Atlee J. Miller
Mrs. Eli A. Mast

1 C. oleo
1 C. white sugar
$^1/_2$ C. milk
Bring to a boil, turn off and add:
1 C. graham cracker crumbs
1 C. nuts

1 beaten egg
1 t. vanilla
a bit of cinnamon

1 C. rolled oats or coconut

Line large sheet pan with grahams. Top with warm filling and spread over entire surface. Top with grahams.

Icing:
$^1/_2$ C. melted butter
1 T. milk

1 t. vanilla
2 C. powdered sugar

Mix oleo, milk and vanilla. Add sugar. Spread over cookies and cut into squares when cold.

CHOCOLATE CRINKLES

Mrs. Fremon Miller

4 squares unsweetened chocolate or
12 t. cocoa and 4 T. oleo
2 C. white sugar
3 C. sifted flour
2 t. baking powder

$^1/_2$ C. oleo
4 eggs
$^1/_2$ t. salt
1 t. vanilla
$^1/_2$ C. chopped nuts

Melt butter with chocolate over low heat. Cool slightly. Blend in sugars. Add eggs one at a time and beat well after adding each one. Add flour, salt, baking powder, nuts and vanilla. Chill for $^1/_2$ hour. Shape into balls and roll in powdered sugar. Bake at 350° for 15 minutes. Baking them too long makes them hard. Enjoy!

CHOCOLATE CRINKLES

Mrs. David Ray Yoder

1 C. cocoa
1/2 C. vegetable oil
2 C. white sugar
4 eggs

2 t. baking powder
2 t. vanilla
1/2 t. salt
2 C. flour

Mix oil, cocoa and sugar. Blend in eggs, one at a time. Add vanilla, flour, baking powder and salt. Chill dough several hours or overnight. Drop by spoonfuls or make balls, roll in powdered sugar, then in white sugar. Bake at 350°. Yields 4 dozen.

HOLIDAY WREATHS

Janice Schlabach

60 large marshmallows
1 C. butter
2 t. vanilla

4 t. green food coloring
7 C. cornflakes

Combine marshmallows, butter, vanilla and green food coloring in top of the double boiler. Heat over water until marshmallows are melted, stirring frequently. Gradually add cornflakes and continue to stir gently (to keep cereal from breaking) until cereal is completely covered. Shape into small wreaths on waxed paper. Decorate with cinnamon candies.

CREAM WAFERS

Mrs. Josiah Miller

1 C. butter
2 C. brown sugar
4 eggs, beaten
2 t. vanilla
4 T. cream

2 t. soda
1 t. baking powder
1/2 t. salt
5 C. flour

Mix ingredients well, use a cookie press. Bake at 350°.

Filling:
8 T. butter
4 T. cream

4 C. powdered sugar
2 t. vanilla

Melt butter then add cream. Bring almost to a boil, add powdered sugar and vanilla. Mix and spread between cookies.

ે

*The recipe for a happy family includes
a heaping cup of patience.*

CREAM WAFER COOKIES

Mrs. David Ray Yoder

1 C. shortening
2 C. brown sugar
4 eggs, beaten
1 t. vanilla

4 T. sweet cream
2 t. soda
2 t. baking powder
6 C. flour

Mix. Press through cookie press. Bake till light brown, cut into 3" pieces and immediately remove from cookie sheet.

Filling:
8 T. sweet cream
powdered sugar till right consistency

4 T. butter, melted
3 T. Crisco

Melt butter, then add cream and powdered sugar, when right spreading consistency add Crisco and beat until smooth and fluffy. Spread between 2 cookies to form a sandwich. I use evaporated milk instead of sweet cream. A favorite with children! Yields 6 doz.

DOUBLE CHOCOLATE JUMBO CRISPS

Joanne Schlabach
Mrs. Josiah Miller

2½ C. oleo
3 C. white sugar
2 t. vanilla
2 eggs
2 C. flour
12 oz. chocolate chips

1 t. soda
1 t. salt
12 T. cocoa
½ C. water
6 C. rolled oats

Cream oleo, sugar and vanilla. Add eggs and beat until fluffy. Blend in dry ingredients, add water. Add oats gradually, then chocolate chips. Drop by spoonfuls onto ungreased cookie sheet. Bake at 350° for 15 minutes. I don't bake them quite so long but then I leave them on the pan for a few minutes.

Filling #1:
5 T. flour
1¼ C. milk

1 C. powdered sugar
¾ C. Crisco

Cook flour and milk until thick, allow to cool. Combine sugar and Crisco, cream well. Add to flour mixture and beat well. Spread between 2 cookies.

Filling #2:
2 egg whites
1 T. vanilla

2 C. powdered sugar
1½ C. Crisco

Beat eggs until stiff, add powdered sugar, and cream, then add Crisco and vanilla.

SOFT SUGAR COOKIES

Mrs. Mark Hochstetler

2 C. oleo
3 C. white sugar
4 eggs
2 C. cream or evaporated milk
1 t. lemon juice or vanilla

2 t. soda
6 t. baking powder
$\frac{1}{2}$ t. salt
10 C. Robin Hood flour

Cream together oleo and sugar. Add eggs and stir well. Add the rest of the ingredients. Chill dough overnight. Bake at 350°. This batter works great for cutouts.

Butter Frosting:
1 C. melted butter
$\frac{1}{2}$ C. hot cream

4 t. vanilla
8 C. powdered sugar

Melt butter, then add cream. Bring almost to a boil. Add powdered sugar and vanilla. Spread on cookies.

CUTOUT COOKIES

Laura K. Miller

4 C. brown sugar
1$\frac{1}{2}$ C. melted butter or margarine
3 eggs
1 C. sweet cream
1 C. milk
pinch of salt

2 t. soda
2 t. baking powder
10$\frac{1}{4}$ C. Robin Hood flour,
   sifted
3 t. vanilla

Mix all together and chill overnight. Roll to $\frac{3}{8}$" thick and cut with cookie cutters. Place on ungreased cookie sheets and bake at 325° - 350°. Do not brown. Makes approximately 100 cookies.

BROWN SUGAR COOKIES (CUTOUTS)

Mrs. Merle Hershberger

2 C. brown sugar
1 egg
1 C. sour milk
1 C. shortening

1 t. soda
1 t. baking powder
1 t. nutmeg
4 C. flour

Mix, then chill a few hours before rolling out. Bake at 350°. Very tasty Valentine cookies.

SOUR CREAM FROSTING COOKIES

Mrs. Roman Coblentz

4 eggs
1 C. shortening
3 C. brown sugar
2 t. vanilla
2 t. soda
Mix and bake at 350°.

1 t. baking powder
5 - 5½ C. flour
2 C. sour cream
dash of salt

Frosting:
1 egg beaten
vanilla
1 box powdered sugar

4 T. oleo
2 t. cream or evaporated milk

Mix and spread on cookies.

BUTTERMILK COOKIES

Mrs. Aaron Coblentz

1 C. shortening
3 eggs
2 t. baking powder
2 C. sugar
1 t. soda

1 C. buttermilk or sour cream
4 C. flour
1 t. salt
1 t. vanilla

Mix sugar and oleo, add eggs, buttermilk and vanilla. Add dry ingredients. Bake at 350° for 15 minutes or till slightly browned. Good with frosting.

SOFT CUTOUT COOKIES

Dorothy Yoder

4 C. white sugar
1 lb. butter
6 eggs
2 C. cream
2 t. salt

2 t. soda
3 T. + 1 t. baking powder
2 t. vanilla
10 C. Gold Medal flour

Combine in order given. Chill at least 8 hours. Roll out to ¼" thick. Bake at 325° until cookie is set, 8 - 10 minutes. Do not overbake. Cool, frost and enjoy! Approximately 10 dozen cookies.

ও

Be patient with the faults of others,
They have to be patient with yours.

SOFT CUTOUT COOKIES

Mrs. Jr. Wagler

2 C. white sugar
1 C. butter
3 eggs
1 C. whipping cream
1 t. salt

1 t. soda
5 t. baking powder
1 t. vanilla
5 C. flour

Mix in order given. Bake at 350°. (Hint, do not overbake!)

Cream Cheese Frosting:
8 oz. cream cheese
1/2 C. butter

5 C. powdered sugar

SPICE COOKIES

Coleen Troyer

2 C. brown sugar
1 C. shortening
1 1/4 C. milk
4 eggs
4 C. flour
2 t. soda

1 t. cinnamon
1/2 t. cloves
1 t. vanilla
1 t. salt
2 t. baking powder

Cream shortening and sugar, add milk, eggs and vanilla. Beat well. Sift all dry ingredients and mix with shortening mixture. Beat well and drop on greased cookie sheet. Bake at 350° for 10 minutes. Let cookies cool just a little, then put icing on.

Icing:
6 T. butter
3 T. hot water

1 t. vanilla

Melt butter, stir in water and vanilla. Add powdered sugar until thick enough to spread.

BUTTER PECAN TURTLE COOKIES

Mrs. Roy Mast

Crust:
2 C. flour
1 C. brown sugar
Caramel Layer:
2/3 C. butter (real)
1/2 C. brown sugar

3/4 C. oleo, softened

1 C. whole pecans
1 C. chocolate chips

Mix crust and pat in 9" x 13" pan. Sprinkle pecans evenly over crust. For caramel layer, cook butter and sugar together over medium heat, stirring constantly. Boil for 1/2 to 1 minute. Pour over crust and pecans. Bake at 350° for 18 - 22 minutes. Caramel layer is bubbly and crust is golden brown. Take out and sprinkle chocolate chips on top. Leave some whole. Do not spread. Cool completely and cut. Rich!

MAPLE PECAN SQUARES

Mrs. Eddie Miller

1½ C. all-purpose flour
¼ C. brown sugar, packed
½ C. butter
⅔ C. brown sugar, packed
1 C. maple or pancake syrup

2 T. flour
¼ t. salt
½ t. vanilla
1 C. chopped pecans
2 eggs beaten

Combine flour, ¼ C. brown sugar and butter in a bowl. With a fork, mix until consistency of fine cornmeal. Press mixture in ungreased 9" x 13" pan. Bake at 350° for 15 minutes. Combine ⅔ C. brown sugar and syrup in small saucepan. Simmer for 15 minutes. Pour over beaten eggs, stirring constantly. Stir in remaining ingredients except nuts. Pour mixture over baked crust, sprinkle with nuts and bake at 350° for 20 - 25 minutes. Cool in pan. Cut into bars.

PECAN SQUARES

Mrs. Willis Karen Miller

Crust:
3 C. flour
½ C. sugar

1 C. butter or oleo, softened
½ t. salt

Filling:
4 eggs
1½ C. light or dark corn syrup
1½ C. sugar

3 T. butter or oleo, melted
1½ t. vanilla extract
2½ C. chopped pecans

In a large bowl, blend together flour, sugar, butter and salt until mixture resembles coarse crumbs. Press firmly and evenly into a greased 10" x 15" baking pan. Bake at 350° for 20 minutes. Meanwhile in another bowl combine first five filling ingredients. Stir in pecans. Spread over hot crust. Bake at 350° for 25 minutes until set. Cool.

PECAN PIE BARS

Mrs. Mark Hochstetler
Mrs. Crist Beachy

⅔ C. white sugar
½ C. butter or margarine, softened
1 t. vanilla
1 egg
1½ C. Gold Medal flour

½ C. light or dark corn syrup
1 t. vanilla
3 eggs
1 C. broken pecans
⅔ C. brown sugar, packed

Mix white sugar, margarine, 1 t. vanilla and 1 egg in a large bowl. Stir in flour, press dough in bottom and ½" up the sides of an ungreased 9" x 13" pan. Bake until edges are light brown, 10 - 15 minutes. Beat brown sugar, corn syrup, vanilla and 3 eggs. With spoon stir in pecans. Pour over crust. Bake until set, 20 minutes. Loosen edges from sides of pan while still warm. Cool and cut.

SOUR CREAM RAISIN SQUARES

Mrs. Mike Schrock
Mrs. Alfred Miller

1 C. butter or margarine, softened
1 C. packed brown sugar
1³/₄ - 2 C. all-purpose flour
1³/₄ - 2 C. quick oats

1 t. baking powder
1 t. soda
¹/₈ t. salt

Filling:
4 egg yolks
1¹/₂ C. raisins
1 C. white sugar

1 - 2 T. clear jel or cornstarch
2 C. sour cream

In a large mixing bowl, cream butter and brown sugar. Beat in flour, oats, baking powder, soda and salt. Mixture will be crumbly. Set aside 2 C. of the crumbs. Pat remaining crumbs into greased 9" x 13" baking pan. Bake at 350° for 15 minutes. Cool. Combine filling ingredients in a saucepan. Bring to a boil cook stirring constantly for 5 - 8 minutes. Pour over crust. Sprinkle with reserved crumbs. Return to oven for 15 minutes. You can substitue ¹/₂ C. brown sugar and ¹/₂ C. white sugar for 1 C. brown sugar.

RAISIN BARS

Mrs. Henry Beachy

First part:
1 C. raisins, covered with 1 C. water, cook until tender. Add ¹/₂ t. soda, ¹/₂ t. salt and ¹/₂ C. oleo. Cool. Cream 1 egg with 1 C. sugar. Sift together 2 C. flour, 1 t. soda and 1 t. cinnamon. Mix flour and raisins with sugar/egg mixture, add ¹/₂ C. nuts and vanilla. Spread on greased jelly roll pan.

Glaze:
Melt ¹/₂ stick oleo and add powdered sugar and water till spreading consistency.

GRANOLA BARS

Mrs. Josie Miller

2 C. brown sugar
1 C. white sugar
2 C. margarine

8 C. oatmeal
3 C. milk chocolate chips
3 C. peanut butter

Mix sugars, margarine and oatmeal until crumbly. Press into large cookie sheet and bake at 350° for 13 minutes. Cool in double boiler melt chocolate chips and peanut butter. Spread on top of first mixture. A half batch fits into a 9"x 13" pan.

GRANOLA BARS

Mrs. Charles Karn

³/₄ C. margarine
1 C. brown sugar
¹/₂ C. white or maple flavored syrup
1 t. vanilla

1 t. salt
3 C. quick oats
1 C. flour
1¹/₂ C. chopped nuts

Cream margarine and sugar, add syrup, vanilla and salt. Add quick oats, flour and nuts. Mix well. Press into well greased cookie sheet. Bake at 425° till light brown and bubbly. Let set a few minutes, then cut while still warm. Let set a few more minutes, remove from the pan before cool.

FRUIT COCKTAIL BARS

Mrs. Willis Wagler

2 beaten eggs
1¹/₂ C. white sugar
1 lb. fruit cocktail
1¹/₂ t. soda

¹/₂ t. salt
1 t. vanilla
2¹/₄ C. flour

Mix and pour into a large cookie sheet, bake at 350° for 25 - 35 minutes.

Topping:
³/₄ C. sugar
¹/₂ C. butter
¹/₄ C. Pet milk or cream

¹/₂ t. vanilla
¹/₂ C. nuts
1¹/₃ C. coconut

Boil first four ingredients for 6 minutes. Then add nuts and coconut, put on top of baked bars. Put in broiler long enough to brown. Takes only 1 or 2 minutes.

DANISH APPLE BARS

Mrs. Ella Miller

Dough:
3 C. flour
1 C. Crisco
7 T. milk

1 t. salt
1 egg yolk

Filling:
1 C. crushed cornflakes
1 C. sugar
1 egg white, beaten stiff

7 C. shredded apples
1 t. cinnamon

Glaze:
1 C. powdered sugar
1 t. vanilla

3 T. water

Mix together flour and salt. Cut into shortening, beat egg yolk into milk, mix and divide dough in half. Roll thin, put in 10" x 15" pan. Sprinkle with cornflakes. Add apples, sugar and cinnamon, roll out other half of dough and cover apples and pinch edges. Cut vents into top. Brush egg whites over crust. Bake at 375° until golden brown. Spread with glaze while still warm. Cut into squares and enjoy.

SAM BARB'S FRUIT BARS

Mrs. Reuben Miller

14 C. Gold Medal flour
4¹/₂ C. white sugar
1 t. baking soda
1 lb. oleo
5 eggs, well beaten
1¹/₂ C. nuts

1 pt. Brer Rabbit molasses
5 t. soda dissolved in
    ¹/₂ C. boiling water
2 lbs. raisins cooked in
    ¹/₂ C. water

Mix flour, sugar, baking powder and oleo. Add all other ingredients. I use my hands to mix it. Then make small long rolls and put on cookie sheet. Press down with the heel of your hand to flatten. Brush with beaten egg. Bake at 400° for 10 - 15 minutes. Do not underbake.

LEMON BARS

Mrs. Mark Hochstetler

2 C. flour
¹/₂ C. powdered sugar

1 C. butter

Melt butter, add flour and powdered sugar. Mix well. Pat into 9" x 13" cake pan. Bake till light brown. Approximately 10 minutes at 350°.

Mix:
4 eggs, beaten
2 C. white sugar
¹/₃ C. lemon juice

¹/₄ C. flour
¹/₂ t. baking powder

Put this on baked crust and bake 20 - 25 minutes. Sprinkle with powdered sugar. Cut.

RHUBARB DREAM BARS

Mrs. Ben Troyer, Jr.

2 C. flour
³/₄ C. powdered sugar

1 C. butter

Mix and press into 10" x 15" pan. Bake at 350° for 15 minutes.

Beat together:
4 eggs
2 C. white sugar
¹/₂ C. flour

¹/₂ t. salt
4 C. diced rhubarb

Spread last 5 ingredients on hot crusts. Bake at 350° for 40 - 45 minutes.

CHOCOLATE MARSHMALLOW BARS

Mrs. Leroy Yoder

1 C. margarine
³/₄ C. white sugar
³/₄ C. brown sugar
2 eggs
1 t. vanilla
1 t. baking soda

¹/₂ - 1 t. salt
1 C. walnuts
2 C. chocolate chips
2 C. mini marshmallows
2¹/₄ C. flour

Combine sugars with margarine and beat until creamy. Beat in eggs and vanilla. Gradually add flour, soda and salt. Stir in nuts, chips and marshmallows. Spread on greased 10" x 15" cookie sheet. Bake at 375° for 20 minutes.

MARSHMALLOW KRISPIE BARS

Mrs. Mike Schrock

1 pkg. Duncan Hines fudge brownie mix
1 pkg. (10¹/₂ oz.) miniature marshmallows
1¹/₂ C. semi-sweet chocolate chips
1 C. Jif creamy peanut butter
1 T. butter or margarine
1¹/₂ C. crisp rice cereal

Preheat oven to 350°. Grease bottom of 9" x 13" pan. Prepare and bake brownies following package directions for original recipe. When finished baking, sprinkle brownies with marshmallows. Put back in oven for 3 minutes. Combine chocolate chips, peanut butter, and butter in medium saucepan. Heat slowly, stirring constantly until chocolate chips are melted. Add crisp rice cereal, mix well. Spread mixture over marshmallows. Refrigerate until chilled, cut in bars.

NUT CHOCOLATE BARS

Mary Ellen Schlabach

1/₃ C. shortening
1 C. brown sugar
1 egg
1 t. vanilla
1 C. all-purpose flour

¹/₄ t. soda
¹/₄ t. salt
¹/₂ - 1 C. chocolate pieces
¹/₂ C. walnuts

Cream shortening and sugar. Add eggs and vanilla, beat well. Sift together flour, soda and salt. Add to creamed mixture, mix well. Stir in chocolate pieces and walnuts. Spread into greased 7" x 11" pan. Bake at 350° for 20 - 25 minutes.

HERSHEY CHOCOLATE MINT BARS

Mrs. Jr. Wagler

1st layer:

1/2 C. soft butter
1 C. white sugar
4 eggs

1 1/2 C. Hershey's syrup
1 C. flour

2nd layer:

1/2 C. soft butter
1/2 t. mint extract
1 T. hot water

4 - 5 drops green food coloring
2 C. powdered sugar

3rd layer:

1 C. chocolate chips

6 T. butter

Beat 1st layer ingredients until smooth, put in 9" x 13" pan. Bake at 350° for 20 minutes, cool. Mix together 2nd layer, spread on cooled first layer, chill. Melt 3rd layer, spread over 2nd layer.

FAVORITE CHOCOLATE CARAMEL NUT BARS

Mrs. Mike Schrock

14 oz. Kraft caramels (48)
5 oz. evaporated milk, divided
1 pkg. German chocolate cake mix
  with pudding

1/2 C. margarine, melted
1 1/2 C. chopped walnuts
1 C. real chocolate chips

Heat oven to 350°. Melt caramels with 1/3 C. milk in heavy saucepan, over low heat, stirring frequently, until smooth. Set aside, mix remaining milk, cake mix and margarine in bowl. Press 1/2 of cake mixture in bottom of 9" x 13" pan. Bake at 350° for 8 minutes. Sprinkle 1 C. walnuts and 1/2 C. chips over crust, top with caramel mixture, spreading to edges of pan. Top with teaspoonfuls of remaining cake mixture. Press gently into caramel mixture. Sprinkle with 1/2 C. walnuts and 1/2 C. chips. Bake for another 18 minutes. Cool, cut into bars.

OOEY-GOOEY CARAMEL BARS

Mrs. Dean Wengerd
Deborah Troyer

2 C. flour
1 1/2 C. brown sugar
2 C. quick rolled oats
1 t. baking soda
1 C. melted butter

14 oz. caramels
5 T. milk, cream or
  evaporated milk
2 C. milk chocolate chips
1/2 C. chopped walnuts, optional

Combine flour, brown sugar, oats, baking soda and melted butter. (If you substitute margarine for butter use 2 T. less.) Press 2/3 of mixture into 10" x 15" pan. Bake at 350° for 10 minutes. Melt caramels and milk stirring constantly. Sprinkle chocolate chips and nuts on hot crust. Spread caramel mixture over top. Sprinkle with remaining oat mixture. Bake another 20 minutes. Cut while warm.

HONEY GRAHAM BARS

Bena Beachy

3 C. honey graham cereal or
   chow mein noodles
3 C. pretzel sticks (broken in ¹/₂)
³/₄ C. raisins
¹/₂ C. flaked coconut

¹/₂ C. M&M candies
¹/₂ C. oleo
¹/₃ C. peanut butter
5 C. marshmallows

Combine cereal, pretzels, M&M's, raisins and coconut. Melt oleo and peanut butter over low heat. Add marshmallows, stir until melted and smooth. Pour over cereal mixture. Mix well. Press into greased pan. When firm cut into bars.

S'MORE COOKIE BARS

Mrs. Joe Miller, Jr.

²/₃ C. butter flavored shortening
²/₃ C. firmly packed brown sugar
1 egg
¹/₂ t. vanilla
1 C. graham cracker crumbs
²/₃ C. flour

¹/₄ t. salt
6 T. whipping cream
9 - 10 oz. milk chocolate
   candy bars, broken up
1 C. miniature marshmallows

Combine shortening, sugar, egg and vanilla in bowl, blend well. Combine graham cracker crumbs, flour and salt. Add to creamed mixture. Spread dough into 9" x 13" pan. Bake at 350° for 13 - 15 minutes. Do not overbake. Cool completely. Heat cream to a simmer. Remove from heat and add chocolate pieces, stir until smooth. Stir in marshmallows. Spread evenly over cooled crust. Refrigerate, cut into bars.

ROCKY ROAD FUDGE BARS

Mary Beth Mast

1 C. margarine
1 C. + 2 T. flour
³/₄ C. nuts
8 oz. cream cheese
¹/₄ C. milk
3 C. powdered sugar
2 eggs

¹/₂ C. cocoa
1¹/₂ C. white sugar
1 t. baking powder
2¹/₂ t. vanilla
6 oz. chocolate chips
2 C. miniature marshmallows

In a large saucepan melt ¹/₂ C. margarine and ¹/₄ C. cocoa. Add 1 C. sugar, 1 C. flour, ¹/₂ C. nuts, 1 egg, and 1 t. each of vanilla and baking powder. Mix well and spread into 9" x 13" pan. In a small bowl combine 6 oz. cream cheese with ¹/₂ C. white sugar, ¹/₄ C. margarine, 2 T. flour, 1 egg and ¹/₂ t. vanilla, beat 1 minute. Spread over bar mixture, sprinkle with ¹/₄ C. nuts and chocolate chips. Bake at 350° for 30 minutes. Remove from oven, sprinkle with marshmallows, bake 2 minutes longer. In a large saucepan over low heat, melt ¹/₄ C. margarine, ¹/₄ C. cocoa, 2 oz. cream cheese and milk. Stir in powdered sugar and 1 t. vanilla until smooth. Pour over marshmallows and swirl. Cool and cut into bars. Refrigerate.

SWEDISH NUT BARS

Mary Beth Mast

1 C. margarine
1 C. pecans
1/2 C. milk
1 C. sugar

1 C. graham crackers
1 C. coconut
1 egg, beaten

Combine margarine, egg, sugar and milk in a saucepan and boil for 1 minute, stirring constantly. Remove from heat and add pecans, coconut and graham cracker crumbs. Mix well. Line ungreased 9" x 13" pan with whole graham crackers. Spread with icing and chill. Pour filling over top of crackers. Put another layer of crackers on top and spread with icing.

Icing:
1/2 C. melted margarine
1 T. milk

1 t. vanilla
2 C. powdered sugar

Mix margarine, milk and vanilla. Add powdered sugar. Spread over nut bars.

WALNUT BARS

Mrs. Willis Wagler

Bottom layer:
1 C. sifted flour
2 T. white sugar

1/2 C. butter or oleo

Mix flour, sugar and butter. I always make a double batch and put them in a cake pan. Bake at 375° for 10 minutes.

Top layer:
2 beaten eggs
1 1/2 C. brown sugar
1 C. nuts
1/2 C. coconut

2 T. flour
1 t. baking powder
1/4 t. salt
1 t. vanilla

Mix together, pour on top of crumbs and bake at 350° for 30 - 40 minutes.

MUD HEN BARS

Mrs. Willis Wagler

1/2 C. shortening
1 C. white sugar
1 egg
2 egg yolks
1 1/2 C. flour
1 t. baking powder

1/4 t. salt
1 C. nuts
1/2 C. chocolate chips
1 C. mini marshmallows
1 C. brown sugar
2 egg whites

Mix first 7 ingredients, press into 9" x 13" pan. Sprinkle with nuts, chocolate chips and marshmallows. Beat egg whites till stiff, fold in brown sugar. Spread on top. Bake at 350° for 30 - 40 minutes.

NAPOLEON CREME BARS

Mrs. Robert Miller

$1/2$ C. butter, softened
$1/4$ C. sugar
$1/4$ C. cocoa
1 t. vanilla
1 egg, slightly beaten
2 C. graham cracker crumbs
1 C. coconut

$1/2$ C. butter
3 T. milk
1 pkg. vanilla instant pudding
2 C. powdered sugar
6 oz. chocolate chips
2 T. butter

Combine first 4 ingredients in saucepan and cook slowly till butter melts. Stir in egg and continue cooking until mixture thickens. Blend in crumbs and coconut. Press into buttered 9" x 9" pan. Cream $1/2$ C. butter, stir in milk, pudding mix and powdered sugar. Beat until fluffy, spread evenly over crust. Chill until firm. Melt chocolate chips and 2 T. butter. Cool then spread onto pudding layer. Chill, cut into bars.

MOUND BARS

Mrs. Robert Miller

1 stick butter
1 can Eagle Brand milk
vanilla

2 lb. powdered sugar
1 large pkg. coconut.

Mix all together and chill, then roll into small balls and dip into chocolate.

1-2-3 COFFEE BARS

Mrs. Willis Wagler

2 eggs
$2^2/_3$ C. brown sugar
1 t. salt
1 t. baking soda

1 C. vegetable oil
1 C. warm coffee
3 C. flour
1 t. vanilla

Mix in order given and put into greased jelly roll pan. Sprinkle with nuts and miniature chocolate chips. Bake at 350°. Cut into bars.

BLONDE BROWNIES

Mrs. John Troyer

$2/_3$ C. margarine
2 C. brown sugar
2 eggs
1 C. raisins or chocolate chips
$1/2$ C. nuts

1 t. baking soda
1 t. salt
2 t. vanilla
2 C. flour

Melt margarine in 2 qt. saucepan. Add brown sugar and stir. Sift dry ingredients and add to butter mixture. Add raisins or chocolate chips and nuts. Bake at 350°.

CREAM CHEESE BROWNIES

Rachel Coblentz

1 cake mix
8 oz. cream cheese
1 egg

1/2 C. sugar
1 1/2 C. chocolate chips

Mix chocolate cake mix as directed on box. Pour into 13" x 18" pan, beat together cream cheese, egg and sugar. Drop onto cake batter with spoon, then swirl with a knife. Sprinkle with chocolate chips. Bake at 350° for 30 minutes or until done.

DAD'S FAVORITE BROWNIES

Mrs. Merle Hershberger

1/2 C. shortening
2 - 1 oz. squares unsweetened chocolate
3/4 C. flour
1/2 t. baking powder
1/2 t. salt

2 eggs
1 C. sugar
1 t. vanilla
1 C. chopped nuts

Melt chocolate and shortening together in double boiler. Cool. Sift flour, baking powder and salt. Beat eggs until light, add sugar, chocolate mixture and blend. Add flour, vanilla and nuts. Pour batter into well greased 8" square pan, or you can double the recipe for regular size cookie sheet. Bake at 350° for 30 - 35 minutes. Cool and frost.

FROSTED PUMPKIN BARS

Ruby Beachy
Mrs. Willis Karen Miller

4 eggs, beaten
1 C. oil
1 C. pumpkin
2 C. sugar
1/2 t. salt

1 t. soda
1 t. baking powder
1 C. chopped nuts
2 C. flour
2 t. cinnamon

Mix together and bake at 350° for 20 minutes in floured cookie sheet.

Frosting:
3 oz. cream cheese
6 T. butter, melted
2 1/2 C. powdered sugar

1 t. vanilla
1 t. milk

Mix ingredients and spread on cake while still warm.

&

It's not so much the load you carry
as how you carry it.

175

- Notes -

Cakes & Frostings

ANGEL FOOD CAKE

Mrs. John Shetler

1 C. sifted cake flour
1½ C. sifted powdered sugar
2 C. egg whites
1½ t. cream of tartar

1 C. sugar
1½ t. vanilla
½ t. almond flavoring

Sift flour and powdered sugar together 3 times. Set aside. Place egg whites, cream of tartar and salt in large mixing bowl and beat till foamy, gradually add sugar 2 T. at a time, continue beating until meringue holds stiff peaks, fold in flavoring, gradually sift flour/sugar mixture over egg whites. Mix gently by hand. Bake in 10" tube pan, at 350° for 35 - 40 minutes or until top springs back when lightly touched, invert on a funnel and let cool.

APPLE CAKE

Mrs. Noah J. Hostetler

Cream:
1 C. white sugar
½ C. shortening

Add:
1 beaten egg

Stir in:
2 C. chopped apples

Add:
1½ C. flour
1 t. baking powder
pinch of salt

1 t. vanilla
½ C. raisins

Put in greased and floured pan and cover with following topping.

Mix:
½ C. brown sugar
2 T. flour
½ C. chopped nuts

3 T. butter
2 t. cinnamon

Pour over first mixture and bake 45 minutes at 350°. Cool and serve with whipped cream.

&

Recipe for happiness -
This day is for beauty . . . Find something beautiful.
This day is for joy . . . Rejoice in it.
This day is for love . . . Show someone love.

BANANA CAKE

Laura K. Miller

Sift together:
2 C. brown sugar
2¹/₂ C. Velvet cake flour

2 eggs
1 C. sour cream
1 t. vanilla
1 t. soda

1 t. baking powder
1 C. mashed bananas
pinch of salt

Add salt to eggs and beat well. Next add sour cream, vanilla, soda, baking powder, bananas and the flour/sugar mixture. Stir well and bake at 350°.

HUMMINGBIRD CAKE

Regina Miller

Combine in bowl:
3¹/₂ C. flour
1 t. baking soda

1¹/₂ t. cinnamon

Add:
1¹/₂ C. sugar
1 C. vegetable oil
8 oz. crushed pineapple, undrained
1 t. salt

3 beaten eggs
1 C. nuts
1¹/₂ t. vanilla
2 C. crushed bananas

Cream butter, vanilla and sugar. Beat till fluffy, add eggs. Blend in dry ingredients. Add the rest of the ingredients and mix well. Grease 3 - 9" cake pans or 1 regular cake pan. Bake at 350° for 25 - 30 minutes and cool. To frost, beat together 8 oz. cream cheese and ¹/₂ C. butter. Add 3 - 4 C. powdered sugar to make desired thickness. Spread over cooled cake.

BLACK FOREST CAKE

Mrs. Matthew Miller

1 chocolate cake mix
1 can cherry pie filling

1 can whip topping
8 oz. cream cheese

Prepare cake mix as instructed, bake in 2 round pans. Put ²/₃ of batter in one pan and ¹/₃ of batter in the other pan. Bake at 350°. When cake is done and cooled completely. Put the thinnest cake on a cake plate. Layer with whip topping and cream cheese mixture, then add a layer of cherry pie filling. Cut other cake through the center lengthwise. Continue layering. When last piece of cake is on, frost all sides with cream cheese mixture. To garnish, take cake decorating bag and flower tip, and trim edges with additional whip. Shave Hershey's chocolate bar and sprinkle over top and sides. Set a few cherries on top. Makes a nice centerpiece.

BUTTERMILK CAKE

Mrs. Willis Wagler

Crumbs:
4 C. flour
2 C. white sugar

³/₄ C. butter or oleo

Reserve 1 C. crumbs, to the rest of the crumbs add the following.

1¹/₂ C. buttermilk
1 t. soda

1 t. cinnamon

Mix and pour into cake pan then top with reserved 1 C. crumbs. Bake at 350° for 45 - 50 minutes.

CHOCOLATE CHIP CHIFFON CAKE

Mrs. David Ray Yoder

Measure and sift together in bowl:
2¹/₄ C. cake flour
1³/₄ C. white sugar

3 t. baking powder
1 t. salt

Make a well and add in order. Beat with spoon until smooth.
¹/₃ C. vegetable oil
5 unbeaten egg yolks

³/₄ C. cold water
2 t. vanilla

Measure into large mixing bowl. Beat until whites form very stiff peaks. They should be stiffer than for angel food cake. Do not underbeat.
1 C. egg whites (7 or 8)

¹/₂ t. cream of tartar

Pour egg yolk mixture gradually over beaten egg whites. Gently fold with rubber spatula just till blended. Sprinkle 3 oz. coarsely grated milk chocolate over top of batter, gently fold in with a few strokes. Pour into ungreased 10" tube pan. Bake at 325° for 55 minutes, then increase to 350° for 10 - 15 minutes.

CHOCOLATE MOCHA CAKE

Mrs. Henry Schrock

3 C. flour
1¹/₂ t. baking powder
1¹/₂ t. soda
¹/₂ t. salt
1¹/₂ t. cinnamon
³/₄ C. cocoa
³/₄ C. shortening

1¹/₂ t. vanilla
2¹/₂ C. sugar
3 eggs
³/₄ C. cooled coffee
1¹/₂ C. sour milk or
  buttermilk

Sift flour, baking powder, salt, cinnamon and cocoa 3 times. Cream shortening, add sugar, gradually. Add eggs, beating well. Add dry ingredients with milk, vanilla and soda. Beat well after each addition. Add cooled coffee. Stir until batter is smooth. Bake at 350°. This is a large cake.

CHOCO-NUT PICNIC CAKE

Mrs. Marvin Wengerd

3 C. flour
3½ t. baking powder
1 t. salt
2 C. brown sugar

1 C. milk
2 eggs
2 t. vanilla
¾ C. butter

Preheat oven to 350°. Sift together flour, baking powder, salt and brown sugar. Add butter and cut into fine crumb consistency. Reserve 1 C. of this mixture for topping. Stir milk, vanilla and eggs into rest of the crumb mixture. Do not beat too much or mixture will be lumpy. Pour into greased 12" x 17" pan.

Crumb topping:
½ C. chocolate chips
¾ C. chopped nuts

3 T. butter

Add these 3 to your reserved crumbs. I usually add a little flour to make it more crumbly. Sprinkle on top of cake and bake about 20 minutes. Be careful not to overbake. Good just plain or lace with brown sugar frosting when cool. See page 195 for brown sugar frosting.

HO HO CAKE

Mrs. Henry Beachy

Bake chocolate cake mix in jelly roll pan.

Topping:
5 T. flour
Cook together and cool.

1¼ C. milk

½ C. oleo
1 C. Crisco

1 t. vanilla
1 C. sugar

Cream together and beat well. Add flour mixture and beat again. Spread on cooled cake.

Icing:
½ C. oleo
1 egg
1 t. vanilla

5 T. cocoa
3 C. powdered sugar
2½ T. hot water

Melt oleo, add cocoa. Beat egg, vanilla and hot water, add to oleo. Add powdered sugar and blend well. Spread over topping. Refrigerate.

JIFFY CHOCOLATE CAKE

Debra Kay Miller

1 egg
1/2 C. buttermilk
1 t. vanilla
1/2 C. shortening
1 1/2 C. sifted cake flour

1/2 C. cocoa
1 C. sugar
1 t. baking soda
1/4 t. salt

In a bowl mix egg, buttermilk, vanilla and shortening, then sift flour, cocoa, sugar, baking soda, salt and add to first mixture. Last add 1/2 C. hot water and beat till smooth. Bake at 350° for 30 minutes.

MOIST CHOCOLATE CAKE

Mrs. Jake Hershberger

2 C. all-purpose flour
1 t. salt
1 t. baking powder
3/4 C. cocoa
2 C. sugar
1 t. vanilla

2 t. soda
1 C. vegetable oil
1 C. hot coffee
1 C. milk
2 eggs

Icing:
1 C. milk
5 T. flour
1/2 C. butter

1/2 C. Crisco
1 C. sugar
1 t. vanilla

Mix dry ingredients in mixing bowl. Add oil, coffee, milk and mix well. Add the eggs and vanilla. Pour into 2 greased and floured 9" square cake pans. Bake at 350° for 35 - 40 minutes. For icing cook flour and milk until thickened. When cool, mix with shortening, sugar and vanilla. Beat 10 minutes or until fluffy. Frost cooled layered cake.

MOIST CHOCOLATE CAKE

Mrs. Ben Troyer, Jr.

2 eggs
1 C. black coffee
1 C. milk
1/2 C. vegetable oil
2 t. vanilla
1/2 t. salt

2 C. flour
2 C. sugar
3/4 C. cocoa
2 t. baking powder
1 t. soda

Beat eggs well, add all liquids and mix. Add all dry ingredients. Batter will be thin, can be mixed with egg beater. Bake at 350° for 35 minutes. This cake gets moister and better if it sets for a day.

HOT FUDGE SUNDAE CAKE

Mrs. Reuben Miller

1 C. flour
3/4 C. white sugar
2 t. cocoa
2 t. baking powder
1/4 t. salt

1/2 C. milk
2 t. salad oil
1 t. vanilla
1 C. nuts

Mix these ingredients well and pour into greased 8" x 8" pan. Sprinkle 1 C. brown sugar and 1/4 C. cocoa on top of batter. Then pour 1 1/3 C. hot water over top, this makes the sauce. Bake 40 minutes. Delicious to eat with ice cream.

BLUEBERRY BUCKLE COFFEE CAKE

Joanna Miller

4 C. flour
1 1/2 C. sugar
5 t. baking powder
1 1/2 t. salt

1/2 C. shortening
1 1/2 C. milk
2 eggs
4 C. blueberries

Blend all ingredients. Beat vigorously for 1/2 minute. Carefully stir in blueberries. Spread 1/2 of batter in greased pan. Sprinkle 1/2 of topping over batter. Add remaining batter, then sprinkle rest of topping on top. Bake at 350° for 45 - 50 minutes.

Topping:
2 C. sugar
2/3 C. flour
Mix together and sprinkle over cake.

1 t. cinnamon
1/2 C. oleo

CHERRY CHEESE COFFEE CAKE

Mrs. Matthias Mast

2 - 8 oz. cream cheese
2/3 C. powdered sugar
1 egg yolk

1/2 t. vanilla
2 - 8 oz. Crescent rolls
1 can cherry pie filling

Mix and drizzle on top:
2 C. powdered sugar

1 C. water

Beat cream cheese, sugar, egg yolk and vanilla until smooth. Arrange 12 Crescent rolls on a round pan. Pinching together to cover completely. Spread cream cheese mixture over dough. Top with pie filling. Take 4 Crescent rolls and cut into 8 strips. Twist each strip and lay over filling and secure ends to bottom Crescent rolls. Brush dough with beaten egg white. Bake for 20 minutes at 350°.

CINNAMON PECAN COFFEE CAKE

Mrs. Merle Hershberger
Mrs. Jr. Wagler
Mrs. Willis Karen Miller

1 stick margarine
1 C. white sugar
2 eggs
1 t. vanilla

1 C. sour cream
1 t. soda
1½ C. flour

Cinnamon mixture:
½ C. sugar
½ C. chopped nuts

2 t. cinnamon

Butter and flour 2 pie pans. Cream sugar and margarine. Beat eggs, add. Mix in vanilla, sour cream, soda and flour. Put in pans. Sprinkle cinnamon mixture on top. Bake at 350° for 15 - 20 minutes. Remove from pans before cooled too much. Makes 1 layered cake.

Frosting:
½ C. Crisco
3 C. powdered sugar

2 t. vanilla

Add milk to make the right texture and spread on cake. Optional: Drizzle with caramel frosting or glaze or fill with favorite filling.

COFFEE CAKE

Mrs. Nathan Miller

1 C. milk
1 stick oleo
½ C. white sugar
1 t. salt

2 beaten eggs
1 T. yeast
3½ C. flour

Crumbs:
⅓ C. brown sugar
⅓ C. flour
3 T. butter, softened

1 t. cinnamon
½ C. chopped nuts, optional

Mix oleo, sugar and eggs together, add milk then add yeast, flour and salt. Mix thoroughly. Put in pans. Mix crumb ingredients together and put crumbs on top and let rise for 30 minutes. Then bake at 350° for 17 - 20 minutes. Fill with your favorite filling if desired, also delicious for strawberry shortcake.

CREAM FILLED COFFEE CAKE

Mrs. Martha Sue Miller

Scald 1 C. milk, add 1 stick oleo
$^1/_2$ C. sugar
1 t. salt

Beat 2 eggs in large mixing bowl and add the above ingredients. Dissolve 1 T. dry yeast in $^1/_4$ C. warm water and add. Mix in 3$^1/_2$ C. flour and let rise in refrigerator overnight. Next morning, work down and put into 3 pans. Spread crumbs on top and let rise. Bake at 350°. Cool, cut each cake in half and fill with gob or whoopie pie filling.

Crumb topping:
$^1/_2$ C. brown sugar $^1/_4$ C. butter
$^1/_2$ C. flour

Filling:
2 beaten egg whites   2 t. vanilla
2 T. milk   2 C. powdered sugar.

Mix 1 C. oleo or Crisco and 2 C. powdered sugar. Add to crumb topping and mix well.

SOUR CREAM COFFEE CAKE

Rosanna Miller

$^1/_2$ C. butter   1 C. sour cream
1 C. sugar   1 t. baking soda
2 eggs $^1/_2$ t. salt
2 C. flour   1$^1/_2$ t. vanilla
1 t. baking powder

Crumb topping:
1 C. powdered sugar   5 T. butter
$^1/_2$ C. flour   2 t. cinnamon

Put ingredients for topping in a small bowl, mix together to make crumbs and set aside. Cream butter and sugar well. Beat in eggs one at a time. Sift baking powder into flour and mix baking soda into sour cream. Stir in half the flour until batter is smooth. Then add the cream and stir in remaining flour, salt and vanilla. Spread batter in greased 10$^1/_2$" x 15$^1/_2$" sheet pan. Sprinkle crumb topping evenly over all and bake in preheated oven at 350° for 20 minutes. Serve warm with fresh fruit and ice cream.

COCONUT PINEAPPLE CAKE

Mrs. John Shetler

2 C. all-purpose flour
2 t. soda
1/2 t. salt
3/4 C. vegetable oil
3/4 C. buttermilk

1 t. vanilla
2 C. sugar
8 oz. crushed pineapple, drained
3 C. coconut, divided
3 eggs

Grease and flour 9" x 13" pan. Combine flour, soda and salt in separate bowl, whisk together with oil, buttermilk, eggs and vanilla. Stir in sugar, pineapple and 1 1/2 C. coconut, mix well and stir in flour mixture. Preheat oven to 350°, bake for 30 - 35 minutes. Toast remaining coconut on cookie sheet in oven for 3 - 5 minutes or until golden. Watch carefully as it browns quickly. Frost cooled cake with cream cheese frosting and sprinkle with coconut.

Cream cheese frosting:
3 C. confectioners sugar
4 oz. cream cheese, softened

5 T. butter
1 T. milk

Beat till smooth and spread on cooled cake.

CRAZY CAKE

Barbara Schrock

3 C. flour
2 C. white sugar
6 T. cocoa
2 t. soda
1 t. salt

2 T. vinegar
2 t. vanilla
3/4 C. salad oil
2 C. cold water

Put everything together except 1 C. water. Mix, then add rest of water. Mix, but do not overbeat. Bake at 350° for 35 - 40 minutes. This can be baked in loaf pan or used for cupcakes.

DOUBLE CHOCOLATE ZUCCHINI CAKE

Twila Beachy

1 1/2 C. white sugar
1 C. oleo
1 T. vanilla
2 eggs
1/2 C. sour cream
2 1/2 C. flour

1 t. baking soda
1/2 t. salt
2 C. zucchini, grated
6 oz. chocolate chips
1 C. walnuts, chopped
1/4 C. cocoa

In a large bowl, beat at low speed, sugar, oleo, vanilla and eggs. Increase speed of mixer and add sour cream until fluffy. Add flour, cocoa, baking soda and salt slowly to mixture. Stir in zucchini, chocolate chips and walnuts with a rubber spatula. Bake at 350° for 40 - 45 minutes. Cool, serve with ice cream.

ZUCCHINI SHEET CAKE

Mrs. Ben Troyer, Jr.
Mrs. Nathan Miller

1/2 C. butter
1/2 C. oil
2 unbeaten eggs
1/2 C. sour milk
1 t. vanilla
1 3/4 C. sugar
1/2 t. baking powder

1 t. soda
1/2 t. cinnamon
1/2 t. cloves
2 1/2 C. flour
2 C. shredded zucchini
4 T. cocoa, optional

Mix well and bake at 350° just until firm. Optional: sprinkle 1/2 C. chocolate chips on top before baking or frost with the following.

8 oz. cream cheese
2 1/4 C. powdered sugar
Mix and spread on cooled cake.

1/4 C. butter
vanilla

ZUCCHINI CAKE

Mary Beth Mast

3 eggs
1 C. oil
1 3/4 C. white sugar
1 t. salt
3 C. flour

1 t. baking powder
3/4 t. soda
2 C. grated, unpeeled
zucchini or squash

Blend together eggs and oil, then add remaining ingredients. Sprinkle with cinnamon, then bake at 350° for 1 hour and 10 minutes.

GRAHAM STREUSEL CAKE

Mrs. Nathan Miller

1 yellow cake mix
1 C. water
Mix together and pour into cake pan.

1/3 C. oil
2 eggs

1 pack graham crackers, crushed
1 C. brown sugar

1 stick oleo
1 T. cinnamon

Mix together and put on top of batter, swirl with knife or spoon. Bake at 350° for 25 - 30 minutes. Remove from oven, cool 5 minutes and glaze with 1 1/2 C. powdered sugar and 2 - 3 T. water mixed together.

CHERRY FRUITCAKE

Mrs. Mark Hochstetler

3 C. all-purpose flour
2 C. white sugar
2 t. baking powder
2 t. salt
2 lbs. pitted dates
²/₃ C. orange juice

2 lbs. candied pineapple, diced
4 lbs. red maraschino cherries, drained
3 lbs. pecan halves
12 eggs

Grease pans and line with foil, allowing 2" overhang and grease again. Sift flour, sugar, baking powder and salt in large mixing bowl. Add fruits and pecans, toss until well coated. Beat eggs and orange juice together, pour over the fruit mixture. Toss until completely combined. Pour mixture into prepared loaf pans, pressing with spatula to pack tightly. Bake at 250° for 1¹/₂ - 1³/₄ hours or until toothpick inserted in center comes out clean. Allow cakes to cool in pans for 10 minutes. Remove from pans. Tear off foil and brush with light Karo while still warm. Cool thoroughly before serving or storing.

FRUITCAKE

Mrs. Henry Schrock

1 C. flour
1 t. baking powder
¹/₄ t. salt
³/₄ lb. red cherries
¹/₄ lb. green cherries

¹/₂ lb. chopped dates
¹/₂ lb. pineapples
2 eggs
¹/₂ C. sugar
4 C. pecans

Mix flour, baking powder and salt, toss with cherries, dates and pineapples. Beat eggs and sugar together, slowly add to mixed ingredients. Add pecans. Line pans with brown paper or waxed paper and press cake in very firmly. Bake at 275° for 1¹/₂ hours. Remove from oven and brush with Karo.

FRUIT COCKTAIL CAKE

Lois Mast

Combine:
1¹/₂ C. sugar
2 C. fruit cocktail
Sift and add:
2 C. flour
¹/₂ t. salt

2 eggs

¹/₂ t. soda

Pour into large baking dish. Sprinkle ¹/₂ C. brown sugar and ¹/₂ C. nuts over top before baking. Bake at 350° for 30 - 40 minutes.

Topping:
³/₄ C. sugar
¹/₂ C. milk

¹/₂ C. margarine

Boil 1 minute, remove from heat. Add 1 t. vanilla. Pour over cake immediately.

GERMAN PEACH CREAM KÜCHEN

Mrs. Marvin Wengerd

2 C. flour
1/4 C. sugar
1 t. salt
1/4 t. baking powder
1/2 C. butter
2 egg yolks, beaten

3 - 4 C. canned peach slices,
    drained
1/2 C. white sugar
1 t. cinnamon
1 C. sour cream

Sift together the first four ingredients. Cut butter into this mixture. Press this fine crumb mixture into bottom and sides of 9" x 9" pan to make a crust. Arrange peach slices over the crumbs as evenly as possible. Combine sugar and cinnamon, sprinkle over peaches. Bake at 400° for 15 minutes. Blend together sour cream and egg yolks, pour on top of peaches. Bake another 20 minutes. Delicious served warm with ice cream.

RIBBON OF FRUIT TEACAKE

Mrs. Jay Mark Martha Miller

2 1/4 C. all-purpose flour
3/4 C. sugar
3/4 C. margarine or butter
1/2 t. baking powder
1/2 t. baking soda
1/4 t. nutmeg

1/8 t. salt
1 egg, beaten
2/3 C. sour milk or buttermilk
1 t. vanilla
1 1/4 C. canned fruit pie filling,
    cherry, apricot, blueberry or
    raisin

In a large bowl stir together flour and sugar. Cut in margarine till mixture resembles coarse crumbs. Reserve 1/2 C. for topping. Take remaining flour mixture stir in baking powder, soda, nutmeg and salt. In a small bowl combine egg, milk and vanilla. Add all at once to flour mixture. Stir just until moistened. Reserve 1 C. batter. Spread remaining batter onto bottom and 1" up the sides of a greased and floured 2 qt. rectangular baking dish. Spread desired pie filling on top. Spoon reserved batter on top of filling. Sprinkle with topping. Bake at 350° for 40 minutes or until golden. Cool. Make icing with 1/2 C. powdered sugar, 1/2 t. vanilla and 1 - 2 t. milk. Drizzle over cake.

PUMPKIN CAKE

Mrs. Charles Karn

2 C. flour
1/2 t. salt
2 t. soda
2 t. cinnamon
1 t. ginger

2 t. cloves
4 eggs
1 pt. pumpkin
1 C. cooking oil
2 C. sugar

Combine first 6 ingredients. Beat eggs until thick and yellow. Add sugar and beat well. Add pumpkin and cooking oil, beat well. Gradually stir in flour mixture. Raisins or nuts may be added. Bake at 350°. Frost with cream cheese icing on page 190.

ITALIAN CREAM CAKE

Mrs. Fremon E. Miller

1 stick butter or oleo
½ C. Crisco or
1 C. Wesson oil
2 C. white sugar
1 t. soda
1 C. chopped pecans

5 egg yolks
1 C. buttermilk
2 C. flour
1 t. vanilla
1 sm. can coconut

Cream butter, shortening, vanilla and sugar. Add beaten egg yolks. Sift flour and soda, add to creamed mixture with buttermilk, coconut and nuts. Fold in egg whites. Pour in greased and floured 8" cake pans. Bake at 350° for 30 - 40 minutes or until done. Ice with cream cheese icing.

Cream Cheese Icing:
8 oz. pkg. cream cheese
½ C. shortening or oleo

1 t. vanilla
1 lb. powdered sugar

Beat cream cheese, shortening, vanilla and sugar for 10 minutes then spread on cooled cake. Enjoy.

JELLO CAKE

Mrs. Mark Hochstetler

1 white cake mix
3 oz. box jello, same flavor as fruit
1 C. hot water

8 oz. cream cheese
1 C. powdered sugar
1½ C. Cool Whip

Bake cake as directed, dissolve jello in boiling water. Poke holes in cake with fork and pour hot jello over cake while cake is still warm. Cool cake. Mix cream cheese and powdered sugar, add Cool Whip and stir. Spread over cooled cake.

Fruit filling:
2 C. water
¼ t. salt
1 C. sugar

3 oz. jello, same flavor as fruit
4 T. clear jel
2 - 3 C. fresh fruit

Bring water, salt, sugar and jello to a boil. Thicken with clear jel dissolved in a small amount of water. Cool and add fruit. Spread over top of cream cheese mixture.

&❧

Hey, diddle, diddle I'm watching my middle,
I'm hoping to whittle it soon
But eating is such fun, I may not get it done
Till my dish runs away with my spoon.

OATMEAL CAKE   Mrs. Leroy Yoder

Mix together and cool:
1½ C. boiling water   ½ C. oleo
1 C. quick oatmeal

Add:
1 C. white sugar   ½ t. cinnamon
1 C. brown sugar   1 t. baking powder
2 eggs   1 t. vanilla
1 t. soda   1½ C. flour
Bake at 350°.

Frosting:
1 C. brown sugar   2 T. milk
½ C. oleo

Cook in saucepan for 5 minutes. Top with nuts and coconut. Broil till toasty brown.

OATMEAL CAKE   Mrs. Nathan Miller

1¼ C. boiling water   1½ C. flour - ¾ C. white and
1 C. quick oats   ¾ C. whole wheat, if desired
½ C. shortening   1 t. cinnamon
¾ C. brown sugar   1 t. soda
¾ C. white sugar   ½ T. salt
2 eggs   1 t. vanilla
1 t. nutmeg

Pour boiling water over oatmeal and let set while you mix rest of the ingredients. Cream shortening and sugar well, add unbeaten egg, one at a time beating well after each one. Blend in oatmeal mixture. Sift or mix flour, spices, soda and salt together and fold in, add vanilla. Bake in greased and floured pan at 350° for 30 - 35 minutes. While cake is still hot from the oven, pour on the following topping and broil for about 2 minutes until browned.

Topping:
⅔ C. brown sugar   6 t. melted butter
¼ C. cream

Bring to a boil, remove from heat then add coconut, nuts and vanilla. Mix well. If you don't have cream, use rich milk or just regular milk.

1 C. coconut   1 t. vanilla
1 C. chopped nuts

PINEAPPLE SHEET CAKE

Mrs. Levi Miller

2¹/₂ C. all-purpose flour
2 C. sugar
2 eggs
1 C. chopped nuts

2 t. baking powder
¹/₂ t. salt
1 t. vanilla
20 oz. crushed pineapple in
heavy syrup, undrained

In large mixing bowl, combine all ingredients. Mix until smooth. Pour into a greased 10" x 15" baking pan. Bake at 350° for 35 minutes. Cool.

Cream cheese icing:
8 oz. cream cheese, softened
3¹/₂ C. powdered sugar
¹/₂ C. butter or margarine, softened

1 t. vanilla
¹/₂ C. nuts

Combine cream cheese, sugar, butter and vanilla in a small mixing bowl. Beat until smooth. Spread over cake and sprinkle with nuts.

ROCKY ROAD NUT CAKE

Mrs. Wally Detweiler

1³/₄ C. sugar
1¹/₂ C. sifted flour
¹/₂ t. salt
4 beaten eggs

1 t. vanilla
1¹/₂ C. chopped nuts
³/₄ C. oleo
4 C. miniature marshmallows

Sift together sugar, flour and salt. Add eggs and vanilla, mix together until well blended, stir in nuts and oleo. Pour into 9" x 13" pan, bake at 350° for 35 - 40 minutes. Sprinkle with marshmallows. This cake does not require baking powder.

Butterscotch Icing:
1 C. brown sugar
¹/₂ C. oleo
¹/₃ C. milk

¹/₄ t. salt
1 C. powdered sugar

Mix brown sugar, oleo and milk in saucepan. Boil for 3 minutes. Add powdered sugar. Drizzle over cake.

POKE-N-POUR CAKE

Yvonne Miller

1 white cake mix
1 sm. box jello

4 C. fruit filling
3 C. whipped topping

Mix cake as directed on box. Mix jello with two cups boiling water. As soon as cake is out of oven take a fork and poke a lot of holes in the cake. Pour hot jello over cake and cool. To serve spread with whipped topping and fruit filling. Use the same kind of jello and fruit filling.

SHOO-FLY CAKE

Mrs. Crist Beachy

4 C. flour
³/₄ C. softened oleo
2 C. brown sugar

2 C. boiling water
1 t. soda
1 C. molasses or light Karo

Mix together flour, oleo and brown sugar, mix thoroughly. Take out 1 C. crumbs for top. To the rest add boiling water mixed with soda and molasses or Karo. Mix well. Pour into greased cake pan. Sprinkle with remaining crumbs. Bake at 350° for 40 - 50 minutes. Needs no frosting.

SELF FROSTING DATE CAKE

Mrs. Paul Mast

Sprinkle soda over dates, then pour boiling water over all. Let cool.
1 C. dates, chopped
1 t. soda

1¹/₂ C. boiling water

Cream and add to date mixture.
¹/₂ C. shortening or oleo
1 C. sugar

2 beaten eggs

Sift:
1¹/₂ C. flour
1 t. salt

1 t. baking powder

Mix all together and pour into greased 9" x 13" pan. Mix the following and spread on cake 6 oz. chocolate chips, ¹/₂ C. brown sugar and ¹/₂ C. chopped nuts. Bake at 350°.

SUNSHINE ANGEL CAKE

Mrs. Nathan Miller

8 eggs
1¹/₂ C. sugar
¹/₂ t. salt
1 C. whole wheat flour

1¹/₂ t. lemon extract, optional
¹/₂ t. cream of tartar
2 T. water
¹/₂ C. chopped nuts, optional

Separate eggs, beat whites until frothy, add cream of tartar. Gradually add 1 C. sugar, continue beating until very stiff peaks form. Beat egg yolks until very thick, add salt, flavoring and ¹/₂ C. sugar. Continue beating add water and flour, alternately. Beat well, fold yolk mixture gently into whites. Fold in nuts, pour into angel food cake pan. Bake at 325° - 350° for 1¹/₄ - 1¹/₂ hours. Put pan upside down and cool for 1 hour. Remove from pan. We really like this cake cut up and fixed layered with strawberry pie filling and whip.

❧

For every minute you frown you lose
60 seconds of happiness.

TURTLE CAKE

Melva Schrock

1 cake mix, as directed
1/4 C. Carnation milk
14 oz. bag caramels

1 1/2 stick oleo or butter
1 C. chocolate chips or nuts
(optional)

Melt together caramels, butter and milk. Put half of cake mix in pan. Bake until done. Pour chocolate chips and nuts on hot cake. Then top with caramel sauce and rest of cake mix, bake until done.

TWINKIE CAKE

Mrs. Crist Miller

1 yellow cake mix
3 oz. instant vanilla pudding
4 eggs

1 C. water
1/2 C. oil

Mix all together and bake in layers or split cake and frost with Crisco frosting.

Crisco frosting:
1/4 C. Crisco
1/4 C. milk

2 C. powdered sugar
1 t. vanilla

A little marshmallow topping added makes it good.

VANILLA CREAM CAKE

Mrs. Mike Schrock

4 eggs
9 T. cold water
1 1/2 C. sugar

2 C. flour
3 t. baking powder
1 t. salt

Beat egg yolks and water with egg beater until light. Slowly add sugar and continue beating. Sift flour and baking powder and add to yolk mixture. Fold in stiffly beaten egg whites and salt. Pour into 2 - 9" x 13" pans, lined with wax paper, dusted with flour. Bake 20 minutes at 350°.

Crumbs:
3/4 C. flour
3/4 C. brown sugar

5 T. flour
2 T. cinnamon

Mix together. When cake is about half baked or firm enough to hold crumbs, spread crumbs on top of 1 cake and return to oven.

Filling:
3 C. scalded milk
1 heaping T. flour
1 heaping T. cornstarch
1 T. butter

1 C. sugar
2 eggs
1/2 t. salt
1 T. vanilla

Melt butter blend in flour and cornstarch add rest of ingredients. Cool and spread between layers of cake. Put cake with crumbs on top. Dust top with powdered sugar.

WATERGATE CAKE

Ruby Beachy

1 white cake mix
1 C. oil
3 eggs

¹/₂ C. chopped pecans, optional
1 C. ginger ale
3 oz. box instant pistachio
    pudding

Bake at 350° for 40 - 45 minutes.

Frosting:
2 envelopes Dream Whip
1¹/₂ C. milk

Beat until forms stiff peaks then fold in 3 oz. box pistachio instant pudding. Spread on cooled cake. Sprinkle with coconut or nuts.

SELF FILLED CUPCAKES

Mrs. Nathan Miller

1 chocolate cake mix
8 oz. cream cheese
¹/₂ t. salt

³/₄ C. white sugar
1 beaten egg
6 oz. chocolate chips

Prepare cake mix according to directions, fill cupcake tins ²/₃ full. Combine cream cheese, salt, sugar and egg, until fluffy. Stir in chocolate chips. Drop 1 T. mixture on each cupcake. Bake at 350° for 12 - 15 minutes.

BROWN SUGAR OR CARAMEL FROSTING

Mrs. Crist Beachy
Mrs. Willis Karen Miller
Mrs. Ben Troyer, Jr.

1 stick oleo
1 C. brown sugar
¹/₄ t. salt

¹/₄ C. milk
powdered sugar

Stir oleo and brown sugar over low heat until melted. Add milk and bring to a boil. Cool slightly. Add powdered sugar to desired consistency.

CRISCO FROSTING

Mrs. Henry Beachy

³/₄ C. water
1 t. salt
1 t. clear vanilla

6 C. powdered sugar
1¹/₄ C. Crisco

Mix the water, salt, vanilla and powdered sugar. Add the Crisco and as much powdered sugar as needed. Make 4 batches for a wedding cake or the sheet cakes.

CHOCOLATE CREAM FROSTING

Mrs. Alfred Miller

3 sq. unsweetened chocolate
1/4 C. butter
2 C. powdered sugar

1/2 C. sour cream
2 t. vanilla

Combine chocolate and butter in saucepan and melt over low heat stirring to blend. Pour in bowl and add remaining ingredients and blend until smooth.

CHOCOLATE FROSTING

Mrs. Robert Miller

1/4 C. oleo
1/3 C. cocoa
1/4 T. salt

1/3 C. milk
1 1/2 t. vanilla
3 1/2 C. confectioner's sugar

In saucepan, melt oleo. Remove from heat, stir in cocoa and salt. Mix in milk and vanilla. In mixer bowl, stir cocoa mixture into sugar. Beat at medium speed until smooth and creamy. Add 1 T. more milk if needed for good spreading consistency.

ONE MINUTE FUDGE FROSTING

Barbara Schrock

1/2 C. cocoa
1/4 C. milk
1/4 C. butter

1 C. sugar
1/4 t. salt

Place over heat, stirring constantly. Boil for 1 minute. Remove from heat and while still warm, beat until icing consistency.

FILLING FOR ANGEL FOOD CAKE

Mrs. Martha Sue Miller

1 C. Rich's topping
8 oz. cream cheese
Cream together and put in middle of cut up cake.

Butterscotch Sauce for top:
3/4 C. sugar
1/2 C. light corn syrup
1/4 t. salt

1 C. cream
1/2 t. vanilla
1/4 C. butter

Cook together to 234° soft ball stage.

- Friendship Cake -

My mother told me how to make
A very special friendship cake,
One I can give to all my friends
Because she says it never ends.
This cake will not get stale or old
Unless I let it get too cold,
You see, this cake is made of love,
The recipe comes from above.
My love cake needs some song and smile
These things will make it quite worthwhile;
And kindness, courtesy and joy
Will satisfy each girl and boy.
Then if I give my cake away
I'll get love in return each day.

❧

- Happiness Cake -

Combine:
1 heaping portion of true love
1 heaping cup of perfect trust and confidence
1 heaping cup of tenderness (the most tender available)
1 heaping cup of good humor (a little extra won't hurt)
1 T. of good spirits (the more spirited the better)

Blend with 1 heaping cup of unselfishness, a dash of interest in all
he does. Add one good helping of work to avoid spoiling the flavor.
Mix all ingredients with a pint of sympathy and understanding.
Flavor with loving companionship. Bake well all your life. Frost with
fond hopes and tender words. This cake keeps well and should
be served often.

- Notes -

Pies

AMISH VANILLA PIE

Debra Kay Miller

1/2 C. sugar
1 T. flour
1/4 C. dark Karo

1 1/2 t. vanilla
1 egg, beaten
1 C. water

Crumbs:
1 C. flour
1/2 C. brown sugar
1/2 t. cream of tartar

1/2 t. baking soda
1/8 t. salt
1/4 C. butter

Combine sugar, flour, Karo, egg and water. Cook over medium heat till it comes to a boil. Add vanilla, let cool. When cool put in unbaked pie shell. Top with crumbs. Bake at 350°. Makes 1 pie.

RHUBARB PIE

Mrs. Aaron Coblentz

1 1/2 C. sugar
3 C. rhubarb

2 T. flour
2 eggs

Crumbs:
1/2 C. flour
1/2 C. brown sugar

1/2 C. oatmeal
1/4 C. oleo

Cut up rhubarb. Mix with sugar and flour, beat eggs and add to rhubarb. Spread into 9" pie shell. Mix flour, sugar, oatmeal and oleo until crumbly. Sprinkle over top of rhubarb. Bake at 425° for 10 minutes, then at 300° for 30 minutes or until desired browness.

PEACH CRUMB PIE

Mrs. Roy Mast

4 C. fresh sliced peaches
2 1/2 T. minute tapioca
3/4 C. sugar

1 T. lemon juice
1/4 t. salt

Crumbs:
1/3 C. brown sugar, packed
1/4 C. flour

1/2 t. cinnamon
2 T. soft butter

Mix peaches, tapioca, sugar, lemon juice and salt. Let stand 5 minutes. Spoon into 9" unbaked pie shell. Sprinkle with crumbs. Bake at 425° for 10 minutes, then bake at 350° for 30 - 35 minutes. A family favorite! Especially good while still warm topped with ice cream.

PEACH CUSTARD PIE

Mrs. David Ray Yoder

2 or 3 peaches
1 1/2 C. milk, scalded
3/4 C. white sugar
1/4 t. salt

2 T. flour
2 egg yolks
2 egg whites
4 T. sugar

Peel and slice peaches into an 8" unbaked pie shell, sprinkle with 1/4 C. sugar. Mix flour, salt and 1/2 C. sugar, add to beaten egg yolks. Slowly add hot milk and mix. Pour over peaches and bake till custard is set. Beat egg whites till soft peaks form, add 4 T. sugar. Pile on pie and bake until meringue is nicely browned.

DELICIOUS PEACH PIE

Mrs. Noah J. Hostetler

2 1/2 C. sliced fresh peaches
1 T. soft butter
1 1/2 C. sugar

2 eggs, well beaten
2 T. minute tapioca

Put 1 T. each of sugar and flour in bottom of crust. In bowl, add sugar, butter and tapioca to beaten eggs. Fold in peaches and bake as a two-crust pie. Bake at 450° for 15 minutes, then at 350° for 25 minutes.

BLUEBERRY PIE

Deborah Troyer

3/4 C. sugar
1 C. sweet cream
3 T. flour

1/2 t. cinnamon
dash of salt
2 C. fresh blueberries

Mix all together and pour into unbaked pie shell. Bake at 350° until done.

STRAWBERRY PIE

Mrs. Firman Miller

6 C. water
2 1/2 C. sugar
1 box Danish Dessert

6 heaping T. clear jel
2 T. strawberry jello
few drops red food coloring

Cook together till clear and bubbly. When cooled add 3 qts. strawberries. Makes 4 pies.

ঌঌ

God gave us the Bible for everyday use,
not just cake for special occasions.

STRAWBERRY PIE
Mrs. Eli A. Mast

1 C. water
1 C. Sprite
²/₃ C. white sugar
2 T. clear jel

red food coloring
pinch of salt
¹/₂ qt. strawberries

Cook first 5 ingredients. Add jello, cool, then add ¹/₂ qt. strawberries and food coloring.

STRAWBERRY EGG NOG PIE
Mrs. Henry Beachy

1 baked pie crust
1 t. Knox gelatin
2 T. cold water
³/₄ C. milk, scalded
¹/₂ C. sugar
2 T. cornstarch

¹/₄ C. milk
¹/₂ t. salt
3 egg yolks beaten
1 T. butter
1 T. vanilla
1 C. Rich's topping

Soak gelatin in cold water. Scald milk, mix ¹/₄ C. milk with cornstarch, sugar and salt. Add to scalded milk, cook, add beaten egg yolks, butter and gelatin and cook again until thick. Cool. Add Rich's topping, whipped. Put in pie crust and let set, when ready to serve add strawberry filling.

Strawberry Filling:
1 C. water
1 C. 7Up
1 C. sugar

2 T. clear jel
3 oz. strawberry jello

Cook then cool and add ³/₄ qt. strawberries.

GERMAN CHOCOLATE PIE
Mrs. Mark Hochstetler

Melt:
1 sq. german chocolate
¹/₂ C. margarine

Add:
2 C. white sugar
2 T. cornstarch
3 C. Carnation milk

2 egg whites
¹/₄ t. salt
1 t. vanilla

Slowly stir some Carnation milk to the chocolate and oleo mixture. Beat egg whites, not stiff, and fold in last. Pour into unbaked pie shell. Sprinkle with nuts. Bake at 450° for 12 minutes, then bake at 350° till done. Makes 2 pies.

TOLL HOUSE PIE

Mrs. Henry Schrock

1 pie shell
2 eggs
1/2 C. flour
1/2 C. white flour

1 C. butter or oleo, melted
6 oz. chocolate chips
1 C. chopped nuts
1/2 C. brown sugar

Preheat oven to 325°. Beat eggs until foamy. Add flour and sugar, beat until well blended. Blend in cooled butter. Stir in chips and nuts. Pour into pie shell and bake 1 hour. Serve warm with whipped topping or ice cream. Makes 1 - 9" pie.

DUTCH APPLE PIE

Mrs. Henry Schrock

4 C. shredded apples
2 C. white sugar

2 T. minute tapioca
1 C. water

Place apples, sugar and water in saucepan. Bring to a boil. Add tapioca and boil 1 minute. Be sure to bring to a full hard boil. Ladle into jars and seal. To use for pie, place in unbaked pie crust, sprinkle with cinnamon and dot with oleo. Cover with top crust and bake.

DUTCH APPLE PIE

Mrs. Henry Beachy

5 C. sliced apples
1 C. water
Heat then add:
3 T. clear jel
2 T. ReaLemon juice
Cook, then add 2 T. butter.

1 3/4 C. white sugar
1/4 C. brown sugar

1/2 C. water

Crumbs:
1 1/2 C. flour
3/4 C. brown sugar
1 stick oleo

1/2 t. cinnamon
1/8 t. salt

Put in unbaked pie crust. Sprinkle with cinnamon, top with crumbs. Bake at 375° till golden brown.

LEMON PIE

Mrs. Jay Mark Martha Miller

1 can sweetened condensed milk
1/2 C. lemon juice
8 oz. whipped topping

yellow food coloring
1 Graham cracker crust

In medium bowl, combine milk and juice. Let stand a few minutes. Stir in whipped topping and a few drops food coloring. Spoon into crust. Chill until firm.

KEY LIME PIE

Mary A. Kaufman

1 can condensed milk
4 egg yolks

$^1/_2$ C. lime juice

Beat one egg white stiff and fold into above mixture. Beat 3 egg whites and gradually add 6 T. sugar and $^1/_2$ t. cream of tartar. Put in baked pie shell and bake at 350° till whites are golden brown.

PUMPKIN PIE

Mary Miller

2 C. milk, heated
3 eggs, save 1 white
$^1/_2$ C. white sugar
$^3/_4$ C. brown sugar
1 t. cinnamon

$^1/_8$ t. Allspice
$^1/_8$ t. pumpkin pie spice
$^1/_8$ t. salt
2 T. pumpkin
1 t. flour

Mix eggs and sugar. Blend well, then add spices, flour and pumpkin. Add heated milk. Beat egg white and fold in last. More pumpkin can be used if desired. Bake at 425° for 15 minutes, then at 350° for 45 minutes.

CARAMEL PIE

Mrs. Willis Wagler

$^1/_2$ C. brown sugar
$^1/_2$ C. white sugar
1 T. flour
2 eggs

$^1/_2$ t. maple flavoring
pinch of salt
2 C. milk

Mix flour, sugar and egg yolks. I always use $^1/_2$ can Pet milk and stir in with the above ingredients. Add 2 C. of milk and beat well. Beat egg whites, add last. Top with chopped nuts. Bake at 300° for 15 minutes, then 325° for 45 minutes.

CUSTARD PIE

Mrs. Henry Beachy

1 C. brown sugar
3 T. flour

2 eggs
2 C. milk

Beat together sugar, flour, 1 C. milk and 2 beaten egg yolks. Heat 1 C. milk and beat 2 egg whites and mix all together. Put in pie shell, bake at 400° for 15 minutes, then at 350° until pie filling is set.

CUSTARD PIE
Mrs. Marcus Mast

½ C. white sugar
2 C. brown sugar
1½ C. Carnation milk
4 C. milk, scalded

8 level T. flour
pinch of salt
8 eggs

Mix in order given. Save 3 egg whites. Beat and add last. Do not over mix once egg whites are added. Bake at 450° for 12 minutes, then at 350° till golden brown. Baking time is approximately 1 hour total. Makes 3 - 8" pies.

PECAN PIE
Mary Miller

2 eggs, beaten
pinch of salt
½ C. white sugar
1 C. light Karo
1 T. flour

1 C. milk
1 t. vanilla
2 T. melted butter
1 C. chopped pecans

Mix sugar, salt and flour. Add beaten eggs, syrup and vanilla. Mix well. Add milk and melted butter. Put pecans in an unbaked pie shell and pour mixture over pecans. Bake at 400° for 15 minutes then at 350° for 45 minutes.

PECAN PIE
Mrs. Allen Beachy

2 eggs
2 T. flour

½ C. white sugar
¼ t. salt

Beat well, then add:
2 T. butter
1 C. light Karo

½ C. cold water
1 C. pecans

Bake at 450° for 12 minutes. Reduce heat to 350° and bake till pretty well set.

PECAN PIE
Mrs. Wally Detweiler

3 eggs
1 C. brown sugar, scant
¾ C. light Karo
vanilla

salt
2 T. oleo or butter
1 C. pecans

Beat eggs, add the rest of the ingredients. Bake at 400° for 10 minutes, then at 325° until done.

PECAN PIE

Mrs. Wyman Wengerd

$^1/_3$ C. vegetable shortening
$^1/_2$ C. brown sugar
$^1/_2$ C. milk
1 C. chopped pecans

3 eggs
$^1/_2$ t. salt
1 C. light Karo
$^1/_2$ t. vanilla

Beat eggs well, then add sugar and beat again, add remaining ingredients and blend. Pour into unbaked pie shell. Bake at 425° for 10 minutes, then at 350° for 25 minutes or until done.

CREAM CHEESE PECAN PIE

Mrs. David Ray Yoder

8 oz. cream cheese
1 egg, beaten
1 t. vanilla
$^1/_2$ C. sugar

$^1/_2$ t. salt
$1^1/_4$ C. chopped pecans
10" unbaked pie shell

Topping:
3 eggs
$^1/_2$ t. vanilla

1 C. light Karo

Cream together softened cream cheese, sugar, egg, salt and vanilla. Spread over bottom of pie shell. Sprinkle pecans evenly over cream cheese layer. Combine topping ingredients and beat until smooth. Pour over pecan layer. Bake at 375° for 35 - 45 minutes until pecan layer is golden brown.

PEANUT BUTTER PIE

Mrs. Nathan Mast

2 C. milk
2 T. butter
2 T. white sugar
2 egg yolks
2 T. cornstarch

1 T. flour
$^1/_4$ t. salt
$^1/_2$ t. vanilla
1 box Cool Whip

Crumbs:
1 C. powdered sugar

$^1/_2$ C. peanut butter

Melt butter in saucepan, add milk and sugar. Mix rest of the ingredients with a little more milk. Add to first mixture and bring to a boil. Remove from heat, cover tightly with Saran wrap. Let cool to room temperature, then add 1 C. Cool Whip. Put crumbs into unbaked pie shell, add filling and top with more Cool Whip and remaining crumbs.

PEANUT BUTTER CREAM PIE
Joanne Schlabach

3/4 C. powdered sugar
1/2 C. peanut butter
3 C. milk
3/4 C. white sugar
3 T. cornstarch
3 egg yolks

1 T. flour
2 T. butter
1 t. vanilla
2 C. Cool Whip
9" baked pie shell
pinch of salt

Cream powdered sugar and peanut butter together until crumbly. Cook other ingredients together until thick. Cool. Sprinkle 2/3 of crumbs into pie shell. Pour cold pudding over crumbs. Add whipped cream, and top with rest of crumbs. Makes 1 pie.

FROZEN PEANUT BUTTER PIE
Mrs. Matthew Troyer

Graham Cracker Crust:
1 3/4 sticks oleo, melted
1 1/2 T. sugar

2 pkgs. crushed
    graham crackers

Mix well and press into 2 pie pans or a 9" x 13" pan.

Filling:
8 oz. cream cheese
2 C. powdered sugar
2/3 C. peanut butter

1 C. milk
9 oz. Cool Whip or
    Rich's topping, whipped

Beat cream cheese and powdered sugar until smooth. Add remaining ingredients and pour into shells. Freeze.

EASY CHOCOLATE PEANUT BUTTER PIE
Mrs. Alfred Miller

2 - 3 oz. chocolate instant pudding
2 C. milk

1 C. ice cream
1 C. Cool Whip

Mix all together with mixer. Mix peanut butter and powdered sugar, put in bottom of baked pie shell, put filling on top, then top with Cool Whip and garnish with chocolate shavings.

🍂

*Hail to the girl who's learned the art of cooking,
her way to her husband's heart.
She gives him roasts and pies for dinner,
He couldn't be happier but he could be thinner.*

CHOCOLATE PEANUT BUTTER PIE
Mrs. Jr. Kaufman

Filling:

4 - 6 T. cocoa	5 T. flour
1 C. sugar	$^1/_2$ t. salt
2$^1/_2$ C. cold milk	2 T. butter
4 eggs, slightly beaten	2 t. vanilla

Add cocoa to sugar and mix well. Stir in 2 C. milk to make smooth mixture and heat in top of double boiler. Beat egg, add flour, and blend with remaining $^1/_2$ C. milk. Add salt and stir into milk/chocolate mixture. Cook until thick, stirring constantly. Add butter and vanilla. Cool.

Crumbs:
$^2/_3$ C. powdered sugar
$^1/_3$ C. crunchy peanut butter

Mix powdered sugar and peanut butter and sprinkle $^1/_2$ of crumbs on bottom of baked pie shell, add cooled filling. Top with whipped cream and remaining crumbs.

RAISIN CREAM PIE
Mrs. Nathan Miller

1 C. raisins
Cover with water and cook until tender, about 5 minutes.

2 C. milk	4 T. flour
1 C. sugar	1 T. butter
2 egg yolks	

Bring milk to a boil. Mix sugar, eggs and flour together. Add a little milk and stir, then mix with milk and cook until thickened. Add raisins and butter. Cool. Add a little whipped topping to make real creamy and smooth. Put into baked pie shell, top with whipped topping and serve. Makes 1 pie.

BASIC CREAM PIE
Mrs. Ivan Miller

2 C. milk	1 T. butter
$^1/_2$ C. sugar	$^1/_2$ t. salt
2 T. clear jel	1 t. vanilla
2 egg yolks	

Scald 1$^1/_2$ C. milk. Combine sugar, clear jel and salt. Stir in remaining $^1/_2$ C. milk and egg yolks. Stir into hot milk and cook until thickened. Remove from heat. Add butter and vanilla. Let cool and use for any cream pie.

NO BAKE CREAM PIE
Anna Fern Troyer

2¼ C. milk
¼ C. cornstarch
¾ C. white sugar
¼ C. brown sugar

pinch of salt
1 egg
1 t. vanilla
1 stick oleo

Bring 2 C. milk to a boil in saucepan. Beat egg, ¼ C. milk and cornstarch and stir into hot milk. Add vanilla and butter. Pour into baked pie crust.

COOKIE ICE CREAM PIE
Mrs. Mark Hochstetler

10 Oreo cookies, finely crushed
3 T. butter or margarine
14 whole Oreo cookies

½ gal. ice cream
½ C. fudge topping
fresh fruit

Combine crushed cookies and butter, mix well. Press into bottom of a 9" pie plate. Stand whole cookies up around edges pressing lightly into crust. Freeze 1 hour. For filling, spread ½ of your favorite flavor of ice cream over cookies. Drizzle ¼ C. fudge topping. Freeze 1 hour, spread remaining ice cream on top. Drizzle with remaining fudge topping. Freeze several hours or overnight. Garnish with fresh fruit or tea. Let pie set at room temperature for about 15 minutes before cutting.

FRY PIES
Lois Mast

9 C. Hilite cake flour
2 T. sugar
1 T. salt

3 C. Creamtex
2 C. water
1½ qts. pie filling

Mix all ingredients except pie filling. Roll out and cut into circles, fill with filling then seal dough and deep fry in Creamtex.

FRY PIE GLAZE
Mrs. Mark Hochstetler

8 lbs. powdered sugar
½ C. cornstarch
⅓ C. Carnation milk

1 t. vanilla
2½ C. water

Mix together. This is enough for a double batch of the above recipe. Glaze fry pies immediately. When storing, don't cover or they will get soggy.

PIE CRUST

Mrs. Wyman Wengerd

3 C. Softex flour
1 C. butter Crisco
1 T. vinegar

1 t. salt
1 egg
5 T. cold water

Blend flour, Crisco and salt until well mixed. Beat eggs, then add water and vinegar, and mix with flour mixture. Makes 4 pie crusts. Bake at 450° till golden brown.

FLAKY PIE DOUGH

Mrs. Josiah Miller

6 C. flaky pie or cookie flour
1 C. lard
1 C. Crisco

1 t. baking powder
1 C. water
dash of salt

Makes 6 pie crusts.

PERFECT PIE CRUST

Mrs. Henry Beachy

Mix:
4 C. flaky pie flour
1 T. sugar

2 t. salt
1 t. baking powder

Add and mix until crumbly:
1³/₄ C. shortening

Beat together in a small bowl:
1 T. vinegar
¹/₄ C. ice water

1 egg

Add flour mixture and stir until moist. Makes 5 pie crusts.

NEVER FAIL PIE CRUST

Mrs. Moses S. Miller

Mix together:
5 C. flour
2 C. lard

1 T. salt

Break egg into 1 C. measure. Add 2 T. vinegar. Then fill cup with water and mix together well. Add this to the flour mixture and mix well. Chill.

NEVER FAIL PIE CRUST

Mrs. Robert J. Yoder

4 C. Softex flour
1 1/4 C. Crisco
1 t. salt

1 egg
5 T. water
1 T. vinegar

Mix flour, shortening and salt together until crumbly. Beat egg, vinegar and water together. Add to flour mixture and mix well.

PIE CRUST MIX

Mrs. Atlee Miller
Mrs. Matthew Troyer
Mrs. Steve Engbretson

5 lbs. + 2 C. Softex flour
3 lbs. butter flavored Crisco

1/2 C. white sugar
2 T. salt

Blend ingredients and store in plastic container. When ready to use add: 2 T. ice water with 1 1/2 C. mix. Proceed as usual to make 9" crust. Bake at 400° for 13 - 14 minutes. For 2 pie crusts use 3 T. water.

PIE CRUST

Mrs. Marcus Mast

Mix well with fork:
3 C. Softex flour
1 1/4 C. shortening

pinch of salt

Beat together:
1 egg
3 T. water

1 T. vinegar

Add the egg mixture to the flour mixture. Do not overmix. Let stand a couple minutes before making crusts. Makes 4 single or 2 double crusts.

THANK YOU PIE FILLING

Mrs. Matthias Mast

1/2 C. sugar
1/4 t. salt
Make a paste of:
1/4 C. clear jel

1 C. water
1 t. lemon juice

1/2 C. water

Add:
2 T. jello
1/2 C. light Karo

2 C. raw fruit.

Heat sugar, water, salt, and lemon juice. Heat until sugar is dissolved. Stir paste into heated syrup bring to a boil. Remove from heat then add Karo and jello. Add fruit when cooled.

PIE FILLING

Mrs. John Mark Troyer

3 T. clear jel
³/₄ C. white sugar
1 C. water

2 T. light Karo
pinch of salt

Bring to a boil. Remove from heat, and add 3 T. jello. Fill pie with fruit and filling. Do not sugar fruit.

STRAWBERRY PIE GLAZE

Mrs. Wyman Wengerd

¹/₂ C. sugar
2 T. clear jel
1¹/₂ C. water

¹/₂ T. ReaLemon juice
2 T. strawberry jello
1 T. Karo

Mix sugar, clear jel and water. Cook until it thickens. Remove from heat and add ReaLemon, jello and Karo.

FRESH FRUIT PIE FILLING

Dorothy Yoder

3 oz. jello
¹/₄ C. clear jel
³/₄ C. sugar

¹/₄ t. salt
2 C. water

Cook until thickened. Cool, then add 1 qt. fruit.

STRAWBERRY PIE FILLING

Mrs. Robert Miller

6 oz. strawberry jello
1 box Danish Dessert
1³/₄ C. white sugar
3 C. Sprite

2 C. water
4 T. clear jel
1 t. lemon juice
4 T. Karo

Cook together. Let cool. Add Karo while cooling.

- Visitors -

Come in! Come in! But don't expect to find
All dishes done, all floors ashine
See crumpled rugs, the toys galore
The smudged finger printed door,
The little ones we shelter here
Don't thrive in spotless atmosphere
They're more inclined to disarray
And carefree, even messy play.

- Notes -

Canning & Freezing

APPLE BUTTER

Mrs. Matthew Troyer

16 C. applesauce
6 - 8 C. white sugar

1 C. cider or diluted vinegar
2 T. powdered cinnamon

Mix all ingredients together in a large pan and put in oven. Bake at 350° for 3 hours. Stir every ½ hour. When done, pour in jars and seal. Makes 5 qts.

APPLE BUTTER

Mrs. Crist Miller

4 qt. applesauce
1 qt. cider
2½ C. white sugar

1 C. light Karo
2 oz. strawberry jello

Cook applesauce and cider until desired thickness. Add 2½ C. sugar, Karo and jello, put in cans and seal.

GRAPE HONEY

Mary Ellen Schlabach

1 qt. grape juice
½ gal. light Karo

½ gal. white sugar

Boil 5 - 10 minutes or till soft ball stage - 240°.

GRAPE JELLY

Mrs. Moses S. Miller

4 qt. Concord grapes
1 C. water

Boil for 20 minutes. Put in cheesecloth and let drip. You should have 6 C. juice. Divide in half and do the following twice. 3 C. grape juice brought to a rolling boil, add 4½ C. sugar. Heat and stir until sugar is dissolved, but do not boil. Put in hot jars and seal.

FAKE RASPBERRY JELLY

Mrs. Atlee Miller

2 C. beet juice
4 C. water
2 pkg. sure-jel

½ C. lemon juice
8 C. sugar
6 oz. red raspberry jello

Heat beet juice, water, sure-jel and lemon juice. Bring to a boil. Add the sugar and jello all at once. Boil 5 minutes, remove and let cool. Freeze or put in jar with paraffin.

REDBEET JELLY
Mrs. Paul Mast

6 C. red beet juice
2 pkg. sure-jel

½ C. lemon juice

Bring to a boil. Add 8 C. sugar, and 1 large box raspberry jello. Boil 6 minutes.

ELDERBERRY PRESERVES
Mrs. Josiah Miller

½ gal. light Karo
½ gal. white sugar

1 qt. juice

Cook for 10 - 15 minutes. Put in jars and seal.

FREEZING DARK SWEET CHERRIES
Mrs. Willis Karen Miller
Mrs. Mark Hochstetler
Mrs. Henry Beachy

5 lbs. cherries, pitted
3 C. sugar

3 oz. black cherry jello
3 C. water

Make syrup as for canning, using sugar and 3 C. water. When hot, add jello and stir until dissolved. Let cool. Place cherries in containers and cover with syrup.

FREEZING DARK SWEET CHERRIES
Twila Yoder

3 oz. black cherry jello
3 C. sugar

6 C. water

Mix jello and sugar. Add 3 C. boiling water and stir until dissolved. Add 3 C. cold water. Let cool. Put cherries in containers and cover with syrup.

FREEZING BLACK RASPBERRIES
Mrs. Mark Hochstetler

black raspberries
3 C. sugar

3 C. water
3 oz. raspberry jello

Make syrup as for canning, mixing the sugar and water. After it is hot add the jello. Stir to dissolve. Let cool. Put black raspberries in containers and cover with syrup. They taste great in mixed fruit or they can be used for pie filling, jello is added already.

FROZEN MELON MIX

Deborah Troyer

Syrup:

4 C. white sugar
2 qts. water

6 oz. frozen orange juice
6 oz. frozen lemonade

Bring water and sugar to a boil, add juice stirring until dissolved.

1 watermelon, balled or chunked
2 cantaloupes, chunked
2 honeydew melons, chunked

3 lbs. seedless grapes
3 lbs. peaches, peeled and sliced

Mix fruits together and put in boxes. Pour syrup over fruit leaving $1/2$" head space. Freeze. Serve partially thawed. Also delicious fresh.

FRUIT SALAD FOR FREEZING

Mrs. Josiah Miller

Stir together:

7 lbs. black cherries
6 lbs. red grapes
$3/4$ bushel Red Haven peaches, sliced

15 lbs. fresh pineapples
7 lbs. green seedless grapes

Fold in:
1 can fruit fresh and sugar to your taste. Divide among containers and freeze. Very tasty when just partially thawed.

GRAPE JUICE

Mrs. Henry Beachy
Mrs. Roy Mast

6 lbs. grapes
5 C. water

3 lbs. sugar

Boil together grapes and water till grapes are soft. Put through a sieve or cloth. Add sugar and boil 5 minutes. Put in jars and seal. Juice should be clear. Add 3 - 4 parts water before serving.

APPLE PIE FILLING TO CAN

Mrs. Nathan Miller

12 C. grated apples
4 C. white sugar

3 C. water
6 T. minute tapioca

Cook water and sugar together just till boiling, then add apples and tapioca. Put in jars and cold pack for 15 minutes. Do not overfill jars, it will thicken while cold packing. Add cinnamon and apple pie spice when making pie. This recipe is simple but good. Yields $4 1/2$ qts.

CANNED APPLE PIE FILLING

Mrs. James Troyer

4¹/₂ C. sugar
2 C. clear jell
3 t. cinnamon
¹/₂ t. nutmeg

3 T. lemon juice
1 t. salt
12 C. water or apple cider
10 apples, peeled and grated

Mix 3 C. water with clear jell. Bring rest of water to a near boil then add clear jell mixture. Stir until thickened. Add sugar, cinnamon, nutmeg, salt, lemon juice and apples. Put in jars, cold pack for 20 minutes.

SNITZ FOR PIE

Mrs. Henry Schrock

³/₄ bushel apples
12 C. white sugar
4 T. cinnamon

2 T. Allspice
2 t. salt
5 heaping T. flour or cornstarch

Peel apples, put through grinder and let stand overnight. Stir a few times in the evening so they will not get brown. Next morning add sugar, spices and salt. Mix well. Add flour mixed with a little water and pour over apples. Stir and mix well. Put in jars and cold pack 1 hour. This should fill a 13 qt. mixing bowl so use apples accordingly.

BREAD AND BUTTER PICKLES

Mrs. John Shetler

1 gal. pickles, sliced thin
8 sm. onions

¹/₂ C. salt

Mix and cover with water, let stand 3 hours, drain well, then add:

5 C. sugar
1 T. mustard seed
1 T. celery seed

1 t. turmeric
2 scant C. vinegar
2 C. water

Bring to a boil and put in jars and seal.

BREAD AND BUTTER PICKLES

Mrs. Matthias Mast

1 gal. sliced cucumbers
4 onions, sliced

¹/₃ C. salt

Cover with ice water and soak for 3 hours. Drain then add:

4 C. sugar
2 C. vinegar
1 C. water

1 t. turmeric
1¹/₂ t. mustard seed
1 t. celery seed

Place drained cucumbers in syrup and boil 5 minutes. Put in jars while still hot. Cold pack for 5 minutes.

CRISPY PICKLES

Mrs. Allen Beachy

1 gal. pickles, sliced and put in 1 gallon cold water with 1 C. salt. Let stand 3 - 5 days. Drain and wash with clear water. Put in boiling water enough to cover pickles and put in 1 T. alum. Boil for 10 minutes. Drain and make syrup. Put in syrup and boil for 10 minutes. Put in jars and seal.

Syrup:
1 pt. vinegar
1 pt. water
6 C. white sugar

Put in bag:
1 T. pickling spice
1 T. celery seed
2 cinnamon sticks

HAMBURGER PICKLES

Mrs. Merle Hershberger

1 gal. cucumbers, sliced thin. Soak 3 - 5 days in salt brine. 1 C. salt to 1 gal. hot water. After 3 - 5 days, drain and wash in clear water about 4 times. Be sure to get all the salt off. Boil in alum water for 10 minutes, 2 T. alum and water to cover pickles. Rinse again in hot water.

Syrup:
2 C. vinegar
2 C. water
6 C. sugar

Put in bag:
1 T. celery seed
1 stick cinnamon
1 T. whole cloves
1 T. mixed pickling spice

Put bag in syrup and cook until clear, about 20 minutes. Put pickles in jar, add syrup and seal.

HAMBURGER PICKLES

Mrs. Willis Priscilla Miller

1 gal. pickles
1 gal. boiling water
1 C. salt

1 T. alum
1 gal. boiling water

Syrup:
1 pt. vinegar
1 pt. water
1 T. celery seed
1 cinnamon stick

6 C. white sugar
1 T. pickling spice
1 T. cloves

Slice pickles thin. Make brine of 1 C. salt dissolved in 1 gallon water. Pour over pickles. Let set 3 - 5 days. Drain and wash off salt 4 times with cold water or they won't be crisp. Boil in 1 gallon water with alum. Drain and wash once. Combine syrup ingredients. Put spices in bag. Boil pickles and spices in syrup for 15 minutes or until pickles are transparent. Put in jars and seal. Yields 6 pt.

LIME PICKLES

Mrs. Merle Hershberger
Mrs. Mark Hochstetler
Mrs. Willis Wagler

7 lbs. unpeeled, sliced pickles
2 C. pickling lime

2 gal. cold water

Soak for 24 hours. Rinse two or three times with cold water, cover with clear water and let soak for 3 hours. Drain then add:

2 T. salt
1¾ - 2 qts. vinegar
4½ lbs. sugar

1 t. whole cloves
1 t. mustard seed
2 t. mixed pickle spice

Soak overnight in this solution. The next morning bring to a boil and simmer for 30 minutes. Put in jars and seal. You can put spices in a bag. Very delicious and crispy. Makes approximately 6 qts.

RED APPLE PICKLES

Mrs. Willis Priscilla Miller

Part 1:
15 big pickles
2 C. lime

8½ qts. water

Part 2:
1 C. vinegar
½ oz. red food coloring

1 t. alum

Part 3:
2 C. vinegar
8 - 10 C. sugar
12 oz. red cinnamon hearts

5 cinnamon sticks
2 C. water

Mix lime and water. Peel pickles and cut into ½" rings. Take out centers of seeds. Put rings in lime water and let set 24 hours, stirring occasionally as lime settles. Drain and rinse until clear. Cover with cold water and let set 3 hours. Drain, mix part 2 and pour over rings in kettle, adding enough water to cover. Simmer 2 hours. Drain. Mix part 3 and bring to a boil. Pour over rings and cover tightly. Let stand overnight. Drain and reheat syrup the next two mornings repeating above procedure. The third morning reheat syrup and rings to boiling. Then pack in hot jars and seal. Makes approximately 10 pts.

REFRIGERATOR PICKLES

Mrs. Levi Miller

7 C. unpeeled, sliced cucumbers
1 C. diced green peppers

1 C. diced onions

Make a brine with 1 C. vinegar, 2 t. salt, 2 C. sugar and 1 T. celery seed. Do not heat. When sugar is dissolved, add celery seed and salt and pour over sliced cucumbers. Refrigerate in covered container. Let stand 24 hours before using.

REFRIGERATOR PICKLES

Mrs. Mark Hochstetler

6 C. cucumbers
1 C. onions
1 C. green peppers
2 C. white sugar

1 T. salt
1 T. celery seed
1 C. vinegar

Thinly slice cucumbers, onions and green peppers. Combine. Mix sugar, salt, celery seed and vinegar. Stir till sugar is dissolved. Pour over cucumber mixture and stir. Refrigerate. They can also be frozen.

SOCIETY PICKLES

Mrs. Robert W. Yoder

2 doz. 4" unpeeled, sliced pickles

Syrup:
1 qt. vinegar
1 pt. water
3 lbs. white sugar
1 T. whole cloves

1 T. whole allspice
1 T. cinnamon sticks
1 T. celery seed

Put pickles in strong brine for 4 days. Stir daily. On the fifth day rinse well. Boil in water with 1 heaping T. alum for 10 minutes. Rinse again. Put in water with 2 T. ginger and boil for 10 minutes. Pour off and add syrup to pickles. Tie spices in bag. Boil till clear in syrup, about 1/2 hour. Put in jars and seal while hot.

SANDWICH SPREAD

Mrs. Paul Mast

6 lg. onions
6 red peppers
6 green peppers

12 green tomatoes
6 cucumbers

Grind all together, add a handful of salt and let stand for 2 hours, then drain. Add 1/2 scant qt. vinegar. Cook for 15 minutes. Add 1 pt. mustard, 5 C. sugar, 1/2 pt. vinegar, 1 C. flour and 2 T. turmeric, boil together 5 minutes. Put in jars and seal.

SWEET PICKLES

Mrs. Reuben Miller

2 gal. sliced pickles
1¼ C. salt
1 gal. boiling water

Syrup:
6 C. vinegar
12 C. white sugar
2 C. water

1 handful horseradish leaves
1 T. alum

4 sticks cinnamon
4 T. celery seed
4 T. whole allspice

Put salt and boiling water over pickles and let stand 7 days, stirring every day. Drain. Add 1 gal. hot water and horseradish leaves, let stand 1 day. Drain. On ninth day add 1 gal. hot water and 1 T. alum and let stand for 2 more days. Drain. Combine syrup ingredients in saucepan, put spices in cloth bag and bring to a boil. Pour over pickles and can or let set for a few days.

CUCUMBER RELISH

Mrs. Roy Mast
Mrs. David Ray Yoder

6 large cucumbers
4 large onions
4 large peppers
2 T. salt
1 T. celery seed

2 C. vinegar
5 C. sugar
½ t. turmeric
2 drops green food coloring
1 T. mustard seed

Grind cucumbers, onions and peppers. Add salt and let set overnight. Drain and rinse, add remaining ingredients. Cook slowly till most of juice has boiled away, approximately 30 - 40 minutes. Pack in sterilized jars and seal. Yields 3 pts.

PEPPER RELISH

Mrs. Willis Karen Miller

2 doz. peppers, chopped
1 doz. onions, chopped

Pour boiling water over to cover. Let stand 15 minutes. Drain and add 1 qt. vinegar, 1 C. water, 5 C. sugar, 2 T. salt and 2 oz. mustard seed. Let cook for 20 minutes. Put in jars and seal.

PEPPER RELISH

Twila Beachy

12 lg. green peppers
12 lg. red peppers
12 sm. onions
5 C. white sugar

3 C. vinegar
2 T. salt
1 T. celery seed

Grind peppers and onions, cover with boiling water. Let set for 15 minutes. Drain 1 hour or overnight. Add sugar, vinegar, salt and celery seed. Boil 20 minutes, put in jars and seal.

PEPPER RELISH

Mrs. Ray Troyer

1 doz. hot peppers
1 doz. sweet peppers

1 doz. onions

Syrup:
1 qt. vinegar
5 C. sugar

2 T. salt
2 oz. mustard seed

Grind peppers and onions. Cover with boiling water and let stand for 15 minutes. Drain. Pour syrup over it and cook for 20 minutes, open kettle. Makes 8 pts.

PICKLE RELISH

Mrs. Matthias Mast

1 gal. ground pickles
1 pt. ground onions
Add 1/4 C. salt and let stand 2 hours. Drain overnight. Then add:

2 t. mustard seed
2 t. celery seed
2 t. turmeric

6 C. sugar
2 C. vinegar

Bring syrup to a boil, then add pickle onion mixture. Put in jars and cold pack for 5 minutes.

SEASONED TOMATO JUICE

Mrs. Mark Hochstetler

6 qts. juice
1 T. garlic salt
1 T. onion salt

1 T. celery salt
1/2 C. white sugar

Cut up tomatoes and cook. Put through Victorio strainer. Add seasonings and sugar to 6 qts. tomato juice. Put in jars and seal, use in soups and casseroles.

TOMATO COCKTAIL

Mrs. John Mark Troyer

1 peck tomatoes
1 t. parsley flakes
2 green peppers

3 - 4 stalks celery
6 sm. onions

Cook and put through sieve. Add:

1 C. sugar
1/4 C. salt

1/2 t. black pepper

Cold pack 10 minutes. This is very good to use for chili.

TOMATO SAUCE

Mrs. Nathan Mast

1 gal. tomato juice
3 lg. onions, diced fine
2 T. salt
1 t. cinnamon
1 t. dry mustard

1/2 t. red hot pepper
3 C. white sugar
1 1/2 C. vinegar
6 T. cornstarch with water
  to make a paste

Boil first 8 ingredients 1 hour. Add cornstarch mixture, boil 10 minutes longer.
Put in jars and cold pack for 20 minutes.

PIZZA SAUCE

Mrs. Dean Wengerd

10 lbs. tomatoes
1 lg. onion
Combine and cook till tender. Put through strainer. To 4 qts. juice add:

1/4 t. Tabasco sauce, more if you like it hot
4 t. salt
2 t. oregano
1 t. pepper

1 C. vegetable oil
1 C. sugar
2 t. garlic powder

Bring mixture to a boil, then thicken with clear jel. Cold pack for 35 minutes.
Makes 10 pts.

ॐ

A man's best friend is his dog, because
he wags his tail and not his tongue.

PIZZA SAUCE

Mrs. Mark Hochstetler

3/4 bushel tomatoes
3 lbs. onions
2 green peppers
2 garlic cloves, chopped
1 pt. vegetable oil
1 1/2 C. sugar

4 T. oregano
2 T. basil
2 T. parsley
6 bay leaves
4 - 6 oz. tomato paste
1/2 C. salt

Cook the first four ingredients together and put through Victorio strainer. I like to add hot peppers too. Add the rest of the ingredients and cook slowly for 1 hour. Remove the bay leaves, put in jars and seal.

PIZZA SAUCE

Mrs. Willis Priscilla Miller

1/2 bushel tomatoes
1 bulb garlic
2 or 3 hot peppers
4 onions
red and green peppers
2 t. oregano
1 t. basil

1 C. brown sugar
3/4 C. clear jell
1 C. vinegar
salt and pepper to taste
2 - 18 oz. tomato paste

Boil cut up tomatoes, garlic and hot peppers until soft. Put through strainer Chop onions and enough peppers to make 1 qt. Add to tomato pulp and simmer uncovered for 1/2 - 1 hour. Add sugar, spices, and seasonings. Mix vinegar and clear jell, stir into tomato mixture, bring to a boil. Add tomato paste and mix well. Cold pack for 1 hour.

PIZZA OR SPAGHETTI SAUCE

Mrs. Marion Miller

3 gal. tomato chunks
3 med. onions, chopped
1 bay leaf
3/4 C. sugar
1/3 C. salt
4 t. ground oregano

2 T. chili powder
2 T. garlic salt
3 1/2 C. clear jell or cornstarch
2 C. or more water
1 T. paprika

Cook together first three ingredients until tender, about 15 minutes. Sieve, add spices, and heat to boiling. Combine clear jell and water, stir until dissolved. Add to mixture, stirring constantly until thickened. Approximately 25 pts.

PIZZA SAUCE

Mrs. Nathan Miller

3 onions, cut fine
1 C. white sugar
1 T. garlic salt
1 large can cream of mushroom soup
3 - 12 oz. cans tomato paste
1 #3 can tomato soup

3 med. peppers
1 t. sweet basil
1 t. oregano
3 qts. tomato juice
4 sm. Jalapeño peppers

Combine all ingredients. Put in jars and cold pack for 30 minutes.

PIZZA SAUCE

1 peck tomatoes
3 onions
1 C. sugar
8 T. flour
8 t. oregano

8 t. salt
2 t. red pepper
2 t. basil leaves
5 - 6 oz. cans tomato paste
8 t. garlic powder

Cook tomatoes and onions and put through strainer. Add rest of ingredients to tomatoes and bring to a boil. Put in jars and cold pack for ¹/₂ hour.

CHILI SALSA

Mrs. Leroy Yoder

14 C. chopped tomatoes
3 C. chopped onions

8 oz. green chilies
¹/₂ C. chopped
  Jalapeno peppers, optional

Mix together and set aside. In separate bowl mix the following:

3 T. salt
1 T. chili powder
5 T. cornstarch
1 T. garlic powder

1¹/₂ t. cumin
¹/₂ C. vinegar
1 C. tomato sauce

Pour ¹/₄ C. seasoning mixture into each pt. jar. Fill jar to within ¹/₂" of top with tomato, onion and pepper mixture. Pressure cook at 10 lbs. pressure for 35 minutes. Yields 8 pts.

❧

*People seldom improve if they have no other
model but themselves to copy after.*

TOMATO SALSA

Mrs. Robert Miller

1 qt. peeled and chopped tomatoes
3 qts. thick tomato juice
12 oz. tomato paste
6 onions, chopped fine
4 C. sweet peppers, chopped

1/2 C. hot peppers, chopped
4 T. white sugar
1/4 t. garlic salt or powder
3 t. salt
1 T. vinegar

Simmer 2 - 3 hours. Cold pack 20 minutes. Yields 8 pts.

CHUNKY SALSA

Mrs. Roman Coblentz

1/2 bushel tomatoes
1 head garlic
hot or red peppers to taste
Cook together 1 hour, then put through blender or sieve. Add:

3 T. chopped onion
8 - 10 green peppers
2/3 C. vinegar
1 t. paprika

5 T. salt
4 T. brown sugar
2/3 C. clear jell
1 T. parsley

Simmer 1 hour, put in jars and seal.

MEXICAN HOT SAUCE

Mrs. Mark Hochstetler

1/4 C. salad oil
3 med. onions, diced
3 lg. carrots, diced
2 minced garlic cloves or
   1 t. garlic powder
2 med. peppers, diced
12 lbs. tomatoes, peeled and chunked

1/4 C. brown sugar
2 T. salt
2 t. oregano leaves
1 1/2 t. basil leaves
1/2 t. black pepper
12 oz. tomato paste

Over medium heat cook onions, carrots, peppers and garlic in oil until tender, stirring occasionally. Add tomatoes and remaining ingredients. Heat to boiling, reduce heat to medium, put lid on halfway or remove. Cook for 2 hours. Cold pack for 45 minutes. If you want to use this as salsa add 4 T. taco sauce to a pint.

ᘒ▲

The glory of springtime is the same to all.
But there are many different points of view.
A child sees it best from the middle of the mud puddle.

BEAN WITH BACON SOUP

Mrs. David Ray Yoder

4 lbs. navy beans
2 lbs. bacon
3 C. chopped onion
8 C. potatoes
4 C. celery

3 qts. tomato juice
3 T. salt
2 t. pepper
2 bay leaves
4 C. carrots

Soak beans overnight, drain and add water to cover, cook till soft. Fry cut-up bacon and chopped onion, add bacon drippings to soup. Cook vegetables till tender, mash or put through blender, also $1/2$ or more of the beans. Combine all in a mixing bowl and add tomato juice which has been boiled with bay leaves, salt and pepper. Pack into jars, and cold pack for 3 hours or pressure can for 75 minutes at 10 lbs. pressure. To serve, mix with equal amounts of milk and heat. Yields 10 qt.

BEAN WITH BACON SOUP

Mrs. Nathan Miller

1 lb. dried navy beans
3 qts. water
1 lb. bacon
2 - 3 C. chopped onion
2 C. diced potatoes
2 C. diced celery

2 C. diced carrots
1 - 2 qts. tomato juice
4 t. salt
$1/2$ t. pepper
1 bay leaf

Combine beans and water in large kettle, bring to a boil, boil for 2 minutes. Remove from heat, cover and let stand 1 hour. Fry bacon until crisp, remove from skillet and add to beans, cook onions in bacon drippings, add to beans. Bring soup to a boil and simmer covered for 1 hour. Put vegetables through grinder, then add to soup. Add remaining ingredients. Simmer till vegetables are soft. Remove bay leaf, and pressure cook for $1/2$ hour. You can also soak beans overnight then add enough water to cover beans. Bring to a boil and add bacon and onions.

CANNED VEGETABLE SOUP

Mrs. Jake Hershberger

1 qt. potatoes
1 qt. celery
1 qt. pork and beans
1 qt. carrots
2 C. onions
3 qts. tomato juice
2 lbs. hamburger, fried

1 qt. beef chunks
1 can beef broth
3 t. chili powder
$1/2$ C. sugar
salt and pepper to taste
2 cans bean with bacon soup,
  undiluted

Put vegetables together raw. Add meat, broth, seasonings and soup. Cold pack for 3 hours. Makes 10 qt.

CREAM OF TOMATO SOUP
Mrs. Willis Priscilla Miller

2 C. butter
1/4 C. finely chopped onion
2 1/4 C. flour
3/4 C. sugar

1/4 C. salt
2 t. pepper
7 1/2 qt. tomato juice

Melt butter, add onions and fry a little, (not brown). Stir in flour, sugar, salt and pepper. Cook until smooth and bubbly, stirring constantly. Remove from heat, add tomatoes. Stir. Cold pack for 15 - 20 minutes.

TOMATO SOUP
Mrs. Ben Troyer Jr.

1 peck ripe tomatoes
3 lg. stalks celery
3 onions
1 bunch parsley
1/4 C. salt

1/4 lb. butter
1 C. sugar
1 C. flour
water

Wash and cook tomatoes, celery, onions, parsley and salt. Put through sieve. Mix butter, sugar and flour. Add enough water to make a paste. Add to other ingredients. Bring to a boil. Put in jars and cold pack for 45 minutes. To serve add equal amount of milk and heat. Very Good!

CHICKEN NOODLE SOUP
Mrs. Nathan Miller

4 chickens
16 oz. noodles
2 qts. carrots

2 qts. celery
2 qts. potatoes
salt and chicken base to taste

Cook chickens and add plenty of water for broth. Cook vegetables in chicken broth. Cook noodles. 6 - 7 qt. water added for broth is about right. You can use legs and thighs and canned chicken broth. Pressure cook qts. 1 1/2 hr., pts. 1 1/4 hr.

CREAM OF CELERY SOUP
Mrs. Henry Schrock

3 T. butter
2 T. flour
1 t. salt
1/8 t. pepper

4 C. milk
1 T. chicken soup base
1 C. diced, cooked celery

Melt butter over low heat in heavy saucepan. Add flour, salt and pepper. Blend until smooth. Remove from heat and stir in milk. Bring to a boil, stirring constantly, boil 1 minute. Add soup base and celery, cook until thick. To can I use only 1/2 of the milk and cold pack for 2 hours then add the rest of the milk when ready to serve. If white sauce is too thin add some clear jel, before adding celery. I use water instead of milk.

CHUNKY BEEF SOUP

Mrs. Ray Troyer

2$\frac{1}{2}$ gal. water
1$\frac{1}{4}$ C. beef soup mix
2 lg. cans beef broth or
   2$\frac{1}{2}$ qts. canned broth
4 qts. tomato juice
2 C. brown sugar
$\frac{1}{4}$ scant C. salt
1$\frac{1}{2}$ lb. browned butter added last
2 lg. onions cut up and fried in butter

3 qt. or 4 - 1 lb. bag peas
1 qt. cooked navy beans
1 qt. celery, barley or macaroni
1 lb. fried, cut up bacon
4 qts. cooked potatoes
8 lbs. fried seasoned hamburger
4 lbs. cooked beef chunks or
   roast
4 qts. carrots, diced

Heat all liquid and thicken with 4 - 5 C. Perma-flo and enough water to make a paste. Add to vegetables and cooked meats. Don't overcook vegetables, not much more than boiling. Put in jars and cold pack for 2 hours.

CHUNKY BEEF SOUP

Mrs. Josiah Miller

Fill 21 qt. canner $\frac{1}{2}$ full with water.
1 C. beef base
2 lg. cans beef broth
2 lg. onions
$\frac{1}{4}$ C. salt and pepper
4 qts. carrots
4 qts. potatoes

4 qts. tomato juice
3 qts. peas
2 qts. green beans
2 C. sugar
1 qt. flour
5 lb. hamburger,
   seasoned and fried

Thicken water, beef base, beef broth, onions, salt, tomato juice and sugar with flour. Cut up vegetables and add salt, cook until tender. Add hamburger and mix all together. Put in jars and cold pack for 3 hours or pressure cook for 1$\frac{1}{2}$ hour.

CHUNKY SOUP

Mrs. Charles Karn

$\frac{3}{4}$ C. beef base
2 lg. cans beef broth
$\frac{1}{2}$ C. butter
4 qts. tomato juice
1$\frac{3}{4}$ C. sugar
$\frac{1}{4}$ C. salt
4 qts. carrots

1$\frac{1}{2}$ qt. green beans
3 qts. peas
4 qts. potatoes
2 qts. flour
8 lb. hamburger
2 lg. onions chopped
salt and pepper to taste

Heat together 2$\frac{1}{2}$ gal. water, beef base, broth, butter, tomato juice, sugar and salt till boiling. Cook vegetables in salt water, then add to mixture. Mix flour with enough water to make a smooth paste add to soup to thicken. Season hamburger with salt, pepper and onion, fry in flour and butter. Add to soup. Some beef chunks may be added instead of hamburger. Cold pack for 2 hours or pressure cook for 40 minutes at 10 lbs. pressure. Makes about 30 qts.

NACHO CHEESE SAUCE

Mrs. Jr. Wagler

3 - 2 lb. boxes Velveeta cheese
3¹/₂ C. cream
¹/₄ lb. butter

1 qt. milk
hot peppers

Melt butter in medium saucepan, then add milk and cream, then slice cheese into mixture. Melt slowly, put in jars and cold pack for 20 minutes.

CHEESE WHIZ

Mrs. Henry Beachy

3 lbs. Velveeta cheese
1 can Milnot milk

1³/₄ C. milk
¹/₂ stick butter

Put together and melt on low heat. Put in jars and cold pack for 15 minutes.

CANNED CORN

Mrs. Henry Schrock

1 pt. corn
2 T. oleo

1 T. flour
¹/₂ T. sugar

Cut corn of cob, whole kernel, do not scrape. Add water to wash all milk off of corn. A lot of silk pieces, etc. will float to the top, remove these. Wash and drain at least 3 times. Fill jars. Add salt and cold water. Put lids on and cold pack for 3 hours. To serve, melt oleo in saucepan, add flour and sugar. Stir until blended. Add corn along with liquid. Heat to just boiling and serve. Boiling too long spoils the flavor.

PORK AND BEANS

Mrs. Robert W. Yoder

8 lbs. navy beans
1¹/₂ lbs. bacon
¹/₃ C. salt
4 qts. tomatoes
2 C. water
1 lb. white sugar

²/₃ C. brown sugar
¹/₂ C. flour
¹/₂ t. red pepper
1 t. dry mustard
1 t. cinnamon
¹/₂ C. Karo

Soak beans overnight. Lightly brown bacon. Pour off grease. Cook beans till nearly done. Add salt, sugar, Karo, spices and tomatoes. Make a paste with flour and water. Bring beans and tomatoes to a boil and add paste. Fill jars and cold pack for 1¹/₂ hours.

CANNING SWEET POTATOES

Mrs. Ray Troyer

Peel and cut sweet potatoes. Pack in jars. Cover with syrup made with 1 C. white sugar and 2 C. water. Do not add salt. Put lids on and cold pack for 1 hour.

CANNED MANGOES

Mrs. Eli Mast

1 peck mangoes, red or green, cut into strips and cover with cold water, bring to boiling point. Drain and put into jars. Cover with syrup made of:

1 pt. light Karo
1 qt. vinegar

1 T. salt
2 lbs. white sugar

Boil this together for 5 minutes. Pour over mangoes and seal.

CANNED MEAT LOAF

Mrs. Eli Mast

15 lbs. ground beef
1/2 scant C. salt
4 slices bread
36 soda crackers

1 C. oatmeal
3 C. water, milk or tomato juice
4 eggs

Mix well and pack into jars. Cold pack for 3 hours. May also be formed into balls and fried before canning.

TENDER BEEF CHUNKS TO CAN

Mrs. Wyman Wengerd

16 lbs. beef chunks
1 C. brown sugar
1 C. salt

1 t. salt petre
2 t. soda
3/4 gal. water to cover meat

Boil brine and let cool, then pour over meat and let stand for 4 days. Remove from brine and rinse to can. Add 1/2 t. salt and 1 C. water to each qt. and cold pack for 2 hours.

PICKLING YELLOW BEANS

Twila Beachy

Blanch beans and drain water off. Boil 2 C. vinegar, 2 C. water and 1 1/2 C. sugar. Put beans in jars and pour hot vinegar solution over beans. Seal.

CANNING PIMENTOS

Twila Beachy

1 1/2 gal. water
1/2 C. salt

2 pt. vinegar
3 lbs. brown sugar

Peel pimentos, cut into quarters. Soak in 1 gal. water and 1/2 C. salt for 3 hours. Drain. Cook 2 minutes in 2 qts. water, 1 pt. vinegar. Drain. Bring 3 lbs. brown sugar and 1 pt. vinegar to a boil. Put pimentos in jars and pour sugar/vinegar mixture over top. Cold pack for 15 minutes.

SAUERKRAUT

Mrs. Josiah Miller

Shred cabbage, put loosely into qt. jars. Take handle of wooden spoon and punch holes in the center of the cabbage in the jar. Add 1 T. salt and fill with boiling water. Seal jars. Let set for 6 - 8 weeks before using.

HOT PEPPER RINGS

Mrs. Mark Hochstetler

Slice hot peppers in rings with seeds. Put in pt. jars. Put 1 t. vegetable oil and 1 t. salt into each jar. Mix 1 pt. vinegar, 3 C. water and 3 C. white sugar and bring to a boil. Pour over hot peppers in jars. Cold pack to boiling, remove immediately. Makes 6 pints.

STUFFED MINI RED PEPPERS

Twila Beachy

1 C. brown sugar
2 C. vinegar
1 t. celery seed

1/2 t. mustard
1/2 t. turmeric
1/2 t. salt

Stuff peppers with shredded cabbage, place into pt. jars. Heat remaining ingredients to a boil. Pour over stuffed peppers in jars. Cold pack for 15 minutes.

The Vegetable Garden

First plant five rows of peas:
    Patience
    Perserverance
    Promptness
    Purity
    Preparation

Next, plant three rows of squash:
    Squash gossip
    Squash criticism
    Squash indifference

Then plant five rows of lettuce:
    Let us be faithful to duty
    Let us be unselfish
    Let us be loyal
    Let us be true to obligations
    Let us love one another

And no garden is complete without turnips:
    Turn up for important meetings
    Turn up with a smile
    Turn up with good ideas
    Turn up with determination

To make everything count
for something good and worthwhile!

- Notes -

Children's Recipes

Ages 7 - 12

KINDERGARTEN COOKIES

Mary Esta Yoder

1 small child
5 - 6 years of tender loving care
1 pound of patience
2 heaping measures of good manners
4 drops of safety rules
$\frac{1}{2}$ t. humor
generous pinch of reading time
10 sticky fingers

If dough is wiggly, add a few extra hugs until desired consistency is obtained. Allow to stand 5 - 10 minutes for proper discipline. Place in desired world with interest and pride. Set goals at a degree that will give a child a feeling of accomplishment. Will produce a creative, enthusiastic, capable child. CAUTION: will crumble easily, must be reassured often.

MORNING EGG CASSEROLE

Julia Michelle Yoder, Age 11

30 saltine crackers
2 C. grated Cheddar cheese
6 beaten eggs
$\frac{1}{2}$ C. melted butter
2 C. milk
$\frac{1}{2}$ C. real bacon bits

Preheat oven to 400°. Crumble crackers and place in bottom of greased 9" x 13" baking dish. Mix remaining ingredients and pour over crackers. Bake uncovered for 20 minutes. Quick and simple.

TACO PIE

Heidi Miller, Age 11

browned hamburger with taco seasoning
sour cream
Cheddar cheese

Layer in unbaked pie shell. Bake till browned, then top with lettuce and tomatoes.

QUICK PIZZA

Regina Beachy, Age 8

bread
pizza sacue
Velveeta cheese
onion salt

Spread both sides of bread with margarine. Place on cookie sheet. Put 2 T. pizza sauce on each slice and spread with knife. Put 1 slice of cheese on top of each piece. Sprinkle with onion salt. Bake until cheese is melted and bread is slightly crisp around edges. Serve immediately. Bake for 10 - 15 minutes at 350°.

EASY BREAD PIZZA

Jeffrey Miller, Age 8

slices of bread
pizza sauce

turkey ham or lunch meat
cheese

Place slices of bread on cookie sheet. Spread each one with pizza sauce. Top with a slice of meat and cheese. Place in 350° oven till cheese melts.

MOCK TURKEY

Mary Beth Kaufman, Age 12

2 lbs. hamburger
1 loaf of bread, cubed or
1 lg. pkg. bread stuffing

2 cans cream of chicken soup
1 can cream of celery soup
4 C. milk

Fry hamburger in butter. Add bread, milk and soups. Mix all together and bake at 350° for 45 minutes to 1 hour.

ZUCCHINI PATTIES

Heidi Miller, Age 11

1½ C. peeled, shredded potatoes
1½ C. shredded zucchini
¼ C. chopped onion
2 T. flour

2 T. wheat germ
1 t. salt
parsley
3 eggs, slightly beaten

Toss or mix everything except the eggs. Beat eggs and add to the mixture. Fry in patties with cheese on top.

CHEX MEX BUDDIES

Matthew David Miller, Age11

9 C. of your favorite Chex cereal
1 C. semi-sweet chocolate chips
½ C. peanut butter

¼ C. margarine or butter
1½ C. powdered sugar

Place cereal in large bowl, set aside. In small saucepan melt chocolate chips, margarine and peanut butter over low heat, stirring often. Remove from heat, stir in vanilla, pour over cereal, stirring until pieces are evenly coated. Place cereal mixture and powdered sugar in large, clean paper bag. Shake until pieces are well coated. Tear bag open and spread apart to cool.

ॐ

All people smile in the same language!

TRIPLE LAYER COOKIE BAR
Rosetta Miller, Age 8

½ C. butter
1½ C. graham cracker crumbs
7 oz. or 2⅔ C. flaked coconut
14 oz. Eagle Brand milk

12 oz. semi-sweet
   chocolate chips
½ C. creamy peanut butter

Preheat oven to 350°, or 325° for glass dish. In 9" x 13" baking pan, melt butter in oven. Sprinkle crumbs evenly over butter. Top with coconut, then Eagle Brand milk. Bake 25 minutes or until lightly browned. Melt chocolate chips and peanut butter in medium saucepan over low heat. Spread evenly over hot coconut layer, cool 30 minutes. Chill thoroughly. Cut into bars. Store loosely covered at room temperature.

CHOCOLATE CHIP COOKIES
Abigail Miller, Age 10

1 C. white sugar
1 C. brown sugar
1 C. shortening, melted
2 beaten eggs
3 C. flour

1 t. soda
½ t. salt
1 t. vanilla
1 t. water
1 C. chocolate chips

Bake at 350° for 10 - 12 minutes. Do not overbake.

CHOCOLATE CHIP COOKIES
Rhoda Ann Miller, Age 12

1½ C. oleo
1 C. Crisco
1½ C. brown sugar
1½ C. white sugar
1⅓ C. dry instant pudding

4 eggs
4 t. vanilla
2 t. soda
6 C. flour
3½ C. chocolate chips

Mix well, roll in balls and bake on ungreased cookie sheet. Do not overbake. Take out before quite done.

CHOCOLATE CHIP COOKIES
Sheila Yoder, Age 12

2¼ C. flour
1 t. soda
1 C. margarine
¼ C. white sugar
¾ C. brown sugar

1 t. vanilla
4 oz. instant vanilla pudding
2 eggs
12 oz. chocolate chips
nuts, optional

Melt butter and mix with sugars, vanilla and instant pudding. Beat and add eggs, then add remaining ingredients. Bake on ungreased cookie sheet at 350°.

OUTRAGEOUS CHOCOLATE CHIP COOKIES

Jolene Renae Troyer, Age 12

2 C. sugar
1 1/3 C. brown sugar
2 C. margarine
2 C. peanut butter
1 t. salt
4 eggs

4 C. flour
2 C. quick oats
4 t. soda
2 t. vanilla
3 C. chocolate chips

Beat eggs, add sugars, margarine, peanut butter and vanilla. Add dry ingredients. Bake at 350°. Do not overbake.

PEANUT BUTTER TEMPTATIONS

Heidi Miller, Age 11

1/2 C. peanut butter
1/2 C. oleo
1/2 C. white sugar
1/2 C. brown sugar
1 egg

1/2 t. vanilla
1 1/4 C. flour
3/4 t. soda
1/2 t. salt

Mix in order given and put in small muffin cups, fill about 3/4 full. Bake at 350° for 10 - 12 minutes. Take from oven and let cool a little, then press peanut butter cups in the middle of each one. Remove from muffin pan.

CAKE MIX COOKIES

Rosetta Miller, Age 8

1 pkg. cake mix, any flavor
1/2 C. cooking oil

2 eggs
1 C. chocolate chips

Mix and drop by teaspoons onto cookie sheet. Bake at 350° for 10 - 12 minutes.

PIG OUT PEANUT BUTTER BARS

Mary Beth Kaufman, Age 12

2 C. peanut butter
1/2 C. butter
3 1/2 C. powdered sugar

3 C. Rice Krispies
1 C. chocolate chips,
   more if desired

Mix peanut butter and powdered sugar thoroughly. Add Rice Krispies and mix again. Press into jelly roll pan with rolling pin. Melt chocolate chips and spread over top. Cool. Cut into squares and pig out.

FLOWERPOT CUPCAKES

Melissa Sue Miller, Age 7

1 pkg. Pillsbury Plus Funfetti cake mix
36 ice cream cones with flat bottoms
1 can pink vanilla Funfetti frosting
assorted candies

Preheat oven to 350°. Prepare cake mix according to package directions. Place ice cream cones in muffin cups or on a jelly roll pan. Fill cones with batter to within 1" from the top. Bake for 20 - 25 minutes. Frost and sprinkle with candy bits.

CINNAMON KITES

Kristine Miller, Age 9

1 pkg. brown and serve dinner rolls
2 beaten eggs
$^1/_2$ C. milk

3 T. cinnamon
$^1/_2$ C. sugar

Preheat oil. Tear rolls into thirds and dip into egg and milk mixture. Drop into oil and fry until golden brown. Remove and sprinkle, or coat by shaking in plastic bag with cinnamon and sugar mixture.

MARSHMALLOW HATS

Hannah Yoder, Age 9

12 Ritz crackers
12 lg. marshmallows
peanut butter

Spread each cracker with peanut butter. Put one marshmallow on each cracker. Put in 350° oven till nicely browned. Enjoy with friends!

MINI CHEESECAKES

Rhoda Ann Miller, Age 12

12 vanilla wafers (round)
2 - 8 oz. cream cheese
$^1/_2$ C. white sugar

1 t. vanilla
2 eggs

Line muffin pans with foil or paper liners. Place one vanilla wafer in each cup. Beat cream cheese until light and fluffy. Gradually add sugar, mixing well. Add vanilla and beat. Add eggs one at a time, beating well after each addition. Spoon cream cheese mixture over wafers filling cups. Bake at 350° for 25 - 30 minutes. Remove from pan when cool. Chill. Top with any fruit pie filling.

LAZY DAISY SHORTCAKE   Heidi Miller, Age 11

4 eggs   2 t. baking powder
2 C. sugar   1 C. hot milk
1 t. vanilla   3 T. melted butter
2 C. flour   1/4 t. salt

In large bowl, beat eggs till lemon colored. Slowly beat in sugar and vanilla. Stir in flour and baking powder. Slowly beat in hot milk, melted butter and salt. Bake at 350° for 35 - 40 minutes. Makes 12 or more servings.

CHOCOLATE CAKE   Ruth Hershberger, Age 10

3 C. flour   2 T. vinegar
2 C. white sugar   2 t. vanilla
6 T. cocoa   3/4 C. salad oil
2 t. soda   2 C. cold water
1 t. salt

Mix all ingredients, add cold water last. Bake at 350° for 35 minutes. Good for cake or cupcakes.

TWINKIES   Rhoda Ann Miller, Age 12

1 box yellow cake mix   3/4 C. water
1 sm. box instant vanilla pudding   3/4 C. oil
4 eggs

Filling:
2 egg whites   2 C. powdered sugar
1 C. Crisco   marshmallow creme

Mix and bake in cookie sheet lined with waxed paper, when cool cut in half then put filling on half and put other half on top. Cut into little squares.

RICE KRISPIE PIE
Julia Michelle Yoder, Age 11

2 C. Rice Krispies
1 T. melted butter
1/2 C. marshmallow creme

Melt the butter and blend with marshmallow creme. Add Rice Krispies and mix. Put in a greased pie pan and shape into crust. Fill the crust with ice cream and freeze. When ready to serve, top with fresh fruit or your favorite ice cream topping.

CARAMEL COFFEE RING
Heidi Miller, Age 11

1/2 C. margarine
1 C. packed brown sugar
2 T. water

2 - 10 oz. cans biscuits
1/2 C. nuts

Heat oven to 375°. In saucepan, melt margarine. Coat bottom and sides of tube pan. Sprinkle 3 T. nuts over bottom. Add remaining nuts, water, and brown sugar to margarine. Heat to boiling. Cut each biscuit in half and shape into ball and place into bottom of pan. Drizzle half of caramel sauce over balls, repeat layers. Bake at 350° for 20 - 25 minutes until golden brown, invert onto wax paper. Remove from pan.

HOT FUDGE SAUCE
Abigail Miller, Age 10

2 C. powdered sugar
2/3 C. semi-sweet chocolate chips
12 oz. evaporated milk

1/2 C. butter or margarine
1 t. vanilla

Combine first four ingredients in saucepan. Bring to boil. Boil for 8 minutes. Remove from heat and stir in vanilla.

PLAYDOUGH
Lena Joy Mast, Age 11

1 1/2 C. water
1/2 C. salt
2 T. alum

1 T. oil
2 1/2 C. flour
food coloring

Heat water and salt to 180° in a saucepan. Add alum, oil, flour and food coloring. Mix well. Knead until color is uniform.

SOFT PRETZELS

Mary Beth Kaufman, Age 12

2 pkgs. yeast
4$\frac{1}{2}$ C. flour

1$\frac{1}{2}$ C. warm water
$\frac{1}{4}$ C. sugar

Knead, let rise 15 minutes, shape dough into rolls. Slice into 20 pieces. Shape into pretzels, then dip into mixture of 1 T. soda and 1 C. water. Bake at 450° for 15 minutes.

ZESTY OYSTER CRACKERS

Lena Joy Mast, Age 11

2 pkgs. oyster crackers
1 pkg. dry Hidden Valley Ranch mix
$\frac{3}{4}$ t. dill weed

$\frac{3}{4}$ t. garlic powder
1 C. vegetable oil

Put in large covered bowl. Mix thoroughly. They get better as they set.

BETH'S DIRT PUDDING

Mary Beth Kaufman, Age 12

1 sm. pkg. Oreo cookies
$\frac{1}{2}$ stick margarine, melted
2 boxes instant vanilla pudding
3$\frac{1}{2}$ C. milk

1 C. powdered sugar
1 lg. container Cool Whip
8 oz. cream cheese

Crush Oreo cookies. Mix with melted margarine and press into 9" x 13" pan. Save some crumbs for topping. Mix pudding and milk. Add powdered sugar, Cool Whip and cream cheese. Spread over top of cookie mixture and top with remaining crumbs. Freeze.

OREO DESSERT

Heidi Miller, Age 11

1 pkg. crushed Oreo cookies
Mixed with one stick oleo.

$\frac{1}{2}$ gal. vanilla ice cream

hot fudge sauce
1 container Cool Whip

cookie crumbs for top

❧

*If you can't say something good about someone,
it is best to say nothing at all.*

PUPPY CHOW

Jessica Lynne Troyer, Age 9

1/4 C. butter
1 C. chocolate chips
3/4 C. peanut butter

8 C. Crispix cereal
2 C. powdered sugar

Melt first 3 ingredients. Pour over cereal, stir well. Pour powdered sugar in a brown grocery bag, add cereal and shake well to coat evenly.

PUPPY CHOW

Lena Joy Mast, Age 11

2 C. chocolate chips
1/2 C. margarine

1 C. peanut butter

Cook on medium high heat for 3 1/2 minutes or until mixture is smooth. Pour over 1 medium size box Rice Chex cereal. Place in large paper bag, add 2 C. powdered sugar and toss until well coated. Spread on cookie sheet and refrigerate until set.

PEANUT BUTTER PLAYDOUGH

Bethany Elaine Troyer, Age 8

1 C. peanut butter
1/2 C. honey

2 C. powdered sugar

In a bowl mix peanut butter, honey and powdered sugar with your hands. Dough should feel soft and pliable, shape into form of your choice. Use a cookie cutter or decorate with raisins. Now eat your playdough. Yummy.

FINGER JELLO

Regina Beachy, Age 8

4 T. Knox unflavored gelatin
3 - 3 oz. any flavor gelatin

4 C. boiling water

In large bowl, combine unflavored gelatin and flavored gelatin, add boiling water and stir until gelatin is dissolved. Pour into large shallow baking pan and chill until firm. Cut into squares to serve.

FINGER JELLO

Heidi Miller, Age 11

3 - 3 oz. jello
4 T. gelatin

4 C. boiling water

Mix together and pour into 9" x 13" pan.

POPSICLES

Ruth Hershberger, Age 10

1 pkg. any flavor Kool-Aid
4 T. any flavor jello
²/₃ C. sugar

1¹/₃ C. boiling water
1¹/₃ C. cold water

Pour in popsicle mold and freeze.

FROZEN POPS

Keturah Engbretson, Age 6

3 oz. any flavor jello
1 pkg. any flavor Kool-Aid
1 C. sugar

2 C. boiling water
2 C. cold water

Dissolve jello, Kool-Aid and sugar in boiling water, add cold water. Pour into ice cube trays, small paper cups or popsicle molds. When partially frozen, insert wooden sticks diagonally. Freeze and enjoy.

POPSICLES

Lena Joy Mast, Age 11

3 oz. jello
1 pkg. Kool-Aid
¹/₂ C. sugar

2 C. boiling water
2 C. cold water

Mix ingredients together and stir until dissolved. Add cold water and stir. Pour into popsicle molds and freeze.

REFRESHING PUNCH

Emily Engbretson, Age 10

¹/₂ gal. any flavor sherbet ice cream
2 liter 7Up

Mix well with egg beater.

ROOTBEER

Heidi Miller, Age 11

2 C. sugar
3 or 4 t. rootbeer extract

1 heaping t. yeast
    dissolved in ³/₄ C. water

Pour everything in 1 gallon of water.

ROOTBEER

Lena Joy Mast, Age 11

2 C. white sugar
2 T. rootbeer extract

1 t. yeast
1 gal. lukewarm water

Set in warm place or sun for 3 - 4 hours, do not turn lid too tight, then cool.

ICE TUPS FOR 18

Heidi Miller, Age 11

1 pkg. jello
1 C. sugar

1 pkg. Kool-Aid
1 C. hot water

Mix well and add 2 C. cold water. Stir and pour into ice tups and freeze.

GOLDEN ICE CUBES

Kristine Miller, Age 9

1 C. orange juice
1 C. lemon juice

1 C. corn syrup
2 C. cold water

Mix everything together. Pour into ice cube trays. Put in freezer until you want to make drinks.

BANANA MILKSHAKE

Heidi Miller, Age 11

Freeze bananas, put in blender, add:
1 C. milk   sugar to taste
1 t. vanilla

Blend together, may add ice cubes to thicken. Can use any frozen fruit instead of bananas.

Handy Hints and Helps

For your Kitchen

To cut down on "back and forth" trips in the kitchen during a backyard picnic, use a six cup muffin tin to hold mustard, ketchup and such.

Instead of throwing your broccoli stems in the garbage, peel them and use the insides.

Tomatoes should never be left to ripen in direct sunlight, as they will lose most of their vitamin C.

Baked potatoes should be pricked with a fork to release the steam as soon as they are finished baking. This will keep them from becoming soggy.

If you burn your tongue, try sprinkling a few grains of sugar on it for instant relief.

Popcorn should always be kept in the freezer. Not only will it stay fresh, but freezing helps eliminate unpopped kernels.

A substitute for corn syrup: use $1/4$ C. water or, other type of liquid called for in the recipe, plus 1 C. white sugar.

Uses for the Salsa Master: chopping lettuce, onions, grating cabbage for slaw, chopping broccoli, chopping cauliflower and making cracker crumbs.

Try using cornstarch to roll out pie crust, rolls or doughnuts. It takes much less than it does if you use flour and it will make your dough as stiff as flour will and is also easier to clean.

1 t. baking powder = $3/8$ t. cream of tartar, or $1/4$ t. soda + 1 t. cream of tartar.

1 C. honey = $1 1/4$ C. sugar + 1 C. water.

1 t. dry mustard = 1 T. prepared mustard.

Stick 2 - 3 pieces of macaroni in the center of the top of a double crust pie. The steam escapes up these sticks and prevents pie from running over.

For sour milk, add 1 T. vinegar to 1 C. sweet milk.

When using instant puddings or powdered whipped topping, use homogenized milk, not raw milk.

To improve the flavor of green string beans, place an onion in the kettle before adding beans.

Egg whites will beat up better if left to warm at room temperature.

When baking bar cookies - the recipes asks for 2 eggs add three. Makes them softer. Don't overbake.

To keep vegetables colorful add a pinch of baking soda to cooking water.

Odorless plastic jugs: put a few drops of vinegar in clean plastic jugs to prevent stale odors from developing.

Orange spice tea: In the winter, when you're eating lots of oranges, save the orange peels. Slice fresh oranges, peel into 1/2" squares. Punch a whole clove into each square. Put these on a cookie sheet and put in a warm place to dry for a couple of days. Store in canister. Drop one in the bottom of a cup or one per cup in a teapot. Tastes like the expensive kind.

A few drops of lemon juice added to whipping cream helps it to whip faster and better.

A lump of butter added to water when boiling rice, noodles, spaghetti, potatoes and similar starches will keep it from boiling over.

To clean a scorched saucepan, just fill the pan halfway with water and add 1/4 C. baking soda. Boil awhile until the burned portions loosen and float to the top.

To can pumpkins: cut up pumpkins, put chunks in jars. Add 1/2 t. salt per pt. Fill with water. Pressure cook for 90 minutes or for 3 hours in boiling water. When ready to use drain water and mash.

When baking a chocolate cake, coat pan with cocoa instead of flour. Eliminates the white spots.

In a hurry to fry hamburgers? When forming the patties make a small hole in the center with your finger. This will speed the frying and it will partially close when done.

When an old recipe calls for butter the size of an egg use 4 T.

To determine if an egg is fresh, immerse it into a pan of cool salted water. If it sinks it is fresh, if it rises to the surface it is not fresh.

For fluffier omelets, add a pinch of cornstarch before beating.

To dry tea or parsley, heat oven to 200° and turn off. Spread tea or parsley on a cookie sheet and place in preheated oven. The tea is usually dry till the oven cools off, if not, heat it again for a short time. Drying this way keeps the green color.

When frosting cookies with brown sugar icing, the frosting will have a glossy appearance if the cookies are frosted while still warm.

To prevent the bottom pie crust from becoming soggy, grease pie pans with butter. The crust will be soft and flaky.

To prevent onions from burning your eyes, hold onions under water when peeling or slicing.

Before melting chocolate, rub the inside of the pan with butter. The chocolate will not stick to the pan.

Add a little salt to applesauce, takes less sugar and makes a richer flavor.

When baking cookies save the crumbs you scrape from the cookie sheet and add to your graham cracker crumbs.

How to keep corn on the cob "garden fresh" for up to a week. Immediately husk the corn and remove silk, then place cobs in Zip-lock plastic bags between layers of paper towels that have been soaked in cold water. Refrigerate. When ready to cook, remove as many cobs as you need and reseal the bag.

Store cottage cheese upside down in refrigerator it will keep twice as long.

To keep strawberries fresh longer. Place them in a Tupperware and cover with a paper towel, and put the lid on. The paper towel absorbs the moisture.

Put the plastic lid from an empty Crisco can on the bottom of the next can. This protects shelves and counter tops from rust marks and scratches.

When using fresh farm milk for instant pudding. Bring milk to a boil and cool before adding it to the instant pudding mix. If you don't heat it first, the pudding will taste soapy.

To keep fruit pies from spilling over while baking, always have pie filling cold, wet the edge of bottom crust. Press bottom and top crust together and bake in hot oven.

Ice cubes made from lemonade will give your iced tea an added punch.

Chopped apples benefit cold dishes such as cole slaw, chicken salad, by adding color and flavor.

Sweeten whipped cream with powdered sugar if dessert serving may be delayed, whip stays fluffy longer than if granulated sugar is used.

If you have a 2 or 3 burner gas hot plate, do your canning outside when its warm. If you have a gas grill that has a burner on one side, you can even use that. Watch that it doesn't tip. Beat the heat!

Add $1/4$ t. soda to cranberries and they will not require much sugar.

To eliminate weeping meringue, try leaving meringue in oven until it cools.

Salt should be added after cooking so it won't draw liquids out of the food.

With your Cleaning

To give copper bottom pans that shiny look, just sprinkle salt on the bottom and wipe with a vinegar dampened cloth.

Club soda will shine up stainless steel sinks in a hurry.

Spots on stainless steel can be removed with white vinegar.

Baking powder will remove tea or coffee stains from china pots or cups.

For a sparkling white sink, place a paper towel over the bottom of your sink and saturate it with household bleach. Let set for 1 hour.

If you have gum or gunk on your clothing, try spraying it with just hot water from your hose nozzle, lay it on concrete and fold clothing so that gum is close to the edge, and spray full blast.

To make your own spray and wash, mix together 1 C. ammonia, 1 C. water and 1 C. Wisk or liquid soap. Spray on soiled spots or dirty laundry.

To make your own window cleaner, mix: 1 pt. rubbing alcohol, 1 T. Dawn detergent and 1 gallon water.

Cold weather window cleaning mix: $1/2$ C. ammonia, 1 C. white vinegar, 2 T. cornstarch and $1/2$ C. rubbing alcohol. Put in bucket of warm water and use to prevent ice from forming on your windows while washing them.

To make your own room air freshener, cut an orange in half, remove pulp and fill peel with salt. Proven effective in absorbing strong odors all around the house.

For a real effective pre-wash spray, mix equal parts of Wisk, Clorox 2 and water. Put in spray bottle and spray spots before laundering. Works well on grass stains, etc.

Piles of clean laundry, boys' pants, underware, socks, etc. will be carried upstairs willing by the owner if they are sorted and placed on each one's assigned stairstep.

If you want to get a soiled spot off of Dacron cotton tablecloths, get a bar of Lava soap and wet the area, then rub with the soap, the soil should come out after washing.

Sparkling clean thermos: Fill the Thermos bottle with water, and add one or two tablets of Efferdent denture cleanser. Let stand overnight, in the morning brush the insides of the Thermos, rinse and you have a sparkling clean Thermos.

Heavy seams: rub seams with a bar of soap to allow sewing machine needle to easily pass through.

Badly soiled canvas shoes can be turned white again when sprayed with foam upholstery cleaner and scrubbed with a brush. For best results let shoes dry and brush again.

Keep flies away from windows in your home, by cutting 2" pieces of a pest strip, then attaching them with a small nail between window and screen.

Perspiration stains on clothes may be soaked in a qt. of warm water with 4 T. salt.

In your Garden

Worms won't bother tomatoes if you plant dill nearby.

To keep sweet corn from being bugged, put a drop of mineral oil on silks when they start out of the shuck.

For a good plant fertilizer, dry egg shells in the oven, then pulverize them in a blender to make a bonemeal.

To clean you gardener's hands, rub them clean with cider vinegar. Let dry and apply hand lotion.

Rub a bee sting with an onion slice for relief.

Cut flowers will last longer in a vase if $1/4$ t. or 20 drops of Clorox bleach is added to each qt. of water.

To keep carrots through the winter. Wash them and leave 1" of the tops on. Put in plastic bag and close tightly. Store in ground cellar.

Mosquitoes can be a sleep wrecker when camping. Put a few drops of camphor on a cotton ball beside your head, they will head in another direction.

Index

Breads, Rolls & Cereals cont'...

Soups, Salads & Salad Dressings

Soups, Salads & Salad Dressings cont' . . .

Meats & Main Dishes

Meats & Main Dishes cont' . . .

Large Quantity Recipes

Large Quantity Recipes cont' . . .

Desserts

Desserts cont' . . .

Cookies

Cookies cont' . . .

Cakes & Frostings

Pies

Pies cont'...

Canning & Freezing

Favorite Recipes

VOLUME I

Cooking with the Horse & Buggy People

A Collection of Over 600 Favorite Recipes from the Heart of Holmes County

From mouth watering Amish style main dishes to kitchen dream desserts, this one has it all. Over 600 made-from-scratch recipes that please the appetite and are easy on the food budget. You'll get a whole section on canning and food preparation. The Amish, long known for their originality in the kitchen, share their favorites with you. If you desire originality, if you respect authenticity, if the Amish style cooking satisfies your taste palate—**Cooking With The Horse & Buggy People** is for you.

Contains 14 Complete Sections:

Breads, Cakes, Cookies, Desserts, Pies, Salads, Main Dishes, Soups, Cereal, Candy, Miscellaneous, Drinks, Canning, Home Remedies & Preparing Wild Game, Index.

· 5¹/₂" x 8¹/₂" · 275 pp · Spiral Bound · Laminated Cover · Convenient Thumb Index

Cooking with the Horse & Buggy People ... Item #164 ... **$12.99**

VOLUME II

Cooking with the Horse & Buggy People

Sharing a Second Serving of Favorites
from 207 Amish Women of Holmes County, Ohio

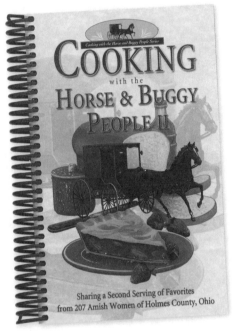

Henry and Amanda Mast, authors and compilers of *Cooking with the Horse and Buggy People Volume II* (as well as Volume I), live close to Charm, Ohio. Their home place is in the heart of the world's largest Amish community. The Masts and their friends worked countless hours in the kitchen to perfect the 600 recipes they chose to share with you.

Good food. Laughter. Compliments. Memories. That's what this new volume of *Cooking with the Horse and Buggy People* is about.

· 5½" x 8½" · 320 pp · Spiral Bound · Extra-Heavy Laminated Cover

Cooking with the Horse & Buggy People ... Item #628 ... **$12.99**

Give Us This Day Our Daily Bread

All the favorites of the Belle Center Amish Community. Over 600 of today's family favorites and even some from Grandma's kitchen. All the usual sections are here. But what makes this one special is the appetizers, large quantity recipes (for weddings, reunions, and other special occasions) and the children's recipe section. The tips, hints, and quotes section is filled with everyday kitchen secrets.

· 5¹/₂" x 8¹/₂" · 263 pp · Spiral bound · Indexed

Give Us This Day Our Daily Bread … Item #733 … $**11.99**

AUTHENTIC AMISH COOKING

The Wooden Spoon Cookbook

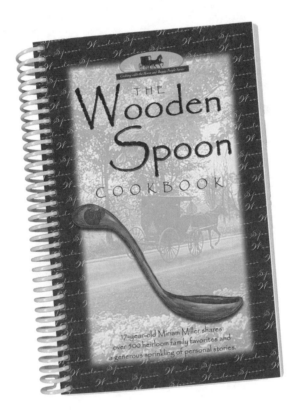

M eet 17-year-old Miriam Miller in the *Wooden Spoon Cookbook*. In additio to sharing her own, her mother's, and her grandmother's favorite recipe Miriam shares childhood memories, stories, and personal details of her life as young Amish girl.

· 5½" x 8½" · 194 pp · Spiral bound · Laminated cover · Double indexed

The Wooden Spoon Cookbook … Item #415 … **$10.99**

Wedding Cookbook

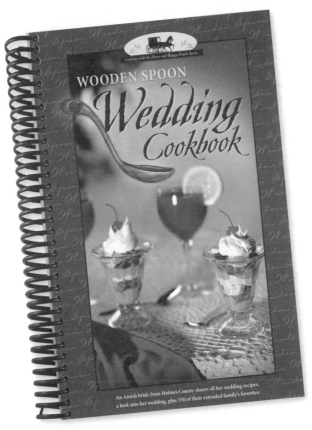

An Amish bride from Holmes County shares all her wedding recipes, a look into her wedding, plus 350 of their extended family's favorites.

Here's a chance to experience the wedding of Amish bride Miriam Miller. Relax and sip the drink served at her bridal table. Enjoy the hearty main dishes and mouthwatering desserts served to her 500 guests. Miriam shares glimpses into the wedding as she talks about the preparation and serving of food on her special day. The icing on the cake with this cookbook is that Aden's (Miriam's husband) family have opened their recipe boxes and shared over 350 of their family favorites!

· 5¹/₂" x 8¹/₂" · Spiral bound · Laminated cover · Indexed

Wooden Spoon Wedding Cookbook … Item #005 … **$12.99**

Table for Two

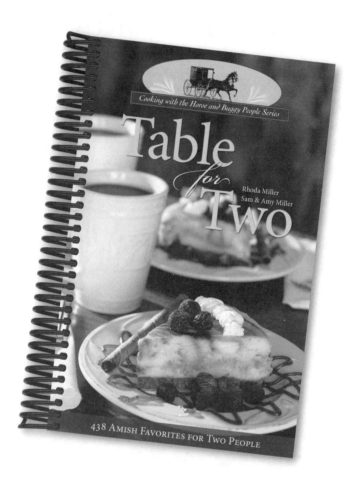

Table for Two sets the table with all the Amish food favorites—just for two! Sam and Amy Miller and their extended family have shared 438 of their best recipes in helpings that won't leave a week of leftovers if there are only two at your house.

Table for Two—mouthwatering food, for just the two of you.

· 5¹⁄₂" x 8¹⁄₂" · 206 pp · Spiral bound · Indexed

Table for Two … Item #021 … **$12.99**

Amish Quilting Cookbook

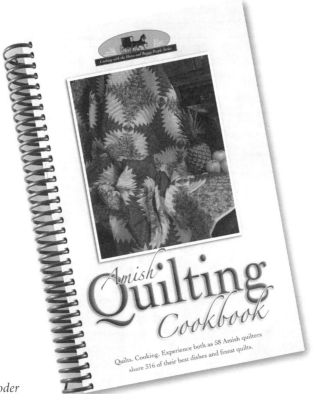

Sara Yoder

Fix up your favorite meal and enjoy the beauty of quilts at the same time with the new Quilting Cookbook. Its 130 pages are packed with 316 favorite recipes from 58 of Lone Star Quilt Shop's quilters. Twenty of their finest quilts are featured in color throughout the book.

· 5¹/₂" x 8¹/₂" · 136 pp · Spiral

Amish Quilting Cookbook … Item #733 … **$12.99**

Healthy Choices Cookbook

*A*re you looking for a common sense approach to a healthier lifestyle? We compiled *Healthy Choices* Cookbook to help you provide nutritious food for your family and friends. The recipes in *Healthy Choices* are sugar-free, use no white flour and don't ask for artificial ingredients. In the long run, no one maintains vibrant, growing health on radiated, fumigated, pasteurized, homogenized, chemical-laden, and nutritionally dead food. Living cells require living foods.

While its sometimes hard to decide the exact place where dead food stops and healthful food starts, and certain foods "don't agree" with some people as they do with others, *Healthy Choices* with its 1,093 recipes offers a wide range of traditional and modern recipes that help you protect, maintain and encourage the good health God gives you and your loved ones. Take the first step toward better health—start with healthy food choices.

7"x10"· 454 pp · Spiral Bound

Healthy Choices . . . Item #126 . . . **$15.99**

Horse and Buggy Montana

In *Horse and Buggy Montana* you'll find the same great home cooking you've come to expect of Amish cooks anywhere, but here it comes with a dash of the West added for good taste. Get fired up for the day with Gold Rush Brunch (page 20), serve delicious Montana Cowgirl Casserole (page 50), or if you prefer, try Cheese-Stuffed Elk Roast (page 55). (Beef works too!) For your family or guests who want something sweet, ring their bell with Huckleberry Roly-Poly (page 86).

5½"x 8½"· 150 pp · Spiral Bound

Horse and Buggy Montana . . . Item #225 . . . . **$10.99**

Keepers At Home

Gluten-Free Cooking

Cookbook series. When we compiled the KAH *Healthy Choices* Cookbook (above) there were so many gluten-free recipes we decided to do a separate cookbook. The 121 recipes in KAH *Gluten-Free* are from KAH readers who want to help others in this special food lifestyle. The "Gluten-Free Cooking Secrets" section is perfect if you're just getting started with gluten-free.

5½"x 8½"· 104 pp · Spiral Bound

Gluten Free Cooking ... Item #119 .... **$8.99**

Homemade Mixes

Prepare and store your favorite mixes, then when you need a quick solution to surprise company or feeding your hungry family, reach for your mix to make your favorites…faster.

Biscuits, Pizza Crust, Breads, Pie Crust, Muffins, Pancakes, Cakes, Soups, Cookies, Drinks

5½"x 8½"· 74 pp · Spiral Bound

Homemade Mixes. . . Item #188 . . . . **$6.99**